White Angel

Edward Farrell

COMING SOON FROM EDWARD FARRELL

Snow Angel

WHITE ANGEL

This is a work of fiction. Names, characters, organizations, places, events, and incidents are either products of the author's imagination or are used fictitiously.

Text copyright © 2018 Edward Farrell
All rights reserved.

No part of this book may be reproduced, or stored in a retrieval system, or transmitted in any form or by any means, electronic, mechanical, photocopying, recording, or otherwise, without express written permission of the publisher.

First Print Edition 2018 Dark Ink Press

www.darkink-press.com

ISBN-13 **978-0-9997016-8-3**
ISBN **0-9997016-8-1**

Cover design by Melissa Volker

Printed in the United States of America

*For Barbara
who makes life good
and has for as long as I remember.*

Author's Note

General Seminary, the setting for some of the scenes in this book, is a real place, a lovely square block in Chelsea. As late as the 1990's, *White Angel's* time frame, there were tunnels under the buildings along its 21st street side. The 1870 incident that the book references actually occurred – you could look it up. Let this be said: other than these facts this is a work of fiction.

Chapter One

NEW YORK CITY - 1991

FRIDAY - 1:02 a.m.

Nothing. There was still nothing. No contact. Michael Powell sat erect on the plain wooden bench, his spine braced against its straight back, his feet flat on the bare wood floor, hands lying loosely on his knees, palms up, fingers slightly curved. In front of him nothing, only the flickering candle and behind it the painted figure of a man, nearly naked, his arms spread, his head hanging heavily, his wrists and feet and face and side dripping with blood. The room smelled sweet and smoky, the odor of burning beeswax. Inside were no sounds. From beyond the walls, beyond the painted glass of the window where the candle appeared in ghostly flickering refraction, came only the city's late night buzz, an ebb and flow of traffic noise and distant sirens and airplanes, of far-off indistinct voices and subway rumbling, all muted by the thick heat of the humid air. Powell tried to tune it out, tried to find the frequency of a different time, listened for different reverberations, the ones that had been there before. The whip's sharp crack. The muffled groans. The harsh clang of metal on metal. And the voice, most of all the voice. Which this time did not speak.

Then words, shouted words, not clear but somewhere close. Powell closed his eyes and leaned forward slightly, easing his back away from the bench. Then a shout again: "Here! Over here!" Car doors slamming, running feet falling on concrete. Powell exhaled, sagged back against the hard wood and opened his eyes. Wrong time. Here and now. Something on 20th Street, probably. Drunks going home from the discos on 11th Avenue. As if to confirm this, the next sound was a low groan and the sound of violent retching. Bright lights, big city, thought Powell. But not like the book. Really, it was kids with not much money and less hope, out to drink and snort and smoke the world away. And then back on the subways, barfing their ways back to Queens and Brooklyn and the Bronx. Outside, another shout, almost a scream: "JESUS CHRIST!"

Powell felt his face begin to form a smile in the darkness. Nothing funny but he couldn't stop. Jesus Christ. What did it mean to scream that in the middle of a New York night? What would the screamer do if J.C. answered? Showed up? Nothing funny. He wouldn't show up. Wouldn't speak. Not tonight, anyway. Just as well to acknowledge that. Powell stood and stretched and blew the candle out. He turned and stepped through the shadows of bench and wall and door; his hand reached up from his side and fell unerringly on the cold iron of the unseen ornate doorknob. He smiled again. How many times? How many times here and in so many other darkened rooms. How many minutes, how many hours? How long since the last time the voice had spoken from stillness? Powell's hand tightened on the knob, now warmed in his grip, turned it, pushed into a hallway, the air damp here, too, but surprisingly cool. Cool and what? Musty? Before the mustiness could explain itself, he had turned left to a paneled door under a red EXIT sign, and pushed through into the sultriness of the city's Indian summer night.

Something wrong. Light was coming and going, and the voices were close. Something crackled. Like a fire but there was no smell of smoke - and there seemed to be a voice in it. The flashing light was blue and came from somewhere around the corner of the high brick wall on Powell's right. Police. Police radio. In the second that it took him to know this Powell had covered half the fifty feet of sidewalk along the side of the looming chapel wall and his pace was quickening, up from a quick walk to a near trot.

"YOU! RIGHT THERE!" Something odd about the voice that came

from near the wall, from a corner where a brick buttress rose. No time to consider this. With the words was the light, a bright beam that caught Powell full in the face and brought his hands up involuntarily to waist height.

"HOLD IT!" Something soft there, even in a shout. The radio crackled again and footsteps clopped close behind him on the stone walk. Powell stepped towards the light.

The stick surprised him. It came back hard against his throat, pulling him back and down, turning the bright whiteness of the light red around its halo rim. Breath going, choked out.

Powell, reacting not thinking, brought his left elbow up quickly and then back in a quick piston motion connecting with a solid ridge of something behind him. Rib cage. Not perfect but the stick loosened and someone groaned. Now his right hand stretched back over his head and caught cloth, a handful of starched cotton somewhere behind his left shoulder. Pivoting left, dropping slightly, he brought Stickman up over his right shoulder and slammed him hard on the pavement and flower bed border between him and the Light.

Which was gliding to his left, now gone arcing up along the wall into the city night sky, now shooting a falling beam at planes and helicopters and stars, now gone in a sharp crack just above Powell's left eye that sent sparks and streaks of color into a descending blackness. Now gone.

Chapter Two

FRIDAY - 10:46 a.m.

Not a typical morning. Before he knew that it was morning, Powell knew that there was nothing typical about it. Typically, the top of his skull did not shoot jagged shards of pain down towards the base of his neck nor did his right arm ache from elbow to shoulder. He forced his eyes open, felt them shut tight, squinted them open again against a strong light. Typically, he woke to colors of grey and black and black going to grey in the sky outside his window, but here there was no window and everything was white. White lights, white walls, tightly tucked white sheets. From somewhere white noise - footsteps, voices, TV music. What time was it? Powell turned reflexively to his right to check the clock radio on the nightstand. Not there; neither stand nor clock. But another surprise. Typically, he woke alone; here next to the bed was a woman.

She was seated in a grey institutional arm chair, a small notebook in her right hand, body turned towards him but eyes right, gazing away towards the barely cracked door. Young, Powell guessed. Maybe 30, probably less. Good looking. Dark hair, dark eyes, dark skin. East Indian? Hispanic maybe. Short, straight nose, high cheekbones, lips glossed and full. Difficult to picture her figure the way she was sitting. Nicely dressed, though. She was wearing a tailored grey suit and a white silky-looking blouse, open at the throat. There was a bright scarf - blues and greens and reds - on the back of her chair. Looking from it back to her face, he found her staring, her eyes full on his and no embarrassed glance away.

Silence for a long moment, which Powell went along with - most people didn't like it but the woman seemed comfortable. Finally, a voice, firm, medium range, a hint of something familiar.

"Mr. Powell?" She knew him but it wasn't what anyone had called him for years. Powell propped himself up on his elbows - the right one sore and swaddled in Ace bandages - and nodded. Awake now, he knew that he was in a hospital, that someone had hit him. But why? And where had he been? And who was this?

The woman reached into a shoulder bag of soft black leather and pulled out a wallet sized case.

"I'm Detective Hernandez." The photo next to the gold shield showed a slightly younger woman in police blues, faced squared off for the photographer, jaw hardened, eyes sparkly hard, lips tight and narrow. Maria Hernandez. The same person who sat back in the chair now, but not quite the same, Powell thought.

"Can you tell me what happened last night?"

"Nope." The pain at the top of his head rose and fell hard on him like a wave crashing on a beach. "Someone hit me and that's about all I can tell you."

"Can you tell me where you were? Where you were going?"

"No." Something not right, something wrong about Detective Hernandez and her questions. "I took a pretty good shot. It's pretty much a blank."

Not happy. Some slight movement in Hernandez's face told Powell that his answer had not been what she wanted. Something off. She glanced down, reached into the bag again, came up with a notebook. "You were brought here from General Theological Seminary, between 20th and 21st on 9th. Does that help any?"

"Yes." It did. The scream. The walk, the stick. Something else, too; something that added to Powell's queasiness. What was it? Something still in the haze. "I was on the walk there, by the chapel. Someone jumped me from behind. We struggled a bit, there was a light, another one – someone else - hit me. That's about it."

"And what were you doing there, Mr. Powell?"

There it was. What she wanted to know. It wasn't about him. Now it came back to him - the flashing light was blue. The police were already there. Stickman was one. The Light was one, too. Something else had happened. Now a voice was there, not the One he listened for, the One that wouldn't speak; this was one of his own, whispering: *careful. Be careful.*

"Mr. Powell? What were you doing there?" A bit of an edge in her tone this time, not cutting, but prickly.

"Aren't you supposed to ask me if I got a look at them? Could I identify them?"

No reaction. That's what she's trying for, Powell thought. Her eyes stayed full on his, didn't back off a bit. No movement of the lips either, but up the jaw just a twinge of movement where a muscle tightened. Got her. Got her now. Try for naive, Powell told himself. Try for dumb. It wouldn't work but it might annoy her in to telling him something.
"Does the police department usually send a detective out on mugging cases? To tell you the truth, I'm surprised to see anyone. What you hear is that the department doesn't give a shit about this petty stuff."

"Mr. Powell, how about I ask the questions? I think this'll go faster that way." A cool forced smile. No score.

Try again, pushier this time. "How do you know my name, anyway? I don't think I had a wallet."

"You didn't. It was on this." As she leaned forward to hand him a scrap of paper her blouse fell away form her throat revealing a loose slip or camisole and her breasts, firm and high, with large dark nipples. She knows, Powell thought as he reached towards her. Knows I'm looking.

Part of the game. He glanced up to find her eyes still on his, narrower now, maybe with a sparkle of something. Taking the paper, a dry cleaner's ticket, he sat back and watched her slowly straighten. Angry? Maybe, but maybe laughing, too.

"Anything else?"

Her eyebrows arched a millimeter. No other response.

"Was I carrying anything else?"

The eye sparkle was hot now. Annoyance, Powell thought. Or the beginning of it. He knew she didn't know it yet - she was only sensing that the situation was slipping out of control. A different room came to mind, whitewashed stone with a simple wooden altar, a room with a door that opened to the greenest tropical greens, a room where questions got away from questioners. Powell felt his tension rising like a tight hot fist, the one that still woke him, not screaming anymore, but whispering "no." No. Shake it off. The fist was not real now. Not here. Here was only a New York police detective, an attractive woman with dark sparkling eyes. Now looking at her notebook, now turning back to speak.

"A book of matches."

That was clearly the answer but what, Powell wondered, was the question? Something he'd said and forgotten, probably something that would increase her annoyance, push it to anger if he asked again. Try conciliation, he told himself. Charm or something. He pushed himself up straight and touch his head, finding a bandage. Good. Now smile. Shake your head.

"I'm sorry. I didn't get that."

"A book of matches. You were carrying a book of matches." Flat tone. She glanced at her notebook again. No softening. "From a place called Jimmy Duggan's. In the Village, from the address."

Powell smiled, a real smile this time. "Jimmy's," he said, mostly to no one. And then caught himself. Explain it. Give her something. "I haven't been there in a while. Great spot, though. Neighborhood kind of place." Jimmy would like that.

"That's very nice to know, Mr. Powell." Not working. Her tone honed a bit sharper now. "But we're not getting anywhere. I'm running an investigation and I need you to tell me what you were doing at General Seminary at approximately 1:15 this morning. So could we skip the restaurant reviews?"

"OK, Detective." Time to change course. Try levelling. "But I want to know what's going on. Suppose you go first."

"All right. I'll go first." She didn't like it. Her eyes had caught fire and her lips had narrowed down to almost nothing. Now she didn't speak. Now she shouted. Now he knew what was familiar about her voice. "What's going on, Mister Powell, is that you are about to get cuffed and taken down to the precinct. Charged with resisting arrest, assaulting an officer, and obstructing an investigation. Is that clear enough?" A pause, and not for effect. The detective, Powell knew, was flat out angry. "Now," she hissed, "it's your turn."

"Thank you, Detective." Now he knew who she was - the angry `right there!' voice   Best try not to make it too much worse. "You're the one who hit me, aren't you?"

No answer. Answer enough.

"It doesn't matter. Somewhere in your precinct house there's a piece of paper that would tell us all about it." Powell let that sink in for a too long moment. "Now let me tell you something else that's going on." Another pause. "Something else happened at the seminary last night. The squad car was already there when I came out. I remember the lights. And whatever happened was something big. Otherwise we would not have had police officers, one a detective no less, hiding in the bushes when they heard a door open. So far, I'm right on the money, we both know that."

He was. The fact that she didn't interrupt said so. "And what's going on right here, just so we're clear about it, is that you think you've cracked it. Whatever happened, you think I did it. But you haven't got much that says so. Almost nothing, since you haven't bothered to arrest me. You're hoping I'll say something that'll put it away for you. That's how the game is played."

"Sounds like you've played before." Tough. Soft voice but tough underneath. Powell liked her and knew that he shouldn't.

"Both sides, Detective. I've played both sides." Hernandez stood up. Now, Powell wondered, now would she back out of her role?

"Michael Powell, you are under arrest for the crime of felony assault." Shit. Going all the way. "You have the right to re-"

"CUT THE CRAP, DETECTIVE!"

"-main silent." Hernandez stopped. Her eyes were still snapping but her lips were pursed tightly. Behind her a fat, black nurse peered around the door frame.

"Thank you, Detective." Powell waved at the black woman. "It's ok, nurse, we'll keep it down." The black face disappeared.

"Now, Detective Hernandez, shall we start again? Or would you rather go through the charade? You know: you arrest me, I file a brutality complaint, I can't make it stick but you get little asterisks by your name in the computer at review time. I'm going to find out sooner or later so why don't you just tell me what's going on?"

"Murder."

Hernandez said it matter-of-factly, like a guy at a bar might say `Budweiser.'

"And I don't know if you did it, Mister Powell, but I know you were there and I don't know why. So now suppose *you* tell *me* what's going on.

What were you doing at General Seminary at approximately 1:15 this morning?"

She's not going to like it, Powell thought. Not going to like it one bit. Still, she wanted an answer, the glowing hot eyes made that obvious.

"I was praying," Powell said.

Chapter Three

THE ANGEL

THE ANGEL REMEMBERED. PREENING A BIT, AS IF SMOOTHING SOFT WING PINNAE, THE ANGEL REMEMBERED THE KNIFE. ANGELS WEREN'T FREQUENTLY GIVEN KNIVES SO IT SEEMED STRANGE THAT IT HAD COME TO HIM. STILL THERE WERE THE SWORDS – FROM THE VERY BEGINNING, IN FACT. AT THE TREE OF LIFE, THAT ONE, THAT ONE HAD A SWORD. BUT THAT WAS IN A TIME WHEN SWORDS WERE COMMON. NOW NO ONE HAD A SWORD. PERHAPS THAT WAS THE REASON FOR THE KNIFE.

THE KNIFE WAS A FINE ONE, THERE WAS NO DOUBT ABOUT THAT. ONE SIMPLE STROKE, THAT WAS ALL IT HAD TAKEN. THEN THE LINE, A THIN EVEN MARK, DARK, ALMOST BLACK, THAT HAD WIDENED MINUTELY BEFORE IT HAD TURNED RED. THEN THE BUBBLES, PINK ONES AT THE CENTER OF THE LINE WHICH NOW OOZED DOWN LIKE A CURTAIN FALLING, A THIN RED CURTAIN FALLING TOWARDS A STIFF WHITE COLLAR. AND THEN THE OBLATION, STILL LIVING, HAD LURCHED BACKWARD AGAINST THE DAMP BRICK OF THE WALL AND THE LINE HAD WIDENED AGAIN, TRANSFIGURED ITSELF REALLY, INTO A CRESCENT. AND FROM THIS MOON BLOOD HAD GUSHED AS FROM A SPRING, HOT ENOUGH TO RAISE STEAM FROM THE COLD STONE FLOOR. "AND THE MOON WILL TURN TO BLOOD."

THE ANGEL CONSIDERED THIS FOR A MOMENT. WASN'T THAT THE PROPHECY? ONE COULD ALWAYS SEE THE RIGHTNESS OF THINGS IF ONE CONSIDERED THE HOLY SCRIPTURES.

STILL, THERE WAS THE QUESTION OF THE KNIFE. IT HAD BEEN PROVIDED FOR HIM; THAT WAS AS IT SHOULD HAVE BEEN. ONE OF THE YOUNG MEN HAD BEEN THE MESSENGER, ONE WHO HAD COME IN THE NIGHT AND WAS GONE WHEN MORNING DAWNED. WAKING, HE HAD FOUND THE KNIFE ON THE FLOOR NEAR HIS CHAMBER DOORWAY, A DULLY GLEAMING, FINE-EDGED, FIVE INCH BLADE THAT DARTED FROM A STEEL HANDLE AT THE TOUCH OF A BUTTON. BUT WHERE WAS IT NOW? NOT IN HIS POCKET OR IN THE CLOTHES HE'D BEEN WEARING NOR ANYWHERE ON EITHER FLOOR OF HIS HOME. THE ANGEL HAD EVEN GONE BACK THROUGH THE LONG DAMP TUNNEL TO THE CRYPT WHERE THE KILLING WALL WAS BUT THE WEAPON WAS NOT THERE. COULD HE HAVE HAD IT AT THE FENCE? HE THOUGHT NOT. THERE WOULD HAVE BEEN NO REASON FOR IT THERE. AND NOW, HE THOUGHT, THE POLICE HAD BEEN EVERYWHERE WITH THEIR SPOTLIGHTS AND FLASHLIGHTS AND SHOULDER RADIOS. HAD THEY FOUND IT? IF HE WENT OUT TO SATISFY HIMSELF THAT THE KNIFE HAD SIMPLY DISAPPEARED AS EASILY AS IT HAD COME IN THE FIRST PLACE, WHAT WOULD HE SAY TO THEM? THE ANGEL CLOSED HIS EYES AND TIPPED HIS HEAD FORWARD, RAISING HIS THIN PALE HANDS AND TOUCHING HIS FINGERTIPS LIGHTLY AGAINST HIS TEMPLES. AND THE WORDS CAME. "DO NOT BE ANXIOUS WHAT YOU WILL SAY, IT WILL BE

GIVEN YOU. THE WORDS ALWAYS CAME, JUST AS THE KILLING WORDS HAD. "FALLEN, FALLEN, IS BABLYON THE GREAT, THE GREAT WHORE, THE FORNICATOR."

Chapter 4

FRIDAY - 2:30 p.m.

The office was just the same, Powell thought. Shelf-lined walls, two filing cabinets next to a nearly bare desk below the tall window. In the corner, a pipe rack and phone answering machine on a low side table just to the right of the easy chair and lamp. But why should it have changed? He half smiled. Only a day since he'd been here. Not even that, not quite. Seemed longer, though. A good sign. Time was changing shape again. Like a channeled river that rose over its carefully formed and measured banks to cut a new path down to the sea. Now a full smile at the metaphor. The Army Corps of Engineers takes on Time. Wouldn't the Corps love that?

Corps or nor, channel or not, it had been a long day. Powell stepped up to the desk and looked at the fading October light in the garden below. Not many blossoms there now.

A few mums lining the brick walk to the patio in front of the wrought iron table but nothing like the profusion of late spring and summer. Still the leaves of the sugar maple just to the left of the window were a brilliant scarlet and the view was as soothing as anything imaginable. Just like yesterday. Perhaps a few leaves had fallen since then, but the scene was substantially the same. He'd been right here before dinner the day before, he recalled, and had been so calmed that he'd decided then to man a listening post, to try again, to open up one more time to the voice. And heard only stillness. And then Stickman and the Light and then the hospital and Hernandez.

She had not believed him. Not at first anyway. Praying? She hadn't had to say anything. A vacant expression had washed over her professionally tough demeanor, obliterating it like a wave over a child's sand castle, leaving only surprise. Now he smiled at the memory and supposed that it was a strange thing for a cop to hear. Praying. A good alibi? Different at least. Hernandez hadn't commented. Finally, he'd filled the silence between them by repeating himself, more or less. "I'm a priest. I was praying."

That sunk in. Or seemed to. It had become more routine then. Where? The oratory? Where's that? Are you there often? Occasionally? How occasionally? Did you see anyone?

Hear anything? Notice anything unusual?

He hadn't helped much. Had seen no one. Hadn't heard anything strange - you always heard people on the steps there but the building was a residence hall, only the first floor space was set aside for prayer and meditation. After a while it was easy to tune out footsteps. There *was* something, though. He hadn't remembered it then in the hospital room and didn't remember it now, except that now as then he was sure there was something. It didn't come.

"Nothing else?" she'd said, provoking a smile and a quick rejoinder:

"If there was, it didn't help my recall any to have you belt me with a flashlight."

She had not smiled but there was a glimmer of something. "No choice. You were taking my partner out. Where'd you learn to fight like that anyway, er, Father?"

Not much of a stumble for her to find the patrinomal. Probably a parochial school girl, he had thought, imagining her in a plaid jumper and a starched white blouse. Her question, though, had not been one he'd wanted to get into. Shrugging as if uncertain about it, he'd told her that he'd been in the army. Those were memories that'd be better knocked out of him. Even now, looking at an autumn garden, he felt his pulse quicken and his breath come up shorter.

Powell looked down from the window to the desktop. Empty but for a small stack of papers in one corner. Mail or messages, Powell thought. Anna would have put them there when he didn't show up for lunch. He smiled at the thought of Anna. She was a short, plump Thai woman whose last name was never used if anyone knew it. Always smiling. Usually humming some song to herself. Powell, she called 'brueddah' because he knew a few words of Thai and knew the town from which her family had come. Brother. Not what they'd called him there, in Khemmarat, a steaming village on the Mekong. There he'd been known as Star Man- the one who leaves at dusk and returns at dawn. The one who walks in darkness.

Shake it, Powell thought. Shake the past. Twenty years was a long time. Long enough. He tried to let the mail on the desk provide a distraction.

Not much there, though. A vestment catalogue, a letter from the archbishop advising caution to all his brothers in Christ in statements on matters sexual, an invitation to conduct a retreat in an upstate town, a circular marked 'Occupant,' offering savings on pantyhose. Powell smiled at that. Anna's doing.

She'd know that he would laugh, and would laugh with him the next time she saw him. "Not joker," was what she said about the other priests in the house to set them apart from him, the one who teased her and accepted her gentle teasing in return.

It wasn't true, really. The others all had fair senses of humor and two of them, Bilodeau and Jordan, were really funny. It was just that they didn't see her. The Society taught you to look inward, not outward, and there was nothing in their pasts that would let a small, diffident Oriental woman register at all. Maybe that was lucky for them. Powell shrugged. The past wouldn't let you shake it; that was the trouble. He turned from the mail to the room, looking for distraction.

A pipe might help. A funny thought, really, to have just escaped the medical profession more or less unscathed and then to turn to one of the few things they all agreed could kill you. Not the time to quit, though. Crossing the room to the table by the easy chair, Powell thought of the dozen or more times he had already stopped smoking, once for a period of years, always coming back to riff-cut burley and straight-stemmed pipes. Because it was stupid, he thought. Because it was something he'd started when he was young enough to believe he was sophisticated. Because he liked the smell of it, the taste of it, the feel of it. Because, as Jimmy D. said, he didn't give a shit.

The red numeral on the answering machine caught Powell's eye as he reached for the round glass humidor on the pipe rack. "3." More messages than he sometimes got in a week. The voice after the first beep was the Provincial's. Which figured. The detective would have called there to verify his identity. There was a slight note of exasperation in the quiet tone. He was to cooperate with the department investigation, the machine said. He was not to talk to the press under any circumstances. He was suspended from all duties and should make an appointment to see the Provincial as soon as possible.

Suspended from all duties. Powell chose a pipe, a low bowled black one with a tapering stem and wondered what duties the Provincial was thinking of. He had little to do in the parish, one of three the Society had in the city, and little else to do at all except write, which was hardly what the provincial meant by "duties." And then there was his 10th Avenue work but–

Another beep and another voice to derail his train of thought. "This is Hernandez." Who sounded mad. And something else. Powell smiled. Sexy? "We need to talk. Stay right there until I find you. Father."

The last word was clipped and bristling. Something had happened, something to do with him, something that got her hackles up. Beeeeep-

"Mick?" The third voice sounded doubtful. Duggan. It was Jim Duggan. Jimmy D. "Mick, are you into something? The cops have been here asking about you. And someone else called, too, a woman, I think. Wouldn't say who she was. What's it about? Shout me."

Shout me. Only Jimmy D., Powell mused. No one else spoke his language. That way even in seminary. But maybe it was time to give James Duggan a shout. Powell eased himself into the chair by the phone, pulled the lid off the humidor with his right hand, holding the black pipe with his left. The fill was automatic, thumb and index finger pinching moist tobacco, pinkie tamping it into place. When he'd put the humidor back on the shelf Powell grabbed the phone receiver, tucked it up under his right ear and began punching up numbers, listening to a familiar sequence of beeps, a post-modern melody of connection. Two rings and a youngish voice, a woman's.

"Duggan's."

"Is Jim there?" Odd that he wouldn't be answering himself, the middle of a weekday afternoon.

"Not at the moment. Can I take a message?"

"Ellen? That you?" Powell knew that it was. Ellen Ames was the final straw, the one that had finally made Duggan see what the rest of the Jebbies already knew- that James A. Duggan

was not cloth that would stay in the shape of a priest no matter how you cut it. But what was she doing there? "Ellen, It's Mick."

"Mickey. This is weird." Ellen stopped, then started again, quickly and softly. "I think Jim's gone to look for you. He called and asked me to watch the place. Said he had to tell you something." Another pause. "And then a minute ago someone else called for you."

Something *was* up, Powell, thought. Ellen was a sculptor, a gifted one, but no head for numbers and no gift for small talk. She had waitressed sometimes between commissions but as far as he knew Jimmy had never asked her to stand in before and wouldn't if could see a way around it. And another call; Jimmy's message had said there'd been one, too. Powell shifted the receiver from his right ear to his left, stretching the cord across his throat and shoulder. "Who called?" he asked.

"I don't know. A man, I think. He wouldn't leave a message."

"You think it was a man?" Odd that she'd put it that way. Hadn't Jimmy's message said, `a woman, I think?'

"I don't know. It was a very soft voice, and smooth, you know, like satin or something." Ellen's own voice was like that usually, Powell thought. But now she sounded flustered. Something though - I don't know what - something made me think it was a man."

"What did he want?"

"Only to know were you here. I told him I hadn't seen you. And then he asked did I know how he could get in touch with you. Said it was important."

"Did you?"

"Huh? Did I what?" Still flustered. Not like Ellen.

"Ellen? I meant did you tell him how to reach me - but you sound like something's wrong. You okay?"

"*YES*, I'm okay. I mean no. I mean it's, it was kinda creepy and something's going on; first Jimmy called and then you and I don't know, you're an asshole, you know that?"

"Well certainly I know that." Now Powell smiled and pictured Ellen at the end of the bar where the phone and register were. "Didn't I ever tell you about my sister?"

A silence of an instant or two, long enough for the gears to shift and then a peevish tone: "No. What about her?"

"I was visiting her in San Francisco once and we were having drinks in this pub looking out over the bay and she told me her first rule of life. `All men are assholes.'" There was a sound in the receiver that was somewhere between a snort and a chuckle, which told Powell that Ellen was recovering equilibrium. "I said, `Even your brother?' and she looked me right in the eye and said, `All men.'"

Ellen laughed out loud and there was a knock at the door.

"Your sister's smarter'n you are, you know?"

"She is. Hang on a second, will you? Someone's here." Turning to the door, Powell said loudly, "What is it?"

The panel inched toward him and Anna's head appeared a foot or so above the doorknob. "Excuse me, brueddah. A woman come here to see you. She is very angry. I tell her to go away?"

"No, Anna. I think she's been trying to reach me. Better show her in."

Anna looked doubtful. Angry women, Powell mused, were not what she was used to in the rectory.

The door swung toward him. Behind Anna and on the right side of the doorway's rectangle were dark hair, a grey-clad shoulder, and the bright red and yellow edge of a scarf. Hernandez. She brushed past Anna and stood in the middle of the polished wood floor while Powell put the phone receiver back to his ear.

"Ellen? I have to go. My caller has just arrived - a police detective, said to be angry"

"Mick, I-"

"Bye now." Powell put the receiver on its cradle and leaned forward to stand. He was less than half way out of the chair when the shouting started.

"THIS DETECTIVE IS NOT JUST SAID TO BE ANGRY. SHE IS SERIOUSLY PISSED OFF!"

Powell, now standing, stood closer to Hernandez than was comfortable for either of them. Make her wonder. Make her think. Get her out of her guts, he thought, and into her head. Behind her he noticed Anna, standing in the doorway, her eyes as round as communion patens.

"Thank you, Anna," Powell said mildly. "That will be all." Anna nodded and disappeared behind the door that she quietly pulled shut as she left. Powell raised his hands to his hips and turned to Hernandez whose eyes still glittered with mad. Now, though, her arms were crossed in front of her. A good sign. A mark of uncertainty. Certainty is not human, Powell reflected. People who were certain were dangerous. Without taking his eyes off the detective's, he continued

speaking in low, even tones. A confessional voice, he thought.

"That woman's house was burned down," he said. "Because she would not tell the Khmer Rouge where her son was. He wasn't Cambodian, he was Thai, is what she told them but they didn't care; they needed him to carry a box of mortar shells that they'd bought off a corrupt Thai lieutenant. They were Thai shells, a Thai should carry them. They laughed at that and burned her house down."

Hernandez pulled her gaze from Powell's and looked at the floor.

"That's not all," Powell went on. "Later, they found the boy in the shed where the village rice was stored. They brought him back to her, to his mother, and put a gun in his mouth and shot him." For an instant Powell stopped, then finished, raising his voice half a tone. "Now, it would be better for her not to hearing people shouting."

Hernandez eyes came back to Powell's. She swallowed and spoke flatly. "What happened to her has nothing to do with me."

"That's one way of looking at it." As he said it, Powell saw something change. Had her eyes narrowed a millimeter? Brow come down? Something.

"Were you there?"

"What?" What was she getting at? Powell thought of a hymn tune, a spiritual. How did it go? `Were you there when they crucified my Lord?'

"Were you there? Were you there when her son was shot?"

Now Powell knew. Now he knew what she'd found out. What brought her here. "No," he said. "I wasn't there then."

"But you were out there, weren't you? Special Forces, right? Green Beret?"

My turn for doubt now, Powell thought. My turn for uncertainty. The past could do that. The past never went away. "It's pretty obvious that you've seen my record, Detective," he

said. "What did it tell you?"

"Tell me something I don't know, Father. At least I don't know it for sure." Powell noticed that her arms had moved. Still crossed but the right one reached inside her suit jacket now. Hand on a gun. Her eyes were still boring full on his face. "Don't they teach Special Forces guys to fight with knives?"

The past. But still with him. "Yes, you do an advanced course in hand-to-hand. Why?"

"Because I've got a dead man whose throat was cut. And this same dead man lived in Bangkok, maybe about the same time you were out there, wherever it was." Powell knew. Hernandez was still talking but Powell knew now. "--Same man apparently irritated some drug folks back then, too."

"Oh, God." His hands fell down to his sides. "Wolfson."

"Can I take it from that that you knew him?" Hernandez's voice was firm but something in her eyes wavered now.

"Yeah," Powell said, "I know him."

Chapter 6

FRIDAY - 2:53 p.m.

Duggan hadn't waited for the door to swing open all the way. Starting with, "Jesus, Mick," as soon as he'd seen Powell, the words had spilled out like rice from a torn sack each one clicking and bouncing into the room toward the place where Hernandez pivoted, trying to gather them in. Cops were asking about him. Someone else, too. What was going on? Was he into something again? What should he, Duggan, say?

With exaggerated dryness, Powell said that he hoped Jimmy would cooperate fully with the inquiries of any law enforcement agency.

Silence. And a question mark glance that fell first on Powell and then, as the door opened wider, moved into the space just over Powell's left shoulder. Where, Powell knew, Hernandez was returning it with a look just as inquisitive and probably a bit more hostile.

"Jim, come in," Powell said. "There's someone I want you to meet." He turned to Hernandez who, as he'd supposed, was glowering. "This is Detective Maria Hernandez of the NYPD. Detective Hernandez, this is James Duggan. He runs a bar."

Neither of them moved.

"The detective is looking into a homicide and thought that maybe I could help." Powell backed away from the door and stepped over to the window and the desk again. "In fact, at the moment, I believe she thinks I did it."

Hernandez gave no sign of having heard. She went on staring at

Duggan and asked, "What did you mean 'into something again?'"

Jimmy said nothing.

"Mr. Duggan is referring to another bit of police business, about a year and a half ago." Hernandez was intent on his words. Not happy, Powell thought, whatever that is. "I got into a bit of a dispute with a Colombian fellow, a guy named Viscarra, about whether he could hit his girlfriend with a car fan belt. She was a whore."

"What happened?" Hernandez voice seemed warmer than it had been, still chilly but maybe thawing. Duggan was looking down, staring at the floor as if it were a treasure map.

"I killed him."

"How?"

Duggan glanced at Powell and then at the door. Powell picked up a scent of something sweet and sharp in the room. Old Spice. Duggan's aftershave, had been since seminary.

"Stabbed him. With a broken bottle."

Hernandez' eyes widened just a fraction, showing just a glimmer more of the white around their dark, liquid centers. Lovely. And a little scary now, Powell thought. Eyes that were on to something. Dark cat's eyes looking for prey.

"Why was he beating her?" Cop's cold voice again. Powell felt his own thermometer pushing up fast.

"What does it matter? You think maybe there's a good enough reason?"

Hernandez shrugged. "Might tell me something about you."

That was it. He leaned back and sat on the desk top. That was it. Some little love thing going on might help her later with the D.A. Hang on. Just hang on and breath.

"It's history now, Detective," Powell said. "Has to be blinking on some computer chip down at HQ right now." Duggan had inched closer to the door and had crossed his arms tightly. "But to save you looking it up, I'll tell you. She wouldn't go back on the street for him. She was pregnant. She had AIDS."

"How'd you know that?"

"She was a friend."

"Was?"

"She died. About six months later."

"AIDS?"

"Crack O.D."

Hernandez bit her lip, looked away briefly, looked back at him. And that was that, Powell thought. The dead woman had come and gone now. Invisible. Like she had been to most people when she'd been alive. Just another slut.

"Mr. Duggan." Duggan kept his head down, still looking for the X that marked the spot. Still said nothing.

"Duggan." Hernandez' voice was tighter now, geared down and whining a bit like a car on steep hill. "How come you came all the way up here? Your place doesn't have a phone?"

No answer still. Powell watched the skin ripple along the back of Duggan's cheek as his jaw clenched and loosened methodically. Bad sign. Bad situation. Better to get him out.

"I'll tell you why." Duggan spoke and moved suddenly. Now he was standing nose to nose with Hernandez, who had not backed away. "I came because I don't like fuckin' cops listening to what I'm sayin!'"

Hernandez' hands were on her hips now, fingers extended like a folk dancer's

"In fact, I don't like fuckin' cops at all."

Powell saw it coming, saw her hands coming up to his shoulders as the dance began, Duggan's voice the only music.

"-of them the worst are fuckin dyke quota cops like - UUURRGHH."

Now the hands were clenching bunched cloth at the shoulders of Duggan's shirt as he bent and sagged, now her right foot was dropping back to the floor. When she let go of his shirt, Duggan staggered back a step and dropped to his knees still bent double so that his head was nearly touching the floor.

Powell, moving to grab Duggan, to hold him, glimpsed Hernandez's right hand sliding under her jacket lapel.

"Go ahead, pull it out," he said over his shoulder. "Might as well ice both of us. That'll make a good headline for the guys downtown."

Easing Duggan up towards the chair, Powell could see her feet behind him. Close together. Not firing range stance. Jimmy sank into the chair, head on his knees, both hands on his crotch. Turning, Powell found Hernandez standing by the desk with her arms folded, a dusky flush spreading across her cheeks.

"I think you're finished here now, Maria. Thanks for coming by."

She moved a step closer to the door, but stopped. She said, "He had it coming."

"Is that what it says in your manual?"

She didn't answer. Powell let the silence build between them like a rampart, punctuated only by Duggan's grunting. Something told Powell that this was the beginning again. Something like the voice whispering about silence and walls, mistaken words and violence and estrangement. The lesser angels marching in force.

"Hey, Duggan?" The cop talking now, talking tough, Powell thought, like a thousand movie cops. Mired in the image like some once graceful antelope going down in a tar pit. Like an art, he mused.

Duggan pushed the syllables of a reply out. "Fuck. You."

"Duggan?" Something gritty in her voice, something determined to hang on, to see the scene through. "Duggan, who's Seymour Case?"

"You want to. Know that look. In the fuckin' phone book."

And she was gone. Powell, watching Duggan in the chair, did not see her go. The door was cracked open and the sound of footsteps on the stairs echoed in and the air was Old Spice and sweat.

"What a smell of. Sulfur," Duggan said.

Powell blanked. And then got it. The Wizard - an old thing from the novitiate. Everything, all of life, was really from the Wizard of Oz. The provincial then had been the bumbling wizard. 'Pay no attention to that man behind the curtain.'

"But was she a good witch or a bad witch?" Powell asked.

Duggan snorted. "I don't know but. She got me and. My little dog, too."

"Toto, too?"

"Toto, too."

They both laughed. Duggan's color was coming back, pasty white going to a fairly florid pink.

"You didn't need to come, Jim."

"No shit." Duggan shifted gingerly in the chair.

"No, I mean I already knew what you were going to say." Powell moved away from him and leaned again on the desk top. "I called and talked to Ellen."

"What's it about?"

Powell gave him a brief fill-in; the walk scene, the hospital, the subsequent interview.

"Wolfson, huh? One of the big guys."

"You know of him?" Powell found it funny and surprising. "You didn't read theology when you were in seminary; you starting now to catch up?"

"Good, Mick. Real good." Duggan's smile was wide screen and genuine. "First the detective busts my nuts and now you're gonna bust my chops."

"C'mon. What do you know about Wolfson?"

"Nothing much about his stuff." Duggan's voice a little defensive. "I know him, though. Customer."

"No kidding?"

Duggan pouted a bit. Just like a barman, Powell thought. Wants you to know who he knows even though you couldn't know.

"C'mon, Jimmy. He doesn't strike me as the pub type."

"Maybe not. But we get a lot of gays. You know that."

That was true. And interesting. Duggan's also got yuppies, Irish zealots, neighborhood rummies, and the egghead stiffs who wandered over from the NYU library. But Jimmy D. didn't put Wolfson with them.

"So he was gay?"

"I don't know about him. But the guys he'd come in with were."

"Howdya know?"

Duggan snorted. "Mick, this is in Greenwich Village. You know that. People don't exactly stay in closets there."

Powell felt himself frowning. What was it about? Just random facts. With a dead man at the center. And, coincidently, he himself just off stage. Both at the scene and at Jimmy's. And something farther down, too. Some current, a dark one, was flowing down closer to the center.

"So how deep are you in this?"

Duggan's voice. The words clear but not registering.

"Huh?"

"How deep're you in? Your detective friend didn't seem to like you much."

"No, I don't think she does." Why should she? Because he wanted her to? And why was that? "I don't think she's got much or they'd have pulled me in on the grill. But I don't think she's got anyone else."

Jimmy grinned. "Love the one you're with, huh?"

No connection. What Duggan said made no sense but there was something familiar about it. What?

His question must have showed; Duggan looked chagrinned. "You don't remember that song? Oh, man. Steve Stills. 'If you can't be with the one you love, love the one you're with.' Nineteen and seventy something."

Powell did remember it. 'The eagle flies with the dove' - that was part of it. Something sad about it, too. But still no connection.
"Jim," Powell said. "What the hell brought that to mind anyway?"

Duggan's look said that Powell was a moron. His voice said, "The dick." He smiled again. "Can that be right? Can a woman dick be a dick?"

Powell felt the piss off level rising. He leaned forward and down toward where Duggan sat. "How about a little focus, Brother James? What the fuck are you talking about?"

"Sorry, Father," Duggan said. He was still smiling but was trying hard not to. "What I mean is if you're not with the one to nail, nail the one you're with. She's got you and she's got a hammer."

Now Powell's smile was coming up fast and he was shaking his head. "Jimmy, how did the Jebbies ever let you go? With a mind that works like yours does, you should have been a goddammed bishop."

They were both laughing now and Powell leaned back on his hands. Duggan was shaking his head. "But they wanted little Toto. To take him to the sheriff and be sure that he's destroyed."

The laughter was good but Duggan was right. Powell looked at the floorboards near the door where Hernandez had been standing. If there was no one else, it was going to be trouble for him. At the scene. Knew the stiff. History of violence. Nail him.

"So who the hell is Seymour Case?" Hearing the words, Powell wondered who had said them. Had he? Duggan sat staring at him expectantly. Had anyone spoken? The question was there, though. Who was Case? No one at the seminary by that name as far as he knew. And if there was, Hernandez'd know it by now.

"Hey, Jim?"

Duggan cocked his right eyebrow.

"The phone book's right there. Under the answering machine."

"Yeah?"

"Look up Mr. Case."

"You kidding?"

"Wasn't that your suggestion? Can't hurt. Let your fingers do the walking."

Duggan lifted the machine and grabbed the bulky blue book, wincing as he moved it to his lap. "After Tinkerbell, nothing's gonna hurt today."

"Hey? I'm sorry about that."

"Don't be." Duggan was flipping pages now. "She was right - I had it coming. Shoulda kept my mouth shut."

Powell turned to the window. The garden below was already shaded but the leaves at the top of the maple still glowed red in the afternoon sun. From the avenue a half block away, city noise screeched and honked and rumbled, one sound really, that rose and fell with the time of day like a tide.

"Ellen said something about someone else having called."

Duggan, still searching the book, did not look up.

"And your message-"

"JESUS H. CHRIST!" Duggan looked up and leaned forward, the chair tipping crazily forward as he did. "He's here. Case is here."

"Let's see." Powell crossed the room and followed Duggan's finger down the page. Seymour Case was there. East Canal Street. Between Case, Samuel and Case Shag Rug Rake Co.

"I'll be damned."

"You probably will be." Duggan was smiling wide. "You gonna call him, Mick?"

Without thinking, Powell had put his right hand on the phone. Now he lifted it and clasped his left hand around it.

"Better not. Might scare him off. And Hernandez'll have this soon." He laughed. "Following your kind advice."

Powell handed the phone to Duggan.

"Call Ellen," he said. "Tell her you'll be needing her tender mercies."

"What are you going to do?"

"Me? I think I'll take a walk."

Duggan put the phone down. "Where to?"

"Where else? To Oz."

Jimmy looked down at the phone book and said nothing. He doesn't like it, Powell thought. Knows where I'm going and doesn't like it. Which was smart, at least. The room still smelled of Duggan's Old Spice but beneath it was another scent, sweet and lemony. Maria Hernandez. Detective and ballkicker and? Woman. Not good. Not good to have that mixed in here.

"Mickey, stay out of it."

"I'm already in it."

"Let me come with you."

"This isn't your scene, Jim. And you've got a license to worry about."

Duggan considered this for a moment, then grinned and said, "You're right."

At the door, Jimmy stopped and turned back. "Can I give you some advice?"

"What?"

The goofy grin again. "Follow the yellow brick road."

Chapter 7

THE ANGEL

SOMEONE KNEW. THAT WAS THE ABOMINATION. THE ANGEL SAT STILL IN HIS SEAT, LEGS CROSSED AT THE KNEES BENEATH THE FLOWING ROBE, ELBOWS ON THE CHAIR'S WOODEN ARMS, HANDS FOLDED BENEATH HIS CHIN, STARING OUT THE NARROW WINDOW INTO THE GARDEN. IT WAS FORBIDDEN BUT SOMEONE KNEW. IT WAS NOT GIVEN TO THEM TO EAT THE FRUIT OF THE TREE OF THE KNOWLEDGE OF GOOD AND EVIL. BUT SOMEONE HAD. THE ANGEL WATCHED THE GARDEN AND CONSIDERED THIS.

THERE WOULD HAVE TO BE EXPIATION; THAT MUCH WAS CLEAR. THERE WOULD HAVE TO BE A SACRIFICE. BUT HOW WOULD THIS COME TO PASS? THERE WAS NO KNIFE NOW AND IT WOULD NOT BE EASY TO GET THE LAMBS TO THE KILLING WALL. THE ANGEL SAT QUIETLY AND LISTENED. THERE WAS NO MESSAGE, NO SOUND EXCEPT THE TICKING OF THE CLOCK ON THE LOW BOOKCASE.

BUT PERHAPS THAT WAS THE MESSAGE. THE ANGEL STIRRED IN HIS CHAIR, SETTLED BOTH FEET ON THE FLOOR, AND LISTENED INTENTLY TO EACH FAINT STACCATO TICK OF THE SECOND HAND MOVING RELENTLESSLY ON TO ITS BEGINNING. TIME WAS THE LORD'S. "AND THEY SHALL BE GIVEN INTO HIS HANDS FOR A TIME, TWO TIMES, AND HALF

A TIME."

THE TIME WOULD COME. THE LAMBS HAD NOT YET BEEN PROVIDED FOR HIM BUT THAT WAS AS IT SHOULD BE. AS WITH ABRAHAM, SO IT WOULD BE HERE. HE WOULD LOOK TO THE THICKET AND FIND THEM CAUGHT BY THEIR HORNS. HAD NOT THEIR NAMES ALREADY BEEN REVEALED?

POWELL AND CASE. POWELL, THE PHONY SHAMAN WITH HIS PIOUS, BEGUILING CLAPTRAP. AND WHO WAS CASE? THAT WAS YET TO BE UNVEILED; NOW HE WAS JUST A NAME. SEYMOUR CASE. BUT HE HAD NOT REMEMBERED WHO POWELL WAS UNTIL THE WOMAN HAD TOLD HIM. THE ANGEL STOOD AND WATCHED THE LEAVES FALLING IN THE GARDEN.

Chapter 8

FRIDAY - 4:36 p.m.

Seymour Case was a bookseller. He lived and worked in a tiny apartment on a block on the Lower East Side that had been overrun by Chinatown, two flights up from a storefront vegetable and seafood vendor. The building reeked of fish. He was a Conservative Jew, went to temple on Fifth Avenue, dealt mostly in Judaica, with a small sideline in Yiddish literature. He was short, white-haired, and plump. Wore half glasses for reading that he pushed up on his forehead when speaking. Was about eighty, maybe a little younger. Had a blue number tattooed on his left forearm. Showed no sign of recognizing Powell and did not believe he had ever heard of James Wolfson, though it was possible that he'd sold him something; the Christian scholars sometimes came to him.

All this was after Powell had intercepted Hernandez. Which was more a matter of coincidence than of intent, but probably for the better just the same. Coming up the steps out of the subway piss-musk to the street, he had seen a big dark blue Ford sliding from lane to lane in the thickening afternoon traffic. Without thinking, he'd broken into a trot on the sidewalk, dodging pedestrians and vendors and setting off a cacophony of horns at intersections.

The car had double-parked in the second block over from the subway. Just as Powell caught up, Hernandez had stepped out and headed for a grimy glass door next to a fish stall, tubs of eels and buckets of crabs jammed next to boxes of ice from which grotesque glassy eyes peered up.

"Hernandez!"

The detective's expression had slid hard from mild bemusement and turned to a hot glare as she'd seen him. She'd stood stiffly next to a crate of turtles while he had approached. Had said nothing.

"I think we're going to the same place, Detective."

No loosening. "And where do you think that is? Father."

Easy here, Powell had thought. No way to win. Just try not to lose too much. "I'm going to see if Mr. Case is home." He tried a smile. "What are you up to? Looking for lemon sole?"

"Not a bad idea. I like sole." No smile, but no snap either. "What makes you think Case'll be here?"

Powell had shrugged then. "I didn't call if that's what you mean. I did look him up, though. Jimmy had a good idea, no?"

"He needs to learn to watch his mouth."

"True."

One of the turtles in the crate had made a strange leap up against its wooden side as though trying to join the conversation. They had both turned to look down at it.

"Must be one of the good guys. Donatello, maybe?"

Hernandez had grinned at his reference to the Teenage Mutant Ninja Turtles and then said, "Look, you're not going up with me. Got that?"

"If that's the way you want it. But it means I'll be going up by myself later."

While Hernandez had considered this, the turtle had fallen to the bottom of the crate, landing on its back and waving its clawed toes helplessly. Grabbing the door handle, Hernandez had said something that sounded like `come on.'

Seymour Case had admitted them without question, had offered them tea, a smoky lapsang souchang which Powell had accepted and Hernandez had declined, had answered all of the detective's questions in a gentle, almost sweet voice, had asked only one just as they stood to go.

"This Mr. Wolfson, he is dead now?"

"Yes, Mr. Case, that's correct." Hernandez's voice had made a soft pair with his.

Case had nodded. "I will pray the Kaddish for him."

Hernandez had been puzzled but Powell knew. "That's very kind of you."

Then a tender smile. "It isn't really for the dead, you know. It's for the living. Mr. Wolfson is free."

Mr. Wolfson is free. Now, in the closeness of the hall, Powell wondered what that meant. It was, he knew, what he ought to believe. But not easy. Not easy to see having your throat cut as a kind of liberation. The warm fish stink rising from the street door brought with it another time, the scent of another place. The room again. The rich, hot smell of blood and the sickening sweetness of dead meat, the knife stuck in the table top and the grinning face above the green uniform.

Powell stumbled. The heat and smell and memory had dizzied him, and his buckling legs pitched him forward into a gathering fog, sending him down past Hernandez towards the stairs. The end of the stair rail came at him like a rocket and he caught at it desperately, hoping that it could pull him up out of the now black clouds, up to the sky. And then it was dark.

When he came to, Powell was sitting half way down the steps, his back against the wall. Hernandez's right arm was under his left, propping him up, and her left hand clutched his left lapel. Her eyes were not a foot away from his, her lips were parted slightly and her teeth were clenched.

"Hey, Powell," she said. "No elevator in this building."

He shook his head to clear it. "Are you sure? Something was going down fast."

"Think you can walk?"

"Maybe. Yeah, maybe."

With his right hand, Powell reached for the railing just over his head. Grabbing it, he pulled and Hernandez boosted him up, pushing him against the wall and holding him there, leaning into him with her left shoulder, the lemon scent of her dark hair blossoming in his face.

"Break anything?"

"Don't think so." Powell felt a thickening knot growing on the left side of his head and there was a ripple of hurt that started in his right shoulder and moved diagonally down across his back. No sharp pain, though, and his arms and legs seemed willing to function.

Hernandez backed off a bit, still keeping a firm grip on his left arm. "You do that often?"

"Never that I can think of." Powell shook his head. "Aftershock of a concussion, maybe."

"You think that'll make me feel guilty, Father?" She was smiling. "'Cause it doesn't. I feel just fine."

"So I see." She did look fine. And Powell knew that he did not want her to slide into the blue PD Ford to leave. "You'd probably feel even better if you bought me a cup of coffee."

"Why?" Eyebrows up, full lips holding the smile.

"Because you're still a good little Catholic girl. Don't let the Padre go without asking for his blessing."

She laughed. "You're fulla shit, Father. You know that?"

"Of course I do. That's what we learn in seminary."

"Okay, I'll buy. Since you admitted it."

Canal Street did not present immediate prospects for coffee. The stalls of the Chinese marketplace tripped over one another on both sides of the street without end. Further down, though, above a pagoda-shaped phone booth, a red sign with yellow arches projected over the confusion of the side-walk.

"Mickey D's?" Hernandez asked.

"That's not coffee. Some kind of petroleum derivative, I think." Powell told himself not to go too far. "I know a place up on Mulberry. Five-minute walk. Great cappuccino."

"You couldn't walk across the hall just now." Her expression was flat as a communion wafer. Then a grin, a slight upturn of lips and a quick sparkle of teeth behind them. "Get in the car, Padre."

Hernandez pulled into the traffic without looking, hung a tight U-turn, caught the light at Mott and turned right on Mulberry a full second into the red.

"They teach you to drive like that at the police academy?"

"Nope." Another brief grin. "I learned that in Puerto Rico."

On Mulberry, Hernandez grabbed the radio mike off the dash and logged into the dispatcher, told her she was finished with Case. Going to go looking for Powell again.

Powell wondered what she was thinking. No way of telling. Wondering why it mattered, Powell could only conclude that it did. He said, "You won't have to look far."

"She doesn't know that."

"Here's the spot."

The bakery was on a quiet corner, catty-corner from a cement park with green benches and a high black iron fence and a pocket playground on one side. Hernandez parked at a fire hydrant on the right side of the street. Crossing to the shop, Powell felt the autumn sun warming his backache. A sweet pungent city smell of wet leaves and garbage and dog shit, tinged by the lemon flavor of Hernandez's perfume, rose like a hand to grab at him. Happy, Powell thought. Doesn't take much.

"What's it gonna be, Padre?"

"Cappuccino. Easy on the cinnamon."

Inside were a counter, a refrigerator case, and three small round wooden tables with wrought iron chairs. A door open to the back room framed steel worktables and mixers and ovens, all dusted with flour. Powell eased himself into a chair at the table closest to the front door. In the park across the street, old women, bundled as if against a blizzard, were feeding pigeons from the benches. Young women pushed toddlers on the playground swings, and the sounds were childish squeals and crying and shouts and laughter. Hernandez joined him at the table.

"We've got two cappuccinos working."

She sat and watched the street and said nothing. Powell thought there was a sadness about her just then, something wistful about her dark eyes, something held back behind them.

"You okay?"

"Hmm?" She turned and remembered he was there and stiffened. "Yeah. Fine. Why?"

"No reason," Powell said. "Just wondered."

A short, dark-haired woman as round as a bocce ball brought two foam-topped, dripping mugs to the table, said to Powell, "Your sister?"

"No, mama. My girlfriend." Powell smiling and the woman smiling wider; Hernandez grinning a bit as well.

"Ah, Father. You break my heart." She left a green sales slip next to Powell's left elbow.

"Ahh." Powell raised his mug. "Bon giorno."

"What's that?"

"Italian. Good day."

The cappuccino was wonderful. Heavy coffee scent, a perfect passing whiff of cinnamon, the sharp taste softened by the milk foam. Setting his mug down, Powell wondered why Hernandez had come. Wanting to believe that it was him. Knowing it wasn't. She wants to find something out, he thought. And I do, too. A good time to try? He watched her lick a trace of milk foam off her upper lip. Good enough.

"Hey, Detective." She turned to him and half smiled. "Can I ask you a business question?"

The half smile disappeared. "Sure. Why not? As long as it's not, `what's a nice girl like you doing in a job like this?'"

"It's not. But that's a good question, too."

Hernandez stared at him and waited. Bad start. Nothing to do now, though, but go ahead. Powell took another swallow of cappuccino and set the mug back down on its wet ring.

"Am I still public suspect number one in this Wolfson thing?"

No answer for a long moment. Then a kind of softening around the mouth, a sort of lip shrug, then tight again and a glance out the door towards the park.

"The book says yes. Possible motive, possible means, on the scene. That's usually the perp."

"Perp?"

"Perpetrator."

Powell nodded. "That's what the book says. What do you say?"

Hernandez tipped her head and looked him over. Her left hand absently pushed a long strand of dark hair off her cheek. "I don't know yet. But I don't think so."

"Why not?"

"Case didn't know you. Even if you set that up, he couldn't have done it so well."

"That's not the reason." Not a good idea to push, Powell knew, but what was the alternative? "If you really thought it was me, you'd never've let me go up there with you."

"That's true, Father, I wouldn't've." Hernandez picked up her mug and took a long drink, held it in two hands for a moment, set it down without letting it go, picked it up and sipped again, put it down. "I called the 10th Precinct after I left you. To check on that pimp you killed."

"And?"

"And I found out that he had stabbed you."

That was what had happened, Powell knew, but it wasn't how he remembered it. He remembered the girl, almost naked, and the blood on her mouth and the angry red welts across her back. And his own rage.

"So what about it?"

"So if you were trying to get out of something, you would have told me that."

"Yeah." Powell looked away, across the street to where a young man was just sitting down with a wine bottle. "I guess I would have."

"Now it's my turn." Something in her voice. Official, but not quite. Something else in the tone, too.

"Okay."

"What were you doing there?"

"Where? At the seminary? I've al-"

"With the hooker." Some urgency in her words, something important about the question.

"It's hard to explain."

"Try me."

"Okay." Difficult to say it, the words never sounded right, even to him. Powell looked away from her, into the kitchen, then at the street, finally resting a long look on the grain of the wooden tabletop.

"I used to see these women, these girls really, and I thought that they'd about hit bottom. And I thought I'd see if I could bring God to them."

Hernandez was staring at him but she didn't say anything. There was a voice, though. From somewhere else. Saying, `tell the rest.'

"And you know what I found out?"

No answer. But something in the depths of her dark brown eyes. Answer enough.

"I found out that God was already there. They didn't need me for that. God was there. Waiting for me."

Chapter 9

FRIDAY - 5:45 p.m.

When she offered him a lift, he'd been quick to accept. Not, he knew, that he was in any hurry. Just that he wanted to be with her. Not surprising. A younger woman, pretty and well put together - the stuff of the dreams of forty-one-year-old men. Even priests could dream. But was there something more, some reciprocation? Powell told himself there was. And wanted to believe it.

"Where to? 16th Street?" The car was stuck on Mulberry behind a huge green garbage truck. On Powell's side, a stone church rose behind a black, wrought iron fence. Old St. Patrick's.

"What? Um, no." Nothing to go back for now except the stares of the other priests around the dinner table. Word would have gotten out. "How 'bout the Village?"

"Ah, let me guess." Was she smiling? "Duggan's, right?"

"Why, Detective Hernandez, what an accusation." It was a smile, a lovely grin that lit her face impishly. "Why would a man of the cloth be going to a hellhole like that?"

"A good question, Father. Why would he?"

"To save sinners?"

Hernandez laughed. In the churchyard an old woman in a bright green coat tottered around the gravestones, dropping flowers here and there among their shadows on the grass.

"No sale, Father. With all due respect."

"No sale? Well, keep in mind that salvation comes in many forms." The garbage truck lurched forward, braked, and lurched again, its twin stacks eructing black clouds of diesel smoke which hung over it for a moment and then dissipated in the city air. "The particular manifestation I have in mind is a cheeseburger on Jimmy's menu."

"A cheeseburger?" Hernandez wheeled the car left on Houston and accelerated.

"With bacon and grilled onions and a side of fries."

"Jesus! Think it has enough cholesterol?"

"Ah, Detective. The mortification of the flesh has long been known among the fraternity of ascetical theologians."

"The mort - what?" Eyes on the road but still smiling.

"The mortification of the flesh. Punishing the body to liberate the soul. Fasting. Whipping."

"People do that?"

"People do." And it works, Powell thought but did not say. The room again, and the heat, and the hunger like a dull knife, and fainting thirst. And the Voice.

"Powell? Hey, Padre?" The car was stopped behind a battered yellow Checker at a stoplight at the corner of Houston and Broadway; Hernandez's face wore a look of something like concern.

"Mmmm? It's okay. Mind just wandered." The light changed and the Checker took off like a rocket, riddled muffler blasting with an explosive roar. "I was gonna say that this burger is so bad for you that it's just like self-flagellation. Only better."

"If you say so." A smile again, but not so true. "Where is this place anyway?"

"Barrow Street. Corner of Greenwich."

"Greenwich and Barrow? They don't intersect."

"Greenwich Street. Not the Avenue."

Now they were moving again. Gas station, office loft, movie center, high rises, and a long row of shops; deli, pizza, drugstore, antiques, hair salon, stationery, arts supplies, deli again. And people everywhere, black, shades of brown, Asian, pinkish Caucasians, green haired kids, and blue haired matrons. People, Powell thought; people were the best part of New York. Always people everywhere, moving fast, moving slow, just standing around.

And some of them were killers. Two or three times a day, someone pulled a trigger or jerked a blade or tightened a grip around a windpipe and left a piece of warm, stiffening meat where a life had been. Powell thought of Wolfson with his odd formal air and stiff manner of speech, thought of blood welling from his throat and of the bubbling struggle for breath and words and then the final fall and the stillness. Peace of a kind. Peace which passes human understanding.

"Hey, Powell?" They were at Sixth now, caught at a light again. Hernandez's sunny smile had faded and some more serious star had dawned.

"Yeah."

"What was Duggan talking about with that not wanting cops listening to what he was saying?"

Powell hesitated. Was something telling him not to trust her? "You didn't call that in to your computer?"

"I did. Nothing came up. Now I'm asking you."

"He's a friend, Maria. He's not in this. Not the kind of guy."

The light changed. Hernandez frowned, checked her mirrors, and eased the car through the intersection. She spoke without looking at him.

"I'm gonna find out. Whether he's your friend or not, you gotta know that. If surveillance was going on at Duggan's place, I'm gonna know about it. I don't know what kind of a guy he is. But I want to find out what he was talking about. And I'm going to."

And what would she find? Powell knew that Jimmy was clean but he'd never been sure what had really been happening at the bar. Hernandez was right, though. She would find out.

Somewhere there was a file and before long it'd be on her desk.

"Okay, I'll tell you what I know."

She glanced at him and then back at the traffic, slowing slightly and steering to the right.

"Which isn't much," Powell said.

Hernandez eased the car to the curb at a hydrant. Shifting to park, she turned towards Powell and rested her left forearm on the steering wheel.

"Tell me."

"To put it simply, it was I.R.A."

"It was what?"

"I.R.A. Not retirement accounts. Irish Republican Army."

Hernandez said nothing. Her dark eyebrows arched sharply and her lips, slightly open, pursed shut in a thin line.

"Jimmy's Irish. Both parents were first generation. He gets into the old sod stuff. You know, St. Patrick's Day and all that." Powell paused and let a silence build for a moment

and then went on. "Anyway, someone thought that Jimmy's place might have something to do with funneling money and guns to the I.R.A. The phone was tapped, and the pay phone, too, and finally there was a raid. Feds - B.A.T.F. or something - and N.Y.P.D."

"And then what?"

"And then nothing. No indictments, everyone released, all the records returned. Nothing happened except that Jimmy's got a serious hard-on about police. As you could see."

"Was there anything to it?"

"I just told you that nothing happened."

"But that wasn't what I asked. Father." Big winning smile. Definitely the good cop side of the good cop/bad cop routine. Definitely alluring.

"Has anyone ever told you that you're dangerous?"

"I'm not."

"You certainly are. And to answer your question, I don't know if there was anything to it. Jimmy's not into it, I can tell you that. Too practical. But some of his patrons strike me as romantic types - if someone passed the hat, they mighta kicked in."

"What about guns?"

"In the place? No way. Was someone buying? Those guys get guns from somewhere."

Hernandez looked away for a moment, first through the windshield, then to the side mirror, then back at Powell.

"Thanks," she said, shifting into drive and pulling away from the curb without looking.

"My turn for a question?"

She didn't look at him. "Sure. Shoot."

"What's it got to do with Wolfson? And how does Seymour Case fit in?"

"That's two questions."

"Figured I'd better take my swings while I had the chance."

Hernandez nodded. The car was bumping through a warehouse district now, close behind a dirty white sign with red letters that said, `Tango Paper Company.'

"I don't know if Case fits in at all. Woulda been better if he'd just sold Wolfson some book that only the two of them ever heard of."

"What about Wolfson and this I.R.A. sting?"

"You read the paper this morning?"

"I was in the hospital this morning. I asked for a Times with my croissant but they didn't bring it."

Without looking at him, Hernandez grinned. "Sorry. Forgot."

"Hey, no problem. I like rough women." Now a look. Smile wider, sparkle in the dark, dark eyes. "What about the paper?"

"Look at it when you get the chance. The Post, not the Times."

"What am I going to find?"

The truck stopped in the middle of a block. Hernandez whipped out around it and then snapped back in front of it, missing by inches a commuter van speeding the other way. Coming to the corner, she eased off the gas.

"This is Greenwich. Right here?"

"Yeah. And up a few blocks."

The landscape changed. Warehouses gave way to loft conversions and they gave way to brick row houses and occasional tenements. How the poor used to live, Powell mused. Now the poor were on the street and you needed at least a half mil to get into one of these places. And more than that to get an answer from a cop.

"Madame Chairman. There's a question on the floor."

Hernandez grinned again. "I know. And if I don't answer it, I won't have anything to deny. In case someone asks. Read the paper."

Duggan's was on a corner, next to an antique store and across Barrow from a shop that sold only wind-up toys. Winders On The World - dumb name, Powell thought, but you did remember it. Beyond it was a wholesale lamp company, a low, white brick building with no windows on the first floor. Hernandez pulled into a loading zone in front of it and shifted to park.

"Do me a favor?" she said.

"Sure. Whatta you have in mind?"

"Take me to dinner?"

Powell felt his gut double clutch. Not a good idea, he told himself. Because you want to too much. He said, "How come this never happened to me when I was twenty?"

"Because you were a nice middle-class college kid then. Probably hung out with a better class of people. No Ricans. No barmen, no cops. No stiffs."

She was right up front: she wanted to use him. And what did he want? Powell knew but did not want to admit it even to himself. It was there, though. Something real, almost tangible. Not just dinner and some conversation with a pretty woman. It was her.

"C'mon, Padre. I go myself, I never even see a waitress."

He wanted her. Her dark eyes were watching him expectantly and her lips, slightly parted, glistened. What was telling him not to? Just convention? The rules? Or something deeper down?

"He's a friend, Maria. I owe him."

"You said yourself that he's not in it. I just want to get a feel for the place."

"Isn't there another way?"

"Sure, there is." Hernandez smiled and swung her door open. "But we're here."

"Hey, I didn't say yes." But we're here. There was the voice - in the moment.

"You didn't say no either." She waited, watching again, and Powell laughed and shook

his head and pushed his own door open.

"You must've hit me hard. I gotta be crazy to even think about this."

It was early - Powell guessed a little after six - and Duggan's wasn't crowded. Three men and two women at the bar to the left, a pair of white-haired codgers in a booth across the divider to the right, two young men at a table between the piano and the door to the beer garden. A scene so familiar to him, it almost didn't register. Pausing just inside the door, he wondered what Hernandez was seeing. A saloon like a thousand others in New York, most likely. Tin ceiling, plank floor, polished wood and brass around the bar, jazz combo posters on the walls and the Kennedy brothers over the cash register, the smell of smoke and beer and food grease.

"Hey, Mickey!" Ellen was waving from the end of the bar. She was wearing a Spandex body suit, teal and pink, and a huge grey sweatshirt that slipped off her shoulder. Definitely good for business.

"Mick?" Jimmy popped out of the kitchen door. "C'mon in Sherlock. Who's your-"

Powell felt Hernandez brush past him lightly and followed as she crossed the room to where Duggan was tight-lipped and waiting.

"Sorry about this afternoon. I was out of line. You were, too." Hernandez stood close to Duggan and spoke in a husky whisper. Jimmy didn't answer but Powell could see his face soften. A sucker for a good-looking woman, he thought. Like me.

"I'd like to have dinner here with the good Father." She'd backed off half a step and raised her voice a bit. Across the bar Ellen was leaning forward and taking it all in. "Okay with you?"

"Why not? Grab a table." Duggan gestured towards a corner past the divider and the old men and the hat rack. No smile, though, Powell noted. No forgiving yet. Or forgetting. "Bring you something to drink?"

"Pint of Harp for me, Jim."

"I'll try that, too."

Hernandez led him towards the table but stopped short at the jukebox, forcing him to brush close behind her and steady himself on her shoulder to get by. Still the lemony smell of her hair and now under his hands the suggestion of firm curves and suppleness. A smile thrown at him over her shoulder acknowledged the touch. With approval? You wish, Father, Powell told himself. Probably more like nonchalance, really. He took a seat at the table, the chair furthest back, and watched her fumbling for coins in her shoulder bag, dark hair waving down around her face, her back arched slightly, calves tight. Bad, man. Got it bad this time. She punched the buttons and headed back to the table, drawing stares from both of the old men in the booth and from two of the three guys at the bar. The music came behind her, a mellow guitar riff, backed by drums and bass and a plaintive rough voice.

"Good box," Hernandez said.

Powell nodded. "Who's that? Springsteen?"

"Very good, Father. I'm impressed. Woulda picked you for a '70's classics guy."

"I'm old maybe. But not dead. What's the song?"

"Called `I'm On Fire.' Big when I was at the academy."

"Nice."

Ellen brought the ale, two tall glasses of gold with foam spilling over the rims. Setting them down, she said, "Been a long time, Mick. I miss you."

"Too long," Powell said. Hernandez was sipping her drink and watching him over the edge of the glass. "Give you a call sometime?"

Ellen shifted her weight and looked away, then back. "That a good idea?"

Powell laughed. "Nope. You know it's not. But then how many ideas are good anyway?"

"Eat shit and die, Father." Ellen was smiling now and Hernandez was showing a bit of grin as well.

"I'm eating here tonight, Ellen."

"S'what I said." She reached across the table, slapped him lightly on the cheek, then turned and walked back towards the bar, shaking her head and smiling still.

"You got a way with the girls?" Hernandez's head was tipped back slightly and her fingers were laced tightly around her glass except the two index fingers which were pointing at him, tips touching. Here's the church, here's the steeple.

"Maybe I'm safe after all."

"You're about as safe as a hand grenade. Try again."

"You're a girl. You tell me."

Hernandez arched her left eyebrow a millimeter and her lips pursed and twisted slightly. "Okay, I'll tell you. Like this: you hold something back. A lotta guys tell you everything they know, which ain't necessarily squat. Five minutes and it's all there, take it or leave it. But you don't say much. So there's something to wonder about."

"Spoken like a detective."

"Shit." A blush rose across her face, followed by a smile. "So is Ellen here a girlfriend or what?"

"A friend."

"C'mon, anyone can see there's more."

"Once there was. When I was still in seminary."

Powell took a long drink and tried not to remember. But the heavy ache just beneath his ribcage was the same now as it had been then. Who was it for? Ellen? No. Watching Hernandez, now lifting her glass, now tipping it at her lips, he knew. No voice to tell him. But the ache itself was an epiphany of a kind. Announcing what? No answer, not just yet.

" - a phone here?" Hernandez was saying. "I'd better check in."

His head was nodding on its own, as if on autopilot of some kind.

"Round the corner." His voice, but from where? "By the back door."

"Be right back."

She slid her chair back, stood, and turned away, and now a voice, a woman's voice, was singing something about a fast car. Ellen was busy behind the bar and Duggan wasn't in the picture. Probably in the kitchen, Powell thought. More people on stools now and another table, one by the window, was full. A third man had joined the codgers, a young guy, jeans, blue aviator shades and a leather jacket. Odd trio, the men as drab as sparrows in worn suits with narrow lapels and now this peacock with them, speaking in whispers, jabbing a finger at the man on his side of the booth.

"Gotta go." Hernandez back now, standing across the table, fumbling in her jacket for car keys.

"Something up?"

"Could be. Maybe a witness up at the seminary. And the Dean wants an update."

"Can't wait til after dinner?"

Hernandez shook her head, her dark hair brushing softly across her shoulders. And then she was gone and the fast car song went on and one of the old men in the booth, the one across from the young guy, was leaning and fooling with his ankle. Powell lifted his glass and took a long slug of lager and a sudden movement in the booth caught his eye. The man leaning down was reaching forward under the table. Powell saw his hand, and in it a pug-short pistol, slide along the peacock's denim leg and stop. The stubby barrel poked into the young man's crotch.

Chapter 10

SATURDAY - 3:40 a.m.

Lethe was dying. Her breathing was shallow and rapid and her whole body seemed to shake, to vibrate really, as if her skin itself was all that kept her soul from surging out of time into timelessness. The end, Powell knew, would come soon. Or the beginning. As she believed. As he had taught her. The last time - when was it? - the time he had found her shivering in graying sheets that she'd soaked with sweat and she had asked him if she was dying.

"Just like we all are," he remembered saying.

"What's gonna happen then?"

"Then you'll be free."

A smile had passed across her features then, lingering for just a moment on her lips and eyes, before the thing that held her tightened its grip and shook it loose.

"Free. How you know?"

"It's promised. God promised."

"Shit. What you know about God?"

"Met him. Met God."

"You're crazy, man."

"You're right, I am. And you're gonna be free. No more johns, Lethe. No more needles. No more streets. Free."

"I been bad."

"Me, too. All of us. That'll be washed away. Do it right now if you want me to."

"Do it."

And he had. Sent Tony, who was her husband or pimp or friend or brother, down the hall with a styrofoam coffee cup for some water. Dredged up from memory as much of the missal baptism service as he could remember. Renouncing Satan, renouncing all his works, turning to Jesus Christ, putting trust in his grace and love. Which had meant what to a dying whore?

Now, tonight, ten or twelve days later, he knew. It just meant waiting. Waiting to cross the thin divide between death, which her days had been, to life, something she had not seen. Just waiting. Accepting the water was accepting the wait and now the wait would be over. For her, anyway.

And him? For him the waiting went on but the Voice had spoken again. As the water had trickled through his fingers onto Lethe's feverish forehead, the voice had said again, "This is my beloved with whom I am well pleased." Now in peace he held her hand and waited, listening to the rattle of her breath and wondering about a dead man and a gun shoved up hard against another man's testicles.

At Jimmy's he had acted without thinking. When the pistol hand had disappeared up the young man's crotch, he had raised and arm and waved it and called to Duggan at the bar, " 'nother Harp, Brother James. And a round for my friends over there."

The old man, Pistol, had pulled back and glanced toward Powell, and the young guy in shades had bolted. At the beer taps behind the bar, Jimmy had watched the whole incident with wide-eyed wonder. Pistol had fumbled his piece back into its ankle holster and the other codger, a wiry coot in a shabby brown suit, stood and limped towards Powell, heavily favoring his left pin, stopping a foot or so from Powell's table.

"You called us friends, friend, but I'm wond'rin' if we've ever met."

"You looked friendly to me." Blue eyes, Powell had noted. Tinged red. Bad teeth, a toothpick planted in the corner of his mouth. Sandy reddish hair on the back of a thin, elegant hand. "I'm sorry your buddy couldn't stay."

"And we are, too." The voice was calm but the blue stare was cold as February. "As luck would have it, we'll not be stayin' either. But I'd like to know who I'm to thank for the offer."

"My name's Powell. Michael Powell."

"Well now, Michael Powell. I had a cousin by that very name in Belfast. He had the devil's own time with minding his own business."

And then the man had turned and limped away, pulling Pistol into his tow like a dinghy trailing behind a yacht. And now Duggan had reached the table, open-mouthed and wondering.

"What the hell was that all about?"

"Don't know really. But Sancho Panza had a gun. Pulled it under the table on the young stud. Who were they anyway?"

"Customers, that's who." Duggan's vocal temperature had been rising. "They come in here all the time."

"Jimmy, customers packing iron is trouble you don't need. You know their names?"

"Daffy." A sheepish note in Duggan's tone now. "The one who was talking to you is called Daffy. The other one has a sort of regular name. Jerry maybe. Don't know the young one. You sure 'bout the gun?"

"Sure." He had grinned then. "Sure as shootin'."

"Funny, Mick. Fuckin' funny as a crutch."

"I'm sorry, Aunt Em. How about a cheeseburger? Would that make you smile?"

"No - but your sawbuck will. 'Nother beer?"

"Why not?" Duggan had turned but Powell remembered calling after him. "Hey, Jim. You got a Post I could look at?"

"Certainly, Father," Duggan'd shouted, "Anything to facilitate your continuing enlightenment."

The beer had come first and had been half gone when Ellen had brought the burger and the paper. She'd set them down in front of him and had taken across the table, where Hernandez had been sitting.

"So who was your friend?"

"Maria? Not sure she's a friend. You might want to ask Jim about that. She's a cop."

"Cops and Jimmy don't mix, you know that." Which meant, Powell had realized, that Jimmy hadn't told her. "When'd'ya meet?"

"Last night. She belted me with a flashlight. Thought I might have killed someone."

"C'mon. Really?"

"Really."

The tease had gone off Ellen's face, no hint of a smile then but only an anxious blankness in her eyes and a trace of worry in the tightening of her lips.

"Is something going on, Mick? Something bad?"

And now Lethe was dying. Something bad? Who was to say? What Powell knew about her was that she was twenty three, born when her mother was fifteen, raised by her aunt, molested

by her step-uncle, on the streets when she was fifteen, herself, addicted at seventeen, turning tricks when she was a year older. What could be bad about leaving that? Twenty three, looked like forty three or older. No one with her except Tony and Jamahl, a black drunk with an attitude who'd come for him. And now even Tony was gone. Where?

"Roach Motel," Jamahl'd said when he had asked him earlier, on the walk over. Nothing else. Roach Motel. A cipher only their clan could decode. Lethe moaned and cried softly now without opening her eyes, and Powell thought about her name. Once he'd asked her what it meant, to see how much she knew about its fit.

"It's a river," she'd said. "My mom thought it was about the prettiest word she ever heard."

"Where's the river?"

"Don't know. Someplace beautiful. Africa maybe."

Someplace beautiful. Powell hoped that it was true. Lethe. River of Forgetfulness. Of oblivion. The one the Trojans drank from when they came again to the world to found Rome. What world, he wondered, waited for this Lethe? And what was it that troubled him now, not remembered but not forgotten, something about Wolfson that would not cross to the wakeful mind?

He didn't know enough about him to forget anything. Nothing about his personal life. A bit about his writings, particularly the sexuality stuff, and some of the Asian essays. Provocative, cutting edge kinds of things when they were first published but lots of folks had pushed past it now. Controversial for a time but even then, not the kinds of things anyone'd kill for. Gays could have holy relationships. Other peoples knew something about God. Well-argued and sometimes edgy in tone. But not dangerous even in the stuffiest Episcopal church.

The I.R.A. connection might be different, though. Ellen had brought the bar copy of the Post with his burger and ale, and the article had been easy to find. The front page was given to a subway shooting – GUNFIGHT AT K TRAIN CORRAL – but page two held the banner PRIEST CRUCIFIED. Few details, the police weren't talking, but a neighbor who'd phoned the precinct was quoted as having seen a naked body tied to the seminary's wrought iron fence, arms spread out in the shape of a cross. The end of the article sketched Wolfson's career, noting that he had participated in a disruption of the Saint Patrick's Day parade as a protest against the violence employed by the Irish Republican Army. A photo showed Wolfson being hustled out of a crowd by two short hairs, probably plain clothes cop types.

And something about it stuck with Powell now. He vaguely remembered the incident, one of a series of disruptions of the parade over the past several years. The handicapped had protested, gays had, pro-choice groups, English skinheads, almost always someone. Perhaps it wasn't so odd that Wolfson would be involved. Just the kind of peevish thing that someone with his officiousness might go for. But would anyone have been mad enough to kill him for it?

Not likely. Most churchmen in Ireland had condemned violence and they were all still standing. Ignored, Powell had reflected, but still there. Just like this side of the pond. Something else. There was something more about it that wasn't getting through the fog.

And then Lethe died. Simply died. No last words or final longing glance. Simply a soft squeeze of his fingers and then a loosening of her grip, a letting go, as if his hand was the last hurdle to jump. A stillness filled the space where her breath had been and there was an echo of the Voice. ~`In the world you will have tribulation, but be of good cheer; I have overcome the world.' Powell placed Lethe's hand at her side, pulled himself up from the room's single rickety chair and went out to the narrow hall.

Which was empty except for a sour smell and a lone low-watt bulb hanging from a cord. A single window in the facing wall reflected him dimly: a tall, haggard-looking man with thinning dark hair and blueblack circles under large oval eyes. Powell considered his image for a moment, shook his head, and wondered where Tony was. Or Jamahl. Someone who knew her should be there. Maybe downstairs.

It didn't take that long.

On the first landing of the dark staircase an arm shot out from the shadows, encircled his neck, and pulled him into darkness. A cold sharp point touched his throat just above the Adam's apple.

"Stay still."

The voice was a hiss but Powell knew who it was. The space they were in was cramped, a broom closet maybe, no room to move. The body behind him stunk of gin and sweat and piss.

"She gone?"

"She's gone, Jamahl. She won."

"Don't say my name!" The grip tightened and the blade flicked slightly through his skin, burning coldly. "What you say she won?"

"She's done losing. She won." Powell tried to speak evenly, to give the drunk something else to think about. He moved his right hand slowly up across his chest towards the fingers that held the knife. "She won - but you're still a loser."

"What you say, motherfuck - aaiiyahhh!"

Fingertips on the wrist, find the nerve, apply sharp pressure, that's what the manuals said. Sometimes it worked. The knife clattered to the wood floor. Powell pulled Jamahl out onto the landing, twirled him like a dancer and twisted his arm up tight behind him. A hard shove with his forearm and knee pushed Jamahl's face into the pocked plaster wall. Something cracked and the wino fell, first to his knees and then onto his side. He lay there groaning with his hands covering

his nose.

"It's broken, Jamahl. Probably stop bleeding in an hour. Hurt like hell for a month or so."

Jamahl said nothing. Stillness recaptured the landing like a pond's surface erasing the ripples where a stone had been thrown. Powell grabbed Jamahl's greasy lapels and pulled him upright, propping him against the wall.

"We need to talk, friend."

"Ain't your friend. Nothing to talk about."

"Talk anyway. Where's Tony?"

Jamahl's hands came down and he looked nervously around. For the knife, Powell knew. Somewhere behind them.

"Where's Tony?"

"Woman's dead. He can't fuck her no more. Why should I tell you shit?"

"Because if you don't," Powell felt the anger coming up like a great sickening wave, "I'm going to start breaking your ribs."

"Fuck you."

The full force of the short swing caught Jamahl just above the gut, taking both breath and bone and dropping him to his side again. When Powell pulled him up, the blood caked face had gone a shade paler.

"Where's Tony?"

"You a priest." Jamahl was breathing hard like a runner after a sprint. "Ain't supposed to do that shit."

"I'm a bad priest. Where's Tony?"

"Told you, man. Roach Motel."

"What's that? A flophouse?"

"No man, ain't you seen the ads? Roach Motel. Roaches check in but they don't check out."

Powell could picture a subway placard. Red and black. A little box. A bug with shriveled antennae. What did it have to do with Tony?

"Tell me about it."

"Don't know much. It's a guy gives good green for some head and a buttfuck. They say you go back, though, you don't check out."

"Who is it?"

"Shit, man. Anyone knew that they wouldn't go."

"Cops asking about it?"

Jamahl laughed then doubled up in a groan. "Cops don't care 'bout street shit like us."

True enough, Powell guessed. Just getting through the day was probably tough enough without pulling open the sewers.

"How do you know Tony went for that?"

"Don't know nothing. But he was tellin' me 'bout some john laid fifty on him for suckin' him off. Dude was wearin' a white dress. Said he needed the bucks to fix up Lethe, her hurtin' so bad. 'Bout a week ago maybe. Ain't seen him since."

Greater love than this, Powell thought, has no one. Even me. Especially me. Nothing to be done now. Except not to let it drop.

"Where's this guy supposed to be?"

"Don't know. Down 'round 23rd Street maybe."

No point in asking more. Jamahl was scared of Powell and scared of whatever happened to Tony and angry and scared about living in general. If he knew more, he wasn't going to say. Powell moved past him to the stairs and reached for his wallet. Sliding a ten out, he turned back to the hunched-up figure on the landing.

"Hey, man."

"Fuck you."

"Sorry about the rib." He held the bill out and watched as Jamahl's hand darted out to grab it like a frog's tongue snatching a fly. Time to go. Time to call the meat wagon for Lethe and get back to the rectory on 16th Street. Get some sleep. Maybe figure out what it was about Wolfson that bothered him. Maybe it would come to him in the morning.

"What about my fuckin' nose, man?" Jamahl called after him. "That's gonna cost something."

"Sure it is." Powell didn't look back. "But I'm not sorry about that."

Chapter 11

SATURDAY - 4:31 a.m.

They were waiting for him. The first car hadn't tipped him off, the one at the corner, but when Powell saw the second blue and white at the far end of the block, he'd known that something was up. Two buildings in from Sixth, he'd heard the footsteps behind him and at the brownstone before the rectory the gunman appeared. Big white guy, almost bald, leather jacket and jeans, badge in one hand and a gun as big as a mule's hind leg in the other, .357 probably, leveled at Powell's face.

"Hold it right there, Father."

Powell held it. The footsteps behind him held it, too.

"They want to talk to you at the station," Jacket-and-Jeans said.

"They need artillery like that to talk, son?"

The gun stayed up. "File says you're dangerous."

"What if I don't want to talk?"

"Then I'm s'posed to arrest you."

"For what?"

"Littering. Disorderly conduct. Don't matter."

If they want you, they get you, Powell thought. *Don't matter.* Same here as in any banana republic only here they weren't as paranoid. The piss-off feeling was rising, up from his gut towards his shoulders, tightening across his back. He said, "What's it about?"

"Don't know. Couldn't tell you if I did. What's it gonna be?"

"Can I tell you something?"

Jacket-and-Jeans tipped his head; there was a minute movement in his eyebrows. The gun stayed up. "Sure. What?"

"I like you. I know you're just doing your job."

Big sheepish grin. "Thanks, Father."

It was Jamahl again. And Manny. The white sanctuary and the colonel. No more violence, he'd said then. But that was then - and now the cold hands were reaching once more. Taking what wasn't theirs and making power the final arbiter. "Now lower the gun," Powell said, "Or I'm going to break your jaw."

The smile was gone instantly, and the voice grew a raspy edge. "Cuff him."

Footsteps again and hands grabbing his arms, pulling them back, cold metal at the wrists, a shove towards jacket-and-jeans. Powell kept his eyes on the gun.

Which eased down, still pointed but not extended. Now the cop was grinning again. Powell hopped on his left foot, kicked the right one out and whirled. His right heel caught Jacket-and-Jeans an inch and a half down and in front of his left ear and the big man dropped like a clotheslined halfback while Powell tumbled back towards the concrete. Now the blue suits were on top of him and a stick was under his chin again. As they dragged him towards a dirty white Chevy, the squad car from the end of the block was racing backwards towards them with its lights flashing. The Chevy's door opened and Powell went in hard face down on the seat. The upholstery smelled of tobacco and motor oil. The door slammed hard at his feet.

Dumb, Powell thought. Real dumb. No matter what it was about they had him now for as long as they wanted. But Lethe was dead and Tony was nowhere and what difference did it make? The Chevy's engine coughed and then caught and the car lurched into motion while Powell tried to swing himself into a sitting position. An arm reached over the front seat and shoved him down and his head banged lightly on the driver's side door. No point in struggling now. Should've figured that earlier. Lethe had. Powell thought of her hand in his and heard his own voice speaking to her. 'Met him. Met God.' How to meet God now? How to meet him on a dirty car seat after you've jammed your foot through another man's face? Not by looking. God was here but looking only turned up your own neuroses. Waiting. That's what it took – Lethe had showed him that. The car turned a corner and accelerated and the radio crackled out something but nobody acknowledged. And then another corner and another and Powell rocked on the seat and waited and felt for all the world like sadness owned him.

A final hard stop which rolled Powell off the seat and into the grit on the floor and evaporated all the sad, leaving a sour residue of scared and tired and mad.

The door swung open and hands grabbed his feet and then his belt and pulled. He came out kneeling, head bent down on the seat and knees on a curbstone. Right position, he mused. Strange temple. From somewhere to his right, screened by the open car door, a radio hissed and called out code numbers. Just behind him voices, words Powell could not make out, and then "this way" from someone and the hands again, four of them up on his biceps, lifting him back and away from the car. Freed from the seat now, the dawning light showed him brownstones and storefronts, cars angled in not parallel, cruisers and a cop van and two three-wheeled cop scooter things. 20th Street, he knew. 10th Precinct.

The hands - uniform cops he saw now - pulled him back towards a building but not into the station room he expected where a sergeant would be waiting behind a huge wooden counter and typewriters would be clattering somewhere and cops and riffraff would be coming and going, muttering and shouting. Powell guessed he'd been in the precinct a dozen times, maybe more, usually with a teary older woman come to see a son in the holding pen, a kid up on assault or robbery or petty drug charges. But never where he was now, at a doorway in the back of the stationhouse garage, in a narrow space between a closed grey door and a blue and white paddy wagon with its left front wheel off. The uniforms set him down as if they were delivering a rug for cleaning, brushed past on either side of him, and disappeared out the front of the garage.

"I'm going to take the cuffs off now."

The voice, a man's but in a high, almost squeaky register, was directly behind Powell. Glancing over his shoulder, he could see only the top of a balding head fringed with greying hair. A hand caught his left forearm and pulled his linked arms back again, this time almost gently. Something clicked and rattled and the hand let go and Powell's arms fell stiffly to his sides. He turned to face a short, muscular man with a red, round face, deep blue eyes and a dark mustache.

"I'm Kelsey," the high voice said. "You can kick me if you want to. Probably be better for both of us if you didn't."

Powell didn't answer. Outside, a car playing ten decibel rap music passed and faded off down the block.

"This door goes to a stairway. Third floor, take a right, second room on the left."

"This the new way in, is it?"

Kelsey opened the door and held it.

"I think the plan was to have no official record of your presence. In case rough stuff became necessary."

"Whose plan?"

Kelsey smiled. "God's."

The short man stepped into the dark stairwell and held the door.

"You comin'?"

"I have to?"

"More or less."

Kelsey followed him up the stairs, not close though, maybe a step or two behind. The space was fairly narrow, lit only by red EXIT signs at the landings, walls smooth stone of some kind. Powell thought of Sean Connery in some movie where he was a monk and a detective, a kind of Sherlock Holmes in a brown hood. Title was something to do with a flower but Powell couldn't bring it to mind.

No one was in the third floor hall. The room Kelsey had designated, take-a-right-second-on-the-left, seemed to be some kind of lounge. Scuffed wooden table with beat up, unmatched, wooden chairs, couch against one wall, no windows, coffee table covered with old papers and magazines, grimy notices on the walls. And in a grey-blue naugahyde lounge chair at the far end of the room, Maria Hernandez.

Who did not speak. Her dark eyes smoldered and her full lips were tightened into an angry line. She was wearing jeans, a grey Knicks sweat shirt, a shoulder holster and no make-up. Hair in a pony tail. Kelsey stepped into the room behind him, and pulled the door shut.

"Take a seat, Powell?"

A question, not an order. Powell pulled one of the chairs out and sat. Kelsey moved around the table and sat on the couch.

He said, "Detective Hernandez has a couple of questions for you."

"You two partners?"

"Nope. I'm just filling in. Her partner's down at St. Vincent's having his jaw wired shut."

Powell nodded. Kelsey was still smiling but his high voice didn't sound happy.

"Where were you last night, Powell?" If Kelsey's was unhappy,

Hernandez' was molten.

"When? And why?" Someone was dead. For anything less, they would have found some less elaborate way of doing things. And it wasn't Wolfson they were thinking of. He'd been stiff for forty eight hours and no one was so hacked off yesterday,

even Hernandez. Especially not Hernandez.

"Between 1:30 and 2:30. And I'll tell you why when you establish where you were."

Who was it? Powell froze for a moment. Duggan. It must be Jimmy. Who else?

"I was in a flophouse on 39th Street. Called the Station Hotel or something like that. Room on the second floor."

"What were you doing there?" Still hostile but a slight softening to the tone. Or maybe just wishful thinking on his part.

"Watching a woman die."

Kelsey leaned forward; Hernandez seemed to blink. She asked, "Who?"

"Woman named Lethe. Hooker. Probably an addict."

"Why?"

"Why what? Why was she a hooker?"

"Why were you there?

"Because someone needed to be."

Hernandez wasn't buying it. Her eyes were still as hot as coals. Not Duggan. She hadn't liked Duggan much. Someone though. Who? Kelsey pushed both arms back on the top of the couch, his face bland and only vaguely interested.

"Anyone see you?" Kelsey asked.

Powell shrugged. "Black guy named Jamahl came for me. A drunk and a druggie, possibly a pimp. Find him he might confirm it. Might not."

Kelsey smiled and shook his head. "Anyone else?"

"I called an ambulance. Probably around four. Guess there'd be some record but they didn't see me."

"Shit." Hernandez was leaning forward now, both arms on the table. "You coulda been anywhere."

"I could have been. But I wasn't." Who was it? A new chill seized Powell. Ellen. Had something happened to her?

"No one in the lobby saw you?" Kelsey seemed intrigued by something, something behind his questions.

"Could be but I doubt it. Not the kind of place that has a concierge." Looked like Kelsey liked the answer, knitting his brow and nodding as if something made a lot of sense. Powell turned to Hernandez who was apparently unmoved. "Your turn now. I told you where I was. Now tell me what it's about."

"I'm not telling you shit."

Don't go for it, Powell told himself, but too late. "That 'cause you're constipated," he heard his voice saying, "or just 'cause you don't know shit?"

She was out of her chair before he finished and her backhand cracked across his mouth while his own arms were just moving off the table. His head spun back and the salt taste of blood welled in his mouth but he caught her arms and pulled her towards him before she'd wound up for a second swing. The chair went over and both of them with it. Hitting the floor, she swung an elbow that caught the bridge of his nose and jolted loose his grip of her right hand. And then she had his hair and his head was swinging up and banging down to the floor and his left fist drove up hard into her midsection, sinking in just below her ribcage and she was falling back and away from him and Kelsey was standing over them pointing a square-looking .45 into his face. Third gun in two days.

"That's enough, kids." His high voice was almost squeaking and Powell saw that he was laughing as he shook his head. The door opened a crack and a man's head peered in.

"Nothing going on in here, Stan," Kelsey said. "In fact, there's no one even in here."

The door closed and the head disappeared. Just like the hospital, Powell thought. He swung his legs off the back of the toppled chair and used the table top to pull himself to his feet. Hernandez was on her hands and knees now, breathing fast and hard through her nose. The Knicks shirt had ridden up in the back, revealing the smooth brown skin of a narrow waist and a small, dark mole on the right just above the belt.

"You gonna puke, Maria?" Kelsey asked matter of factly, slipping the automatic back into his jacket and handing Powell a handkerchief, a white and grey designer job.

Hernandez shook her head and sat back on her heels for a moment before pushing herself erect in a motion as easy as a dancer's. No sign of heavy breathing now, Powell noted. Good shape. She stepped up to him, close, in his face, near enough to present him again with the lemony smell, this time tinged with an air of menace.

"Next time," she said, "it'll be different. Father."

"Enough, okay?" Kelsey said like a dad moving farther down towards the limits of patience. "We don't need a next time right now."

Powell turned and reached down to pick his chair up and Hernandez shouldered past him just as he straightened, moving him back a fraction and somehow pulling something inside him toward her. Next time different. He knew now that he wanted a different next time and knew that he shouldn't. And wouldn't. The lure of forbidden fruit was precisely that- it was forbidden.

" - try again," Kelsey was saying, "shall we?" He sat on the couch and crossed his legs and Powell saw that he was orchestrating the whole thing - maybe including the fight - and orchestrating well, pulling it off, setting both him and Hernandez up for something. Good at it, Powell thought. Good at what he does. And now he and Hernandez were sitting, too, and Kelsey was talking in a perfectly even voice like a doctor explaining inoperable cancer to a patient.

" - in her shoes for a minute if you can. She's got a body and she's got you. Not much to put the two together but that's what detection is about, right? Got a name, too. On her way to see the guy, she finds you going there. Interesting. You go together, right? Nothing happens. 'Cept maybe the detective starts to think you're not in it which I guess I would've, too. And then you part company and here's the good part: she gets a call about three o'clock this a.m. that her name's been iced."

"Case?"

Kelsey nodded. Hernandez's eyes still glittered hot. Powell thought of a white-haired man with reading glasses pushed up on his forehead and a blue number on his arm. For a moment there was no sound except a weird buzz from the room's fluorescent fixture overhead.

"You're in this business a while you see all kinds of shit." Kelsey's voice was soft now, still high-pitched but not squeaky. "You stay, you just accept that there wasn't nothing you could do about it. You accept it or you get out. Then one comes along you think maybe you could have prevented. Then you don't accept it and you don't get out. You get mad."

Had to be true, Powell thought. All the Lethes and Jamahls and Tonys and not a damned thing you could do. And the room again, the sweat beading on your forehead and the blood and still nothing but to watch. Why do You let it go on? But no answer. Never any answer.

" - why I sent Arnie for you," Kelsey was saying. "I send Maria, you're dead right now."

Powell looked at Hernandez for an instant, met her gaze, and saw that Kelsey might be right. Too much death for her. She was almost dead herself, now. Dead enough anyway for her to send someone along.

"It wouldn't have helped," he said simply. "It wasn't me."

"Fuck you, Father." Now she had something in her hand, something square in a plastic bag. "What about this?"

The bag hit the table about halfway between them and slid to within a six inches of Powell's seat. The square was a book of matches, brown with gold letters. From Duggan's. Powell looked at Hernandez's volcanic glare and then back at the bag and the matches and then over to Kelsey.

"Found at the scene. The murder weapon, you might say. Goddam strange coincidence, no?"

But something was taking shape. On the table behind Hernandez, the Post with the picture of the shot-up subway car was on top of the pile of papers and Powell saw it and saw himself in his office patting pockets and coming up dry and thought of the limping man at Jimmy's.

And said: "I know who did it now."

"Do you now?" Kelsey looked surprised. "Well, we think we do, too. If your prints turn up on that matchbook, you'll be going away for a long, long time."

"My prints *are* on there. Probably are, anyway."

Now even Hernandez looked jolted. Kelsey put both feet on the floor and leaned forward.

"And yours are, too, Maria."

"The fuck you tryin' to pull?" She was hot and boiling over but still in her seat. "I'm not the one without an alibi, amigo."

"You don't need one. But someone you know does."

"Okay, wiseass. Who?"

"Don't have a name. But I know it was a cop."

Chapter 12

THE ANGEL

NOW THE REST HAD BEEN REVEALED. WHO AND WHERE AND HOW. CASE HAD BECOME REAL, AN INFIDEL AMONG INFIDELS WHO HAD TO BE DESTROYED. THE WOMAN HAD DISCLOSED HIS WHEREABOUTS JUST AS SHE HAD ALSO NAMED HIS NAME. THE ANGEL PICTURED HIM AMONG HIS BOOKS, PICTURED THE FLASH, AS OF LIGHTENING, THE SMOKE CURLING OVER PAPER. "AND AT THE EAST HE PLACED THE ANGEL, AND THE FLAMING SWORD TURNED EVERY WAY."

STRANGE HE HAD NOT THOUGHT OF THIS BEFORE, WHEN THE WOMAN HAD PROVIDED THE FIRE. IT HAD BEEN THERE WITH HIM, AND HE, UNSEEING, HAD NOT HEEDED. PERHAPS THIS, TOO, WAS AS IT SHOULD BE. PERHAPS THE TIME HAD NOT BEEN RIGHT. REVELATION HAD ITS SEASON, AS DID SACRIFICE. "A TIME TO EVERY PURPOSE UNDER HEAVEN." AND NOW IT WAS ACCOMPLISHED.

AND WAS NOW THE TIME TO CONSIDER THE WOMAN. WAS HER PURPOSE NOW FULLFILLED? HE SAW HER AGAIN, SITTING BEFORE HIM, HER HAIR UNCOVERED, HER BREASTS, FULL AND DISGUSTING, JUTTING LIKE A SLUT'S. SHE WAS A MESSENGER, THOUGH. THROUGH HER CAME THE WORD. AND AT THE TIME APPOINTED THE WORD WOULD CONSUME HER. NOW HE IMAGINED HER END, IMAGINED UNCOVERING HER SHAME, BARING THE DEPRAVITY THAT

SHE HINTED AT AND STRIKING IT, STRIKING AGAIN AND AGAIN UNTIL THE PERVERSION WAS OBLITERATED. THE PICTURE OF IT EXCITED HIM, AND THE ANGEL COULD FEEL THE THRILL OF THE SPIRIT UPON HIMSELF. BUT THE TIME WAS NOT YET COME.

FIRST CASE. THE FIRE HAD COME DOWN. AND NOW POWELL. WHAT PENALTY WOULD BE REVEALED FOR HIM? THE ANGEL CROSSED THE ROOM, FROM THE CONFERENCE TABLE TO THE DESK, AND SAT IN THE HIGH-BACKED LEATHER CHAIR BEHIND IT. MIGHT NOT THE WOMAN HAVE ANOTHER MESSAGE ABOUT POWELL? THIS MUST BE WEIGHED. THE RIDER OF THE HORSE OF THE THIRD SEAL HAD IN HIS HAND A BALANCE. HER VOICE AND HIS DEATH WOULD HAVE TO BE WEIGHED.

Chapter 13

SATURDAY - 9:26 a.m.

Now Powell sat alone. The Post was on the table and there was a styrofoam cup holding just the residue of the vile coffee they'd sent up. The matches in the plastic bag, they'd taken with them. The room smelled like stale cigarettes and sweat, his own and others. Kelsey and Hernandez had been gone a while, a long while, and the space was quiet except for the buzzing light but Powell guessed there was someone, maybe one of them, maybe a blueshirt, leaning on the wall just outside the door.

Fatigue had overtaken him. The vigil with Lethe and the night in the hospital hadn't added up to much in the sleep column. The coffee sat sour in his stomach and his head was throbbing and most, maybe all, of his muscles were sore from scuffles they weren't used to any more. His mind was scrolling on a strictly random basis now, throwing together thoughts of God and images of Case and snatches of a Billie Holliday song and a memory of barfing once in the second grade, Mrs. Thiel's class, right on his desk.

He asked himself what that was doing there, but the question only made the scene more vivid. Math time. Mrs. Thiel with her big arthritic knuckles writing numbers on the green chalkboard, and his workbook open to a page with pictures of circus animals, and Karen Mitchell's long braided pigtails hanging down in front of him. If there are sixteen elephants in the tent and twelve of them leave, Mrs. Thiel is saying, how many are left? The room is suddenly hot and his much younger self is dizzy and Mrs. Thiel cannot see that he has raised his hand and he starts to stand and the vomit comes. His desk and workbook and one hand are covered, a snapshot that turns his stomach ninety degrees even now. But that isn't the worst part. The worst part is Karen, whose back and hair have been splattered. She is angry and crying and screaming something at him as Mrs. Thiel leads him from the room.

Karen has something to do with something but now God went by and Billie Holliday sang again, "Ain't nobody's business if I do." God was there, must have been there. Must have been in that second grade classroom and must be here. But here just the song, just that and a thought about Hernandez that streaked by too quickly to be identified. Sleep would help, Powell knew. Some sleep would slow down the parade of thoughts and images and help him get a grip on them. Not in the picture, though. The picture now was waiting and wondering, odd thoughts, and beneath them a chilling kind of fear that some killing thing was out there and that it somehow involved him. Him. The one who'd fled from violence and killing, from the demons, as he himself had thought of them.

First the pimp, a year ago. And now three times with cops. And Jamahl. And the old gunman at Jimmy's. And only a little way off, Wolfson hanging on a fence. And Case. The demons were close now.

But they could be found. If something was close, you could grab it before it grabbed you. And would they? Would they find it? Were they looking in the right place?

Kelsey apparently thought so. At least enough to check. Powell thought about the silence that had followed his assertion, "I know it was a cop," and then about Kelsey's response.

"Okay, your Eminence. Why?"

"Coupla reasons," Powell had said. Hernandez was still glowering but did not interrupt. "First, it's gotta be someone who knew you wanted to talk to Case. I knew it, but I know it wasn't me. Hernandez knew it but she knows it wasn't her. Duggan maybe knew it if he remembered but I'm guessing he was at his place 'til closing. Other than that, who coulda found out except someone on your team?"

"Unless Case really did know something," Kelsey had observed.

"No way. But what did Hernandez tell you? Was Case in it?"

She shook her head without speaking, lips still tight.

"You said a couple of reasons. What else?"

"Those matches. Maria took those off me at the seminary, the night before last. You run the prints, you'll find that out."

"The hell you talking about?" Hernandez had found her voice now, angry but unsure.

"The hospital. You knew who I was by the cleaning ticket. I have that now. Asked you if I was carrying anything, else you checked your notebook, told me matches, and described them. Didn't give them back. When you came to my office I was fumbling around for a match."

"That right?" Kelsey speaking now, his high voice mild but insistent.

"Could be." Hernandez had puzzled it over, brow knit, even white teeth working over her lower lip. "Sounds about right. But a place like that probably gives out a thousand books of matches in a week. He coulda got them another time."

"I could have. But then you'd still have the ones you took, somewhere. And if I could have, so could a lot of other folks. You, for one. And Wolfson. Jimmy says he was fairly regular."

That got both of them. Hernandez had looked over to Kelsey, who had met her glance and twisted his jaw thoughtfully, and then turned back to Powell.

"And let me show you someone else who could have," Powell had said. Their eyes had followed him around the table to the stack of newspapers. He'd put the Post on the table between them, Kelsey up on his feet no and leaning forward to see. The picture was the shot of Wolfson, hands behind his back, being hustled out of a crowd at the St. Patrick's Day parade.

"See that guy, the plainclothes guy on his right? He was at Duggan's last night, came in when you were on the phone. Talking to a couple of guys, one of them Irish."

Kelsey's voice, squeaking now, "You sure?"

"Very. They were an odd mix, and the conversation wasn't friendly."

"What's that mean?"

Hernandez had asked this question evenly, a pro again, dispassionately collecting data. Only the facts, Powell remembered thinking. He had described the incident, the ankle holster, the stubby gun and where it went, his intrusion and its aftermath. As he finished, Kelsey and Hernandez were looking at each other and not at the paper. They knew something. Something they weren't likely to tell him, he knew. So, what the hell - take the long shot.

"You didn't turn anything up, did you, Detective?"

She hadn't replied but her face said he was right. Best to get it right out on the table.

"You tried again and still couldn't turn up anything about an investigation at Duggan's."

Silence for a long moment, then Kelsey's squeaky alto breaking it up. "What'd that guy say to you, Powell? Something about trouble minding your own business?"

"Which may be true, I guess," he had replied, "but when people hit my cranium with dull objects and point guns at me and tell me I'm going away for a long time, then that's my business."

Kelsey had straightened and stepped back, glaring. Hernandez, still seated between them, had not quite believed it. Her dark eyebrows had gone up an inch at least and her lips had parted. She had glanced at Powell and then turned towards Kelsey. Who smiled. The tightness around the clear blue eyes had crinkled and his mouth had pushed the mustache up.

"Guess that's right," he had said, "when you put it like that."

Hernandez had not liked it, Powell recalled. Her mouth had gone taut and her brow furrowed into chasms. Had said nothing, though. Kelsey had ignored her and gone on squeaking.

"If you'll excuse us, Monsignor, it appears that Ms. Hernandez and I have some checking to do." His hand had swept past her face and gestured, like a maitre'd's, towards the door. Then in a quieter, harder tone: "Stay put."

And Powell had. Staring at the dingy walls, leafing through the Post without seeing any of it, drinking the bitter coffee when the stone silent uniform had brought it in, trying to nap on the decrepit couch, failing, finally wondering what God meant by all this.

God was there, he knew that. Somewhere. Some strand tied it all together: Wolfson crucified, and his aching head, and Duggan's saloon, and the whitewashed room in the tropics, and, Karen Mitchell, and Mrs. Thiel, and Seymour Case, and Lethe, and Jamahl, and Maria Hernandez. Something there. But no answer now. No voice.

And then they were back.

Kelsey came in first like a doctor briskly entering an examination room, carrying an inkpad and a white fingerprint card, Hernandez behind him still looking tense but different, alert but not angry.

"Okay, Powell, time to get on with it." He sat on the edge of the table, set the card next to Powell's chair, pulled the cover off the inkpad and set it down, too.

"Get on with what?"

"At the moment, with your prints. We need 'em."

"And if I say no?"

"I bust you for assault and battery. On Arnie. Which I don't want to do."

"I'd make bail."

"And before you did, I'd have your prints. Anyway, the Army's got 'em, right?"

Powell laughed. "Good luck with the Army. But it sounds like checkmate."

"It is." Kelsey was smiling. "You play chess?"

"Some."

"Ranked?"

"Sure. Advanced mediocre."

A chuckle. "Me, too. Have to play sometime."

Kelsey lifted Powell's fingers one at a time, pressed them onto the inkpad and then onto the card, rolling each slightly to flatten out the print.

"Shit." A chuckled squeak. Powell's hands, fingers inked, were palm up on the table.

"Forgot the towel."

Hernandez liked the joke, smiled widely. Funny little cop gag, Powell thought. Probably did it all the time. Got to watch some young punk or old tough guy squirm and curse and rail. He felt the temptation to grab Kelsey's denimed leg, rub ink all over it quickly. But didn't. Not the way.

"No problem." Powell lifted his blackened hands and looked them over carefully, then began wiping them deliberately on the front of his shirt, a powder blue striped polo from Sears or someplace like that over at a Jersey mall. Neither detective was smiling now; both were staring, Kelsey's mouth lost in his mustache, Hernandez gnawing at her lower lip.

"There. Now what?"

Kelsey shook his head. "You're a crazy sumbitch, Powell. You know that?"

"Depends what you mean by crazy." His grin pulled a faint smile from Kelsey. "Now, where are we?"

No response. Kelsey hefted himself up from the table, took a step towards the door and turned. Bad news, Powell thought. Body language says bad news. Establish some distance. But Kelsey opened up his stance, lifted a foot to a chair, rested his hands on his hips. Mixed message.

"Where we are is the book says you're still suspect numero uno. Presence, yes; means, yes; motive, unknown."

"You believe the book?" Standing on the far side of the table, Hernandez was impassive.

"Nope."

"You believe me?"

"Maybe."

"Why?"

"Dunno." Kelsey ran his right hand over his bald pate. "What we can check, checks out. Not that it proves anything. Ambulance call. Dead woman. Don't mean much. But the guy in the picture, guy named Zang, he WAS at Duggan's last night."

"How do you know?"

"He's a looey now. Bumped up a few months ago apparently. He's on duty, he's gotta tell someone where he's going. Last night it was your buddy's place."

"How'd you find that out?"

"Lucky shot. Called his unit. Said we had a message for him here last night; asked was he supposed to be by."

"Why lucky?"

"He might not've been on duty. And they probably shouldn't't've told me, anyhow."

Hernandez was standing with arms crossed in front of her, face still blank and untelling. Kelsey dropped his foot to the floor and slid his hands into the pockets of his jeans. "All of that is interesting but it doesn't add up to much. But there's one more thing."

"What's that?"

"Credo quia absurdum."

Powell smiled. "`I believe it because it is absurd.' Where'd you hear that?"

"Fordham. Philosophy of Religions. Old Father Morton. He woulda been a good dick."

"I had him in seminary. Died a couple of years ago." A white-haired man always in black clericals, Powell recalled, with a good sense of humor and a love of learning a mile wide and just as deep. "What's absurd about this Zang anyway?"

"Nothing. It's you." Kelsey rocked back on his heels. Hernandez was leaning on the table now, watching him, interested, still solemn. "Your whole shtick is absurd. At one murder and you're praying. Not at another one and you're watching a hooker check out. She dies, and THEN you call an ambulance. Doesn't make sense."

"So you believe it?"

"Don't know. Could be true, though."

"What about you, Detective?"

Hernandez turned his way. Looked at him as if he were an object, not a person. Shrugged.

"She's burnt," Kelsey said. "She-"

"Shut the fuck up, Kelsey!" Hernandez was on her feet and squared towards him across the table. "I wanna tell him how I feel, I'll tell him!"

Kelsey looked down, crossed his arms again, shifted his weight to his left foot, looked over the table at her. "Okay, Hernandez. You want to tell him, you tell him. You're gonna have plenty of opportunity for that."

"Why's that?" Her tone was still defiant but a faltering note had crept into the question.

"'Cause he's yours for the next coupla days. Wherever you go, he goes."

"No fuckin' way! He's not coming to my place."

"I don't care where you take him, but he's yours." Kelsey's voice was a full-throttle squeak now. "IF someone inside is in this, the good Father here may be next on the hit list."

"Thanks for the offer," Powell interjected. Bad scene. Getting ugly. "I can take care of myself."

Kelsey ignored him and continued speaking to Hernandez. "And if there is no insider, maybe, just maybe you'll be able to keep him from offing another witness."

"I'm not taking him. No way." Chastened but not backed down. Tough. Something tough there, Powell thought.

"Find a way, Maria. Find a way. Unless you want me to have one of the guys do it?"

Verbal kidney punch. Kelsey knew it, too. Powell watched him pull himself up a little straighter and pull his shoulders back a little further. Hernandez said nothing, squared her jaw and glared, her eyes sparkling and on fire now.

"Count me out," Powell said. "Got other things to do."

"Your choice, mister, is to go with her or head right down to the holding pens. And don't be thinking bail, either, 'cause I think our phones are gonna be out of order for the next two, three days. But if some cop's looking for you, you'll be awful easy to find."

"You always a prick, Kelsey? Or are you making a special effort?"

Kelsey tightened his hands into fists. Kept his arms crossed. Headed for the door. Said evenly, "Man, Padre, you are something else." After the door slam, silence. Hernandez was still standing, bracing herself with both arms on the tabletop, staring at its scuffed and scratched surface.

"I don't know what to say, Maria. I'm sorry."

Head shake, no answer.

"Better get me locked down then. Tell him I wouldn't do it."

"NO."

Now she looked up. Lips tight again, a blush under her brown skin darkening it more, eyes hot and wet. "No, he's right."

And Powell knew what to ask. "What happened with Case?"

Hernandez shook her head again, straightened, locked her thumbs into her hip pockets, and looked away.

"How did he die?"

Now her voice, held tight as a climber's rope. "Tied his hands. Shoved him into his own oven. Turned on the gas."

Powell saw the matches now, heard Kelsey's voice, 'The murder weapon, you might say.' Saw the blue numbers tattooed on the frail, white wrist.

"Burned him to death," Hernandez said.

Chapter 14

SATURDAY - 10:41 a.m.

There was not much more. The fire department had gotten there quickly; not much of the place had burned. No sign of a forced entry. If there had been a struggle, the hoses had washed every trace of it away. The other occupants of the building were Chinese, didn't speak English. They were still being interviewed through interpreters; so far, no one had seen anything. They were probably all too scared to say. Hernandez spoke vacantly, as if her voice were somehow unconnected to her person. Then a long silence.

Which Powell finally broke. "It's over now, Maria. Past."

A quick glance over her shoulder but no other response. It had her, Powell knew. Just like it had him. The past was heavy baggage, a concrete block in a locked suitcase that you lugged on forever. A whitewashed sanctuary that he had never left. And now, for her, a burned-out apartment above a fish market that would keep them from ever really being in the present. But the doors were open.

"You have to come back."

"What're you talking about?" She had turned, now was facing him, the moisture in her eyes evaporated replaced by heat and sparkle.

"To now. Where you can do something."

"This some kind of priest shit?"

"Nope," Powell said. But maybe it was. You couldn't be redeemed in the past and the future never arrived. Redemption was in the present. And

God? Maybe God, too.

"'Cause if it is, I don't want to hear it."

"Nobody wants to hear it, Detective. Everybody wishes something different had happened once or wants to wait 'til something different does happen because then everything'll be all right and they won't have to get off their ass and do anything!"

"Fuck you!" She was up now and leaning towards him, hands on the table and black eyes snapping. "That old man is dead and you don't give a shit even if you didn't do it."

Powell waited, then spoke quietly. "That old man, Detective, started dying fifty years ago. He just finished it last night. And I want what started it and I want what finished it. As much as you do. More."

"The hell you talking about?"

"That number on his arm. Auschwitz, Treblinka, Dachau, one of the camps. Case was there."

Hernandez rocked back on her feet, turned away, turned back. Said nothing.

"At the end of the war my father was attached to the British unit that liberated Bergen-Belsen. Had stories about it, pictures. You might say I grew up with it. Hating it."

"That why you became a priest?

"No. That's why I joined the army. Became a priest when I finally figured out that grunts had the wrong kind of guns."

"Say what?"

"You can't shoot evil with an M-16. Only people."

"And you like people." Hernandez's eyes were cooling now, just a trace of a sarcastic smile at the corners of her mouth. "So why'd you clobber Arnie?"

"Because I'm a bad person." Powell felt a grin coming and tried to get hold of it. "And because he was pointing a great big gun at me when I asked him not to."

"Arnie likes to think he's Dirty Harry."

"Yeah. Works better in the movies."

Her smirk turned into something genuine, a flash of teeth and something different around the eyes. She turned away and tossed her head, picked up the paper, glanced at it, set it back down, and Powell felt the pull again, wanted that smile and a touch and knew it was time to move on.

"We staying here?"

"Can't for long. Precinct commander'll throw our butts outa here soon."

"Where to then?"

"No idea. You?"

"I'd invite you over to my house," Powell said, smiling now, "but I don't think the other guys'd go for it."

"Good. And I'm sure not inviting you to mine."

"Hotel?" Not the answer, but one was forming, the seed was there, not an idea yet but coming.

"You buying? We're not authorized on this."

"Meaning what?" Clearer now but not quite distinct.

"Meaning the department hasn't agreed to pay. Meaning the city's in a fiscal crisis and we have no extra dinero. Don't you read the papers?"

And then the solution. "How about the seminary?"

"Say again? How about what?"

"General Seminary. They have a suite for visiting religious. I use it to meet students. Never stayed there but the out-of-town spiritual directors do. The guestmaster'd let me have it if no one else was in there."

"Great. Who you gonna say I am? Your mother?"

"Not going to say anything. They're used to seeing you around. I'll check in and you can just come on up."

Hernandez bit her lip. Not what she had in mind, Powell could see. But she didn't have anything in mind. Finally, she shrugged.

"You're sleeping on the floor."

"Has two beds."

"Let's make the call." She gestured towards the door.

Moving towards it, Powell wondered if anyone would be in the seminary offices. In this crappy, sealed lounge there was no way of guessing how close they'd be to office hours.

"What time is it, anyway?"

Hernandez raised her right wrist, glanced down. "Ten to ten."

"Jesus. How long've I been here?"

"'Bout five hours since delivery."

Hernandez led him down the stairs, front stairs this time, to the main desk. No one there but a tall, bald sergeant who still looked fresh shaved and morning pressed. He carped at the request for a phone line but pushed the instrument across the scarred wood counter and found a file to shuffle through while Powell punched up the number.

The guestmaster, Brother Donald, an ancient Anglican monk from Wales, was in. It'd be fine if Father Powell used the suite. He would have the linens changed. Would have the keys left at the lobby desk. Would have some coffee supplies left there if Powell would like. Would love to have a chance to talk to him while he was staying.

Loved to talk to anyone, Powell thought. Forty five years of the Great Silence could do that. He thanked the good Brother and turned to Hernandez, who stood with her back against the counter, watching him intently.

"He's a little person, isn't he?" she said.

"Who?" The question a surprise.

"Whoever you were talking to."

"Donald? Not really. Five-eleven maybe. Skinny, though."

"Not what I mean. I mean little, not a big shot."

Powell slipped his hands into his front pockets and shrugged. "Yeah, I guess maybe he is. Why?"

"You like 'em. Little people. Sound different when you talk to them. Like that woman in the bakery. Like this guy."

Funny thing to notice, Powell thought. And true? Could be. "Maybe we're all little people. Some of us just hide it better."

Hernandez was grinning, liking it. "Okay, little guy. Let's get going. Car's in front."

"Leave it here. Seminary's only two blocks. We can walk."

"Gee, that's a great idea, Father." She was headed out the door, turning, walking backward, turning again just at the threshold. "'Cept we're both gonna need a change of clothes. And I live in Queens."

The blue Ford was angled into the sidewalk about fifty feet east of the precinct door just in front of a double storefront, one side offering colorful embroidery and tie-dyes from Haiti, the other the services of Madame Clio, reader and advisor. Which Powell liked. Clio, the muse of history if he was remembering his mythology well. He could use some advice from her. Who couldn't?

By the time Powell slid into the passenger seat, Hernandez was belted in and gunning the engine. She backed out of her slot carefully, then pounded the pedal and took off for the corner to try and beat the light that was yellow before she'd shifted from R to D. The sedan hit the intersection, horn blaring, a full second after the red and was just missed by a battered Checker zooming south on Seventh.

"Jesus. I forgot about your driving." The speedometer hit fifty and they made the light at Sixth, turning left in a screeching wide arc. "Must have suppressed it."

"Hey, it's good for you. Get your 'drenalin going."

"If it doesn't kill me."

"That might be good for you, too."

Powell wondered what that meant but didn't ask Hernandez, who had them on Twenty Third now, weaving in and out of the two lanes of eastbound traffic past the Flatiron and Madison Square and the gold-domed MetLife tower, across Park and Lex, turning left again at Third, gunning up to catch the uptown lights and sailing now with four lanes to play in, hard to starboard at Thirty Seventh and finally a full stop at Second where two limos and an airport bus were clogging the approach to the Midtown tunnel like leaves in a drain.

"Too bad," Powell said. "If you'd been a little faster we mighta got here before them."

Hernandez was still smiling, flushed a little with the energy of the race, no sign of the hate and anger Powell had seen at the station house earlier. Which was still there, he knew. Hate, like love, liked to hang on tight. Had tentacles. A hell of a grip. Like that space thing in the movie, he thought. Jesus, years ago, twenty or more now. The one with Sigourney Weaver where the creature, *Alien*, that's what it was called, wrapped itself around you and sucked itself in and everything seemed to be all right except later it came out and tore you to pieces. And now they were moving again and Powell pushed the movie back under a rug somewhere in his consciousness and watched the walls rise around them as they dropped down towards the tube at the river's bottom. In the tunnel's orange light, Hernandez seemed to glow, looked happy, looked pleased to be driving this big ass car on a pleasant fall day even if they were underwater and pulling in fumes from the thousands that had been there already this morning. Doesn't take much, Powell conceded to himself. Not much at all.

And then the light again. Hernandez waived a badge at the toll booth and they were coming up into sunshine, both squinting, and Powell looked back at the skyline spread in front of a blue morning sky like the Emerald City in the *Wizard of Oz*. Duggan would appreciate it, he thought, and wondered what he'd be up to now, and Ellen, and thinking of her brought his mind back to his driver, who looked more serious now, racing

a delivery van coming off an entrance ramp for possession of the right lane.

She won. Powell said, "So, Detective."

Hernandez glanced his way, eyebrows up, looked back to the road, and swung the car into the center lane an inch or so ahead of an express bus. "What."

"What's the story?"

"What story?"

"With this Zang guy. And Wolfson. And Case. How's it hang together?"

Something amused her. Her eyes and mouth said so. A quick smile and a crinkling of skin just below her temples. She watched the road and shook her head and said, "If I knew, why would I tell you?"

"Why not?"

"'Cause you're still all mixed up in this and I don't know who the hell you are."

"What's to know? I'm your typical Jesuit priest and murder suspect. Pretty uncomplicated."

"No sale, Mickey. Jungle fighter, classified operations, priest; hanging out with pimps and hookers and saloon keeps. Uh-uh. Uncomplicated is not the word."

"Maybe a better word than you think." The first name thing got him. He liked it, wanted to be 'Mickey' with her, wanted again what wasn't his to have, said, "You really want to hear about it?"

"Yeah." She was nodding and looking at him. "Yeah, I do."

Powell looked out his window, watched the buildings and cars going by, pondered how one begins to say who he is. Was it, he wondered, simply the sum of the thousand thousand moments that went before this present one? Or was there something more, something unpredictable, which made this *now* different from the million *thens*? And knew that he had no answer and that one would not come.

"Okay," he said.

Which surprised her. Her eyes had widened and her lips parted a bit and she hid it by looking away and swinging out to the left of a low riding, rust-pocked Chevy Malibu with honest to God fake fur dice swinging in front of the driver, a young white guy with slicked back blonde hair.

"My dad's dad was a farmer, hogs and corn, and he held the family place together all through the Depression but he wanted something else for his son. Sent him to college, which was pretty rare for a farm kid in the '30's. He graduated from the University of Illinois in May of 1941 with a B.A. and a new wife, a graduate student in classics from Cairo, the town banker's daughter. Her dad wanted him on the farm but by then, everyone saw what was coming. They spent the summer at home and he enlisted in the fall, wanted to be a pilot but couldn't see quite well enough and so he got into something new, something called airborne."

They were out there now, approaching the big red and white tanks in Elmhurst, still sailing in moderate traffic.

"And the war defined him. And me, too, maybe. He went overseas a sergeant and came back a captain and I was born in April, 1946. And he went in to banking with his father-in-law and did it well for thirty years but the war was what made him who he was.

"And I grew up in a big brick house in Cairo and heard about it. Not all the time and not even often really. But now again he'd get the pictures down and tell the stories and you could hear in his voice that it meant a lot more than loans or deposits or mortgages.

"And I played baseball and basketball and went to school and to church on Sunday and knew from him that some things were wrong and that when the time came you had to do something about it. And my time came in 1967."

Powell stopped. His palms were moist and his heart rate had picked up as though someone had clicked up the rheostat on a rhythm box. The past, he knew. Never let go. They were well out on the L.I.E. now, coming up on Flushing Meadows, where the World's Fair had been, and there were houses and duplexes sprinkled in among the light brick apartment buildings and Powell felt like crying.

"Best to take a break now, Padre," Hernandez said. She didn't turn towards him but he felt her peripheral glance and appreciated her discretion. "Anyway, we're almost there."

She eased the Ford off the expressway at Woodhaven and headed south in an all-American landscape. Gas stations, fast food, strip malls, houses, trees, funeral homes, diners; except for the license plates it could have been any one of a million streets in any one of fifty states. Something comforting about that, Powell thought. And something sad, too. And then they'd turned again and were winding through a residential area, Kew Gardens he guessed, and stopping in front of a two-story semi-detached place with a sprinkler whirling in the front yard and a fiery red maple tree like the one out his office window on the right where a little girl swung on a steel-pipe swing set.

"Home?"

Hernandez nodded but didn't need to. The girl was off the swing and at the fence and waving. Powell felt his smile building and Hernandez was saying something and had gripped his left arm, guiding it gently towards her as he turned and " - not going to like this - " was the end of the phrase and the handcuff clicked on.

The other cuff was on the steering wheel before he could pull his hand away. Hernandez pushed her door open and stood and leaned back into the car.

"Sorry. No chances."

And she was gone. Powell watched her go, and felt his anger rising like steam in a pipe. But something stopped it. Too nice a day. Here was a lovely woman running through a sprinkler towards a tidy home on a beautiful autumn day. Settle for that. Grace, he reflected. What kept anger from tying you to some ugliness of a moment past.

He tipped his head back and leaned on the seat, taking a deep breath and rattling his cuffed arm as he did so. The cool dampness from the sprinkled lawn carried some message of menace, something below the surface of his memory that he needed to know. But now was not the time. Now he shook the handcuff again and smiled. Now he said to himself, "My name is Michael F. Powell. My rank is lieutenant. My serial number is 34061044T44."

Now he was asleep.

Chapter 15

SATURDAY - 12:22 p.m.

The car was cruising in the tunnel again when Powell came to. The orange ceiling lights repeatedly rolled their glare over him like lurid waves coming up over a flat blue beach. The handcuff still encircled his left wrist but the other link was loose and his arm was lying on the grimy vinyl of the seat. Hernandez was driving one-handed, her left at the six o'clock position on the wheel, her right stretched across the seat back behind his head, fingers tapping gently. Different clothes now, grey linen pants and a hot pink blouse and a plaid jacket of blue and green and white and pink silk, like something a dance band saxophone player might wear if it weren't for the gun underneath.

"Nice threads," Powell said, not turning his head. "Singing somewhere tonight?"

Hernandez glanced his way, smiling, then back to the windshield. "Funny. And thanks."

"I been out long?"

"About twenty minutes since I came out. Maybe a while before that."

Powell straightened and stretched, rattling the cuff, now off the wheel but still on his wrist. Hernandez slid her arm down past him, reached into the side pocket of her jacket, produced a small key on a ring.

"Here. Sorry for that."

He felt himself smile. "True repentance requires amendment of life. You gonna do it again?"

A matching grin. "Probably."

"I thought so. Woman, you are going to spend some time in purgatory."

The car came up out of the tunnel into the sunlight and wheeled into the left lane, turned left, and then hard right, accelerating all the while, then braking hard for the red light at Third. Hernandez raised her elbow to the seat back again and turned towards him, smiling.

"You talk in your sleep, you know that, Father?"

"No. All the girls say that."

"It's true."

"What'd I say then?"

"Bunch of numbers. Then `Maria, Maria.' Pretty flattering, no?"

Powell smiled and felt a blush rising. "Probably an invocation of the Blessed Virgin."

"Really? Then why'd you say 'sell her' next?"

"Come on. Sell her? You making this up?"

"No way." The light flashed green and the Ford jumped forward. She shook her head. "And I thought it was me. That you liked me."

"How could I not? Every guy likes a lady who hits him on the head and hand-cuffs him to a car."

"Only in the line of duty, Father."

They were screeching left on to Lex now, hurtling south towards Thirty Fourth, fast, not quite out of control but close, close enough, close enough to make you scream like on a roller coaster or laugh at the sheer wildness of it. Which Powell did. Head back and laughing, but beneath it he heard 'sell her' and felt something ominous with it but they were across Thirty-Fourth and flying now, literally in the air as they came off the crest, and then banging down hard on all four wheels and shimmying side to side some but still not quite unglued, and then Thirty Third and Thirty Second and all down through the Twenties past East Indian spice shops and restaurants and weaving lane to lane and then a red light at Twenty Third and a long hard stop behind a huge orange van with Nice Jewish Boy With Truck scripted in white on the back end.

"God, that's wild!" Powell was still laughing and Hernandez was wearing a smile wider than the street. "Why do you do that?"

"I just like the way it feels." She shook her head and Powell watched her dark wavy hair flip out over her eyes and back again. "Probably kill myself someday."

"Just hope you don't kill someone else first."

"Worried?" The light turned green and Hernandez eased the car around the struggling truck and rolled it sedately across the intersection.

"Nope. Big parts of me are dead already. Don't think there's too much left to go."

Hernandez turned and stared and then looked away, her face as simple and serious as rain. For a block or two she was quiet. They were turning onto Twenty first, by the leafy park there, all in colors and dappled with light, when she spoke.

"You said something like that about Case, something about being dead already. What's it mean?"

"I don't know really." But she wanted an answer. And he did, too. "Something about being caught by a moment or a time."

"Sorry, Powell. I don't get it."

Powell felt his brow gnarling and his teeth clamping lightly together. How to say? "It's like at funerals maybe. You see people mourning there but it's not just the dead guy, maybe he'd been sick, cancer or something, good in a way for him to go. What's getting 'em is that they're in there, too, in the casket or whatever, some piece of their own life is in there, too, frozen there. And it's like that piece has died, too. And that's what they're sorry about."

"Okay, maybe. Maybe so with funerals or whatever but-"

"No." Powell interrupted; felt silly but pushed in anyway. "It's not just that. More than that."

"What?"

"Doesn't have to be about death, itself. Maybe something else." They were sliding by a church now on his side where a thin young man with curly hair and wire-rimmed glasses knelt, working in a fenced garden. "Maybe you got beat up or something as a kid. Or maybe even something good. Like say a hotshot high school basketball player, local hero when he's seventeen. But then that's it. Never makes it in college, and never gets over it. Part of him just dies back there."

"And so what are we, like some zombies or something?" She had both hands on the wheel now, was leaning forward and turning to him. "Like walking around with little bits of dead hanging on us?"

"Something like that."

"And that's it?"

"I don't know." He felt her attention, wanted acutely for her to understand, knew that he didn't understand, himself. "Maybe it can be redeemed. Maybe that's some of what resurrection is about."

Hernandez didn't respond. But at least, Powell thought, she's not laughing. She angled the car around a truck off-loading pallets of paper at Sixth, gunned up a block, and

headed south. Just before Sixteenth, she pulled it to the curb at a fire hydrant.

"Close enough," she said.

"You mean you're not coming over?" Powell unsnapped his seat belt and reached to the door handle. "Don't you want to meet my parents? They like to know who I'm going out with."

"You are cute. Like a cockroach." She smiled a phony smile and pushed her door open. "And, yeah, I'm coming."

"Then why not put it in front? There's a No Parking zone there, too."

"Because maybe Big Brother is watching. And maybe it'd be better if you didn't get into something that even a moron could make as a cop car. So maybe another piece of you won't get dead."

Something about her voice was grim, there was weight in it, a solid block of something somber. Powell got out and caught up with her on the curb.

"You talked to Kelsey, didn't you?"

"Yeah. From my place."

"And something IS up?"

"Could be. He got hold of a buddy of his in ATF. There was an op going at your pal's. Got nothing on the house wire but a lot of action on the pay phone. And then the city shut it down. Wanna guess who made the call?"

"Zang?"

"Bingo. And something else. Seems like maybe he's just moved to new digs."

"How do you know that?"

"We don't. But a friend of his said something to Kelsey about it, nothing definite, but interesting anyway. Know where?"

Powell shrugged. They were moving towards the corner now and Hernandez had her hand on left his arm just above the elbow, a light grip around his triceps.

"West side. Lincoln Center."

Whistle time, a low one, almost involuntary. "Pricey, no? What's a police lieutenant make?"

"Not that much. But maybe he's just renting it."

"So how do you find out?"

"Good question. If we can get a little more, I guess we go to I.A.D."

"Como esta?"

Hernandez smiled at his bad accent and they turned the corner onto Sixteenth. "Internal Affairs, Padre. The cop cops."

There was almost no one on the street. At the far end of the block a man with a suit bag slung over his shoulder was hurrying toward Sixth Avenue and closer in, across from the rectory, a white-haired woman was walking her dog, a lumpy looking golden retriever. Looks like it always does, Powell thought. Rows of facing brownstones, their high steps angling down past garbage cans to the walk where trees stretched up in their wrought iron fences towards the light, cars bumper to bumper along the curb except in the spots where the hydrants were, occasional traffic passing, cabs and vans and now a Toyota blaring rap.

And maybe someone watching. That possibility changed things. Made the cars and the windows and the vans and the steps somehow malign, threatening, a jungle and not a street. A jungle of the mind.

"Hey, hang on a minute." Hernandez was half a step ahead of him, already round the corner. She slowed, stopped, half turned. "If it's not a good idea to be getting in a cop car, why's it smart to be walking down the street with a cop?"

"Oh, man." Pretended offense in her voice. "You sayin' I look like a cop?"

Powell had to smile. Not many cops out there in plaid silk. "What if it's someone who knows you?"

"Someone who knows me that good already knows how to find me. And you. And there's no one here anyway, they'd have to know what Kelsey was working on which is unfuckinglikely since he just got on it this morning and there's no paper trail of that yet. We're just being careful which is never a real bad idea. And finally, it ain't gonna be someone who knows me; we're looking for someone from the polsec, they don't mix with us common street types. Satisfied?"

"Almost. What's polsec?"

"The political section. Spy stuff, terrorists, crap for the mayor and the commissioner. What Zang does."

"Like extra security for St. Paddy's day?"

"If there's some kind of political threat, yeah. A demonstration or something." Hernandez had crossed her arms tightly in front of her and was biting the inside of her cheek like a schoolmarm talking down to a particularly dense pupil. "Anything else?"

"No, Professor." Powell grinned and swept his right hand out in front of him. "Maybe we could get going if you're done talking."

"Jesus, you're an asshole."

And she was off, a half step ahead of him again, and the street looked better now, like a place you'd want to be, a city postcard scene on a nice fall day, and Powell felt his emotional barometer rising as he caught her and matched her leggy strides, and he thought then that the day might be okay.

Until the empty hall. Which maybe shouldn't have bothered him but did. Anna should have been there. Her room, her office she liked to call it, was right inside the door and she always popped out to see who was coming in, even when the doorbell didn't ring. Powell caught himself listing the places she could easily be. Upstairs cleaning some-where. In the kitchen, setting up lunch. Out at the market. In the small chapel at the back of the first floor, lighting a candle and watching it quietly. No problem, just a feeling, a projection of his own fear.

Which Hernandez seemed to sniff out.

"You can wait here," he'd said at the foot of the staircase but she hadn't heeded him, had been right behind him looking up into the quiet house.

"Hey, you know the other guys aren't necessarily going like you up top. How about I get my stuff and meet you?"

"How about I'm coming up whether they like it or not?" Her voice was adamant, no point arguing.

And there was nothing there but stillness. No sound of Anna or the other priests. Who should be gone by now, off to the big church on Fifteenth or the parish house or hospital or nursing homes or diocese or any one of a dozen other places the call took them. Hernandez waited in the fourth floor hall while he pulled a soft-sided overnight bag from his closet and pulled open a dresser drawer for briefs and socks.

"How long we gonna be gone, anyway?"

"I brought enough stuff for a couple of nights. After that we come back for more or send Kelsey to the laundry."

The sound of her words echoed in from the hall over the tightly spread bed, off the bare walls, a warm living thing in an icebox. A long time, Powell found himself thinking. How long a time it's been. Hurrying to finish now, he slammed the drawer and pulled a shaving kit and folded shirts from a shelf in the closet. Too long a time.

"Ready?"

"Probably forgot something, but this is enough to get by."

Hernandez was leaning on the wall between a picture of an archbishop now long dead and an uncurtained hall window that looked out over treetops and roofs. Looking good. But now was not the time to be moving that thought in. Something else. Find something. But what came was laughter, a crazy kind of high-pitched laugh, like in the car but up the register somewhere towards a giggle.

"You see something funny about me?" Her tone between amusement and annoyance. "What?"

"You. Me." She was staring at him now, hands frozen in front of her. "I mean, what I mean is I came out and you were there and, you know, looking good and nervous, me, I was, and well, something just got me laughing."

"Yeah." She shook her head and brushed her hands lightly across the front of her thighs. "I mean, should I say thank you or what?"

"Don't say anything. Let's just go down to my office. I want to get a book."

She was behind him on the stairs down to the second floor talking to herself for his benefit. "Crazy. He's crazy. First he's laughing like a lunatic. Then he tells me I'm looking good. Now we're gonna spend the night together and he wants a book. Crazy."

Just then, he would know later, he was happy. On the stairs with the woman, still aching with laughter. Wolfson and Case were gone and Kelsey and Arnie and the rest of it. Just then was a Kingdom moment, the way it was supposed to be. And then the office door.

Which was, strangely, ajar. Along the hall the rest of them were closed but his was standing open. He stopped and started again, quicker now and behind him, Hernandez moving quickly, too. No one there but the screenless window opposite the doorway was open wide and a light breeze blowing through had sent papers sailing, scattering them on the bare wood floor.

"Everything here?" An edge in the question. Or wariness. Or fear. Whatever it was, Powell felt it himself, a rising tightness moving up from his gut to his ribcage.

"Can't tell. Looks like it, though."

"Let's get your book and get out of here then."

"Forget it." He moved around the desk to close the window. Outside, the crimson leaves were shining in the midday sunlight. Fewer than before, though. Noticeably fewer. Winter coming. Putting his hands on top of the window frame to push it shut, he looked down now to the garden walk, the brick path edged in mums, the blossoms still there, more visible now through the gaps in the maple's foliage. And something else.

A shoe. A single woman's shoe in the middle of the walk. Balancing lightly on the frame of the still open window, Powell raised himself to tiptoes for a better view. And saw the rest. An unshod foot, and then a leg, and then the torso from which it jutted at a crazy angle, a plain black skirt ridden up to its hips.

Anna.

Chapter 16

SATURDAY - 3:21 p.m.

From the window, things looked calm, almost tranquil. Students passed, book-laden, leaving the plain brick building to the left where the seminary library was, following the slate path around the edge of the quadrangle past the Victorian row houses where some of the faculty dwelt in the drafty elegance of a long-gone era, finally disappearing past the facade of the chapel which neatly split the campus, the Close they called it, in two. The golden leaves yet on the trees shimmered in the faint breeze, occasionally relaxing their grip and drifting in slow fits and starts to the grass below.

What you saw, Powell reflected, was peace. It was what you didn't see that tore you up. Like Anna. He couldn't see her, wouldn't see her again. Would only remember that blood flowing slow and thick beneath her hair and from one ear, the lips laboring to speak, the eyes blinking, puzzled, and finally rolling back as the struggle ended. Only that picture and the words now. "Angel," Anna had whispered, "angel." Simple faith, he thought. Maybe the only kind that mattered.

And Hernandez? Where was she? His eyes swept the Close again, hoping to see her step out from a doorway or from behind the thinning screen of leaves. Not there. In memory she was behind him, first pounding down the rectory stairs, then at a back window, banging out the screen for the short drop down the garden door, then next to him as Anna spoke and died, then pulling him roughly up, both hands on his arm and her face stuck close to his.

"Mick, get out of here."

"No way." Trying to shake free, failing. "She-"

"She's dead." Unable to hear that then, grabbing her jacket as if to throw her off. "She doesn't need you now."

"I'm not leaving." He had pulled her toward him, close, as if to embrace her, but had only hissed with hatred. "I'm going to find out-"

"It was supposed to be you."

That had stopped him cold, frozen him there like an ice sculpture, not the words she'd said but the ones she wasn't saying. `If you stay, they'll find out where you are.' Hearing the unsaid, he had eased his hold on her, had touched her softly, had knelt beside Anna and dipped his thumb in her blood and traced a crude cross on her forehead with it whispering a prayer of peace for her soul.

Had turned back to Hernandez. "Where?"

"The seminary. Might as well." She had been breathing hard, as angry or scared - or both - as he was. "Still no reason to think anyone'd look there."

"Okay. You'll get there?"

"Soon as I can. How'll I find you?"

"You know the big lobby off Ninth? Go through it and it's the first building on the right. Pintard. Third floor, left side. Act like you know where you're going and no one'll stop you."

"All right. Now go."

Below the window, she had laced her fingers into a stirrup and given him a quick boost up to the sill, and he had pulled himself into the grey stillness of the chapel where a flickering candle in a red glass cylinder signed the presence of the Blessed Sacrament. The Body and the Blood. Looking back at Anna and the darkening pool on the walk, it was hard to know what that meant. And then Hernandez's voice to jerk him back to the temporal.

"Powell. Pull me up." She had locked both hands onto the wrist of his extended arm and had scrambled up the wall like a commando.

"You're not going to leave her-"

"No." Both her palms softly resting on his shirt. "But I gotta call from somewhere. Then I'll go back."

"Phone in the front. In Anna's . . . in the room by the door."

"Good. Now get the fuck outa here."

"I think-"

"Don't think. Right now I'll do the thinking. Go."

Now he didn't remember getting to the door or through it or down the steps. Only that somewhere in the time before he had, he'd heard her voice again.

"Hey, Mickey? I'm sorry."

Sorry. It was a word about pain. And that seemed right. Powell felt a soreness in his chest like a muscle pull, a cramped tightness across his lungs and heart. Not physiological, he knew, but nonetheless real for that. The ache for Anna there with a growling stomach and a tingle along his left wrist where he'd scraped across the windowsill and a sleepless stinging in his eyes and a slightly panicked breathlessness and a pleasant tumescence between his legs from wanting Hernandez.

He did want her, he knew that. And wanted not to. Now he wanted to remember Anna, her gentleness and humor and humility, but what came instead was the soft touch of hands on his chest, a body standing close to his, a low voice, a dark face framed by darker hair, the scent of lemons. Not wrong to want that, inhuman not to. But impossible.

Watching the walk, he thought of the house in Queens, the lawn, the maple tree, the girl on the swing. No place for him in the picture. And in his own frame? Only images of emptiness, shadows of empty rooms, empty time, empty prayer. And a voice, accented, from a retreat or a conference or somewhere: 'We must empty ourselves to be filled by God. Even God cannot fill what is full.' Plenty of emptiness now. And where was the filling? Where for Wolfson and Case and where for Lethe and where for Anna? Where in the whitewashed sanctuary where the blood splattered in neat rows of red droplets on the walls before it rolled down in even rills toward the red tile floor?

No answer, of course. Powell knew there would be no answer. None for either the psalmist or the man on the cross who shouted his words: 'Why have you forsaken me?' Never any reply. He watched the walk where a cat stretched on a sunny bench and a bald man in clericals passed and then Hernandez stepped out from the lobby into the sunshine and looked up towards where he was waiting and hurried towards the door.

He could hear her taking the wooden steps two at a time, her footfalls echoing up the narrow stairwell louder as she came nearer, and then the sound of her breathing, even, not in gasps, and then a hand at the top of the rail and then in an instant she was pushing past him and easing the door closed behind her. Her eyes scanned the bedroom, ran over the twin beds and the desk and chair, the dresser and the pictures, both framed photos of angels in dark carved wood, and she ducked into the kitchenette out of his sight, and then back and into the bathroom and out again, stopping close to him, close enough that he could see her agitation, the flighty movement of her pupils glancing here and back, here and back, the minute tremor of her hands held now at her sides, then rising to brush lightly across her lapels, then up to the lower part of her smooth brown cheeks, then down again to rest on her hips.

And a smile, tentative at first, then wider, and her voice, warm but pitched up a half note higher than usual. "You okay?"

"Yeah." What to say? I'm scared? I want you? But what came out was, "Find anything out?"

Hernandez backed away, sat on the edge of the nearer bed, shook her head. "The forensic guys got there but they didn't see anything we didn't see. They're going over the room for prints and hair and fiber but it'll be a while before we know anything. We got people knockin' on doors but so far no one seems to have seen or heard a thing."

"You get to Kelsey?"

"Yeah." Her eyes met his, then turned towards the windows. "Zang's missing."

"Missing?"

"Shoulda been on today. Something doing at the U.N. Didn't show for his shift. I guess he called in for messages, Kelsey said something like that, but he never showed."

Something kinked tight in Powell's gut, a spiral of tension like a serpent that wound up from his intestines and pushed sharply against his back and kidneys.

"So he would've known that Kelsey was looking for him?"

"Yeah." She did not look at him. "Probably."

"And me. Could he have known that you guys were looking for me?"

Now she looked at him, pale and miserable, not wanting to answer. "I don't see how. There's no record or anything.""

"Is it possible? People at the precinct knew. Then you brought me in the back way so somebody might not've known you had me."

"It's possible."

"And Case?"

"Maybe him, too." Her eyes swept down to the polished wood floor and came back up at him hot and angry. "It could be someone inside but it's not the only way, okay?!"

Her words punched him hard and he felt an instinctive kickshit response rising along the tight coil inside him, felt it and caught it, held it till it spent itself like a wave on a beach, rolling in then pulling itself back out, leaving just a glistening shadow on the sand.

"I'm not accusing anyone, Maria. But someone seems to be trying to kill me." Still a trace of pissed off but not, he hoped, too much. "Do you have someone else have in mind?"

"Don't know." Hernandez relaxed a little, leaned back on her arms, her jacket falling back to show the curves of a body in pink and a leather holster strap crossing one shoulder. "How 'bout that guy at Duggan's? The old guy you saw Zang with?"

Now he heard the man's voice again. 'I'd like to know who I'm to thank . . .' " Heard his own reply, his name passing through the air like a casual invitation. To murder. He had not been afraid to tell. And that dumb macho fearlessness might have left Anna dead on a brick sidewalk. And blood on whitewashed walls. And now he knew what Hernandez had been feeling, sitting pale on the bed. My fault. My hand in this. But not the one who pushed. Not the hand that struck the match. Still no backing away, no way out. The sick remembered feeling of responsibility. Oh, God. Was he speaking or just thinking it? Oh, God.

"Yeah." Hernandez's voice, a little snide now. "Where was he?"

Dizzy still, denying, resentful. "Who?"

"God," she said, "Where's your God now?"

And then the voice, just a whisper and gone. 'I have overcome the world.' And calm coming then, the coil loosening. And his voice calm too: "I'm not gonna bite on that, Detective. Been through all that before you got here. God was right where God always is. On that walk. In that oven. Hanging on that fence."

She didn't know what to make of it, he could see that. Lips pursed, thin lines predicating furrows on her brow, eyes searching and uncertain.

Not surprising. Did anybody really get it?

"Sorry," she said, "it was a cheap shot."

"It's okay. I know what you meant. I've always wanted a God who'd make things right. Get the bad guys. Zap, zap, zap. Instead I got a dead carpenter who tells me to surrender when he says anything at all."

"He talks to you?" She was leaning forward now, legs crossed at the knees, fingers laced tight around her shinbone.

"I told you that. Call it praying. No burning bush, no pillar of fire. Too bad, though. It'd make a better movie if there were."

Big smile and a shake of her head, dark hair flowing like water in a wave. "You're fuckin' weird, you know that, Father?"

"I s'pose so. Could be that's better than 'normal' if you think about it."

Powell crossed the room then, past her, past the second bed, across the oval rag rug between the desk and the easy chair, back to his watching post by the window. No one on the walk. Nothing doing at all. Just a black and brown cat asleep on a stone bench in the sun and behind him, Hernandez still sitting, facing away, looking towards the kitchen and hugging her knee.

"Hey, Powell?" Even speaking she did not turn his way.

"Yeah?"

"Tell me the rest of your story."

The serpent tightening its hold again, the past hanging on, pulling him back toward a dark maw. But no way out. Say it and let it go. The principle of confession. Hernandez turned towards him now, face over her shoulder, right hand on the bed. Eyes somehow urgent. Or was that his own projection? No matter now.

"Okay." So easy to agree. "How about a cup of coffee first?"

"Yeah." So easy with her.

They found a jar of Folger's crystals in a cupboard and mugs on a shelf over the small table. Powell started the kettle boiling and watched Hernandez dig spoons out of the back of a cluttered drawer. Waiting for the water's whistle, she kicked her shoes into the main room and when the mugs were brimming settled the question of where they'd sit by leading him to the windows - his lookout post before - and sitting cross-legged on the thick rug. Joining her there, he stared at the leaves out the window and at the brick projects rising behind them a block or two away and wondered what to say.

"You left off with the Army. I think so, anyway." Her voice soft and encouraging. "1967."

"Yeah. I got out of college in May. Took a trip to New Mexico with my girlfriend. Enlisted in June."

"What'd she think?"

He shook his head and took a long sip of coffee - too hot and too weak but it gave him some space. What had Nancy thought? Nancy, a thoughtful, artistic type who wrote good poetry and like to make love in the middle of the afternoon thought then what Maria Hernandez was thinking now. `Fuckin' weird,' though Nancy would never have put it that way. In New Mexico when he'd told her, on a mountain up near Bloomfield where they were headed to find some Anizazi ruins, she'd pushed him hard and gone on climbing by herself. He'd caught up with her at the summit but she wouldn't speak. Had been crying and would not say a word. Angel's Peak it was called. But where had the angels been? Why hadn't they told her what he'd always heard about duty? About freedom? Why hadn't they explained how the past had hold of you? He thought of Anna's whisper and knew that they had been speaking to him in Nancy's silence but then he'd still known the rightness of it.

"She didn't get it. Not many people did."

"What happened to her?"

"She got married. Had two kids. Boys. Got divorced. Now she teaches English at a college in Macomb, Illinois. Still hear from her now and then."

"And you?"

"Me? I did Basic and volunteered for Airborne. Did that and volunteered for Special Forces. That was where you wanted to be then. Finished that and shipped out. Vietnam. And that's where it gets funny."

"Funny?" Hernandez had slipped the plaid jacket off and the shoulder holster too, hanging the jacket on the back of the desk chair. The gun was on the floor beside her.

"Yeah, funny in a way. You read about Green Berets and you think about methodical killers, counterinsurgency experts, all that stuff. And we were trained for that. Only I never even pulled a trigger. In country a year and I never fired my weapon except once at a snake in my hooch."

"You kidding?"

"I wished I was then. I wanted some action. And it was there. I did two tours in the highlands with the Montagnards and there was plenty of action. Just never where I was. I'd hear it and go out but when I got there nothing. Spooky, huh?"

"I guess."

Now she was leaning forward, elbows on thighs. The smooth cloth of her blouse had fallen away from her chest, revealing brown skin and cleavage and white lace. Powell remembered the hospital and her ploy then but guessed that it wasn't conscious now. And half wished that it were.

"So there was nothing to shoot at. I thought I'd try a few salvos with a typewriter, started sending reports. Said the V.C. were evil but so was the Republic of Vietnam. Said we ought to get out of there since we didn't have anything to give 'em.

"Suffice to say the brass didn't like it. But one guy did. Guy named Kinlock. C.I.A. Got me seconded to the agency. Said they needed someone like me to work the boondocks of Cambodia and Laos. They were both still neutral or supposed to be but Kinlock said it was only a matter of time.

"And so I went to Thailand, a place called Khemmarat, on the Mekong. My assignment was to cross the river or to float down it to places where the Pentagon was telling Congress we had no people. Go to the villages, teach them how to fight, gather information, report in from time to time.

"I was there six years. Sometimes I thought they'd forgotten me. No one ever came out. I was never called in. There was a woman there, a French doctor, older than me, who ran a clinic for one of their aid outfits. Other than that, no Caucasians. Twice a year I went to Bangkok. Once Kinlock was there but the rest of the time no one."

Powell stopped and slugged his coffee, which was warm now, verging on tepid. Hernandez was staring like someone entranced, eyes rapt, mouth slightly open, still leaning forward, motion-less. What would she do with all these words, he wondered. File them somewhere? Forget them? Shape them into something else? No telling. Now, she blinked as if waking, lifted her cup to her lips and drank, set it down on the bare floor under the window, stretched her legs out in front of her so that they almost touched his knees, leaned back on her arms. Behind her, the sun struck the pink brick of a building beyond the window touching it with gold.

"Then what happened?"

Powell took a moment to frame a reply. How to tell it? Maybe no point in elaborating.

"I fell in love with the doctor and we had an affair," he said. "And she left. And I wrote my reports and they were ignored and the people in the villages got killed."

"How old was the doctor?"

That was the striking thing, wasn't it? Not the villagers; they were as invisible to Hernandez as they had been to everyone else. You teach them how to fight and they do fight; you don't help them and they lose. Everything. Homes and families and lives. But no one sees it and it seems not to have happened.

"The doctor?" Powell felt a smile coming. "I said she was older, didn't I? I was twenty-five; she was in her forties. About the same as I am now."

Hernandez considered this, nodded, and picked up her cup. "And then you went to seminario, yes?"

His grin was full now, a laugh there waiting. Masking, Powell knew, a scream. "Jilted lover seeks comfort in God? Nope. Seminary was later. That wasn't it."

"How then?"

Why not answer? The coil was squeezed, killing tight and the pain had risen up through his chest and throat to a small space just behind his eyes. Why not tell her and let go of it? The principle. The words came but the voice was someone else's, not his, how could he make these sounds?

"For that I watched a priest have his skin pulled off and he thanked me and I shot him."

Chapter 17

THE ANGEL

THE ANGEL CONSIDERED THE SMALL WOMAN AND WEPT. SHE HAD GAZED UPON HIM WITH KIND EYES AND HAD OBEYED HIS VOICE AND YET HAD BEEN DESTROYED. BUT SO IT WAS WRITTEN: "DO NOT LOOK LEST YOU BE CONSUMED IN THE PUNISHMENT." IT WAS NOT GIVEN TO MANY TO LOOK UPON THE GLORY, AND FEW WHO SAW IT SURVIVED.

AND IT WAS NOT THE SMALL WOMAN FOR WHOM HE HAD COME. HER DEATH MUST BE IMPUTED TO POWELL IN WHOSE PLACE SHE HAD FLOWN. THE ANGEL SIGHED. THE PLAN HAD BEEN SO SIMPLE AND SO NEAT. HERNANDEZ, THE HARLOT, HAD MADE IT CLEAR THAT THE TEMPORAL POWERS WOULD BE SATISFIED WITH POWELL, HER QUESTIONS ABOUT HIM INDICATING THAT HE WAS THEIR SUSPECT. HIS DISAPPEARANCE, OR BETTER, HIS SUICIDE WOULD HAVE TIED TOGETHER ALL THE THREADS. "IT IS EXPEDIENT THAT ONE SHOULD DIE AND THE WHOLE NATION NOT PERISH." THAT WAS HOW IT WAS WRITTEN.

"HE COME BACK SOON," THE SMALL WOMAN HAD SAID, BUT HE HAD NOT. THE ANGEL HAD WAITED AND HAD DONNED HIS CELESTIAL RAIMENT BUT POWELL HAD NOT RETURNED. INSTEAD THE SMALL WOMAN HAD RETURNED,

SO QUICKLY OPENING THE DOOR THAT HE HAD CAREFULLY LOCKED BEHIND HIMSELF THAT THERE WAS NO TIME FOR HIM TO DO ANYTHING BUT TO STAND SILENT BEFORE HER AS SHE BUSILY ENTERED.

SHE HAD GASPED. AND NO WONDER. WHO COULD SEE HIM IN SUCH SPLENDOR AND NOT RESPOND? OFTEN THE YOUNG MEN GASPED, AND SOME OF THEM EVEN SQUEALED IN JOY. AND WHEN HE SAID, "COME" SHE HAD, AND WHEN HE INDICATED THE WINDOW, SHE STOOD BEFORE IT, AND WHEN HE PUSHED, HER BODY OBEYED, ARCING SILENTLY INTO THE TREETOP AND DOWN. THE EASE OF IT, HE KNEW, INDICATED ACCORD WITH THE DIVINE WILL WHOSE AUSTERE HARSHNESS BROUGHT HIM TO TEARS NOW.

AND YET THAT WILL BE DONE. THE ANGEL'S WEEPING CEASED AS HE AGAIN CONSIDERED POWELL. CLEARLY THE TIME HAD NOT YET COME. ANOTHER SIGH. CERTAINLY HIS DESTRUCTION WAS ORDAINED BUT IT WAS SO HARD TO KNOW WHEN. AND YET IT HAD ALWAYS BEEN SO; THERE WAS SOME CONSOLATION IN THAT. IT WAS WRITTEN THAT "OF THAT DAY OR THAT HOUR NO ONE KNOWS, NOT EVEN THE ANGELS .... AND WHAT I SAY, I SAY TO ALL: WATCH."

Chapter 18

SUNDAY - 1:06 a.m.

Besides the two men, no one was on the street. They were standing at the edge of a streetlamp's yellow circle, a Mutt and Jeff pair, the tall man in a long sleeveless coat like a cloak and an odd broad-brimmed hat with the edges turned up a touch, the shorter man, curly-haired, suddenly embracing the other, looking up towards his face, the tall man pushing him away, fumbling in an overcoat pocket, handing his companion something that even Powell could see was money. And then, abruptly, he was gone, moving quickly back towards the avenue and across to the near side of the street, out of the line of Powell's sight. The short man stayed in the lamplight for a moment counting the bills and smiling so broadly that Powell could see the white of his teeth from the window.

The man did not look like Tony but the money and the situation brought him to mind and Powell wondered where he was and where Lethe was, too, and what it would be like to take a handful of bills to have someone else's sperm spurt into your mouth and throat, and what or who the Roach Motel was about. And then the man who was not Tony began to whistle and, whistling, walked away, west on Twenty First into the shadows of the trees, leaving Powell nothing to look at but a dark street and nothing to think about but Hernandez.

Who was sleeping now in the next room. Whose breathing he could hear from where he sat by the kitchen window, softly soughing above the city's night hum, whose dark hair lay on the white pillowcase, a contrast he could make out even in the lightless suite. To whom he had made his confession, with whom he was falling in love.

How typical to fall for a confessor. It had happened often to him, to most priests really, perhaps more often since Vatican II had opened up the confessionals and put you face to face with penitents. You knew things: that was how it happened. You knew that they couldn't always control their tempers with the kids, or that they lied about late meetings to spend some time in a bar, or that they'd had an affair with someone they'd met at the supermarket, someone who listened, you know, don't you Father, or that they pretended to be asleep when their husbands got into bed. Sometimes you even knew their dreams, the tales their psyches told as it came clearer and closer that all life's promises weren't really there. You knew things and you couldn't walk away, no matter how loathsome or banal they were, and it seemed to them that you understood. And for that they loved you.

Hernandez had cried but had she understood? He thought of the two tears tracking across her cheeks, felt again the touch of her hand on his wrist, remembered the shock hot in her eyes when he'd mentioned the priest and his thanks and the shot. Had she understood?

"Where?" was all she'd said. And numbly he had gone on.

"El Salvador." The Savior. Strange to think that it might have worked out that way. "1975 when I went there. Vietnam was sinking like a rock and everyone knew that Laos and Cambodia would be right behind it. I was telling the villagers to get out but they wouldn't, most of them. Or couldn't – nowhere to go, really. And then Kinlock came down to Khemmarat.

"He'd never been there as far as I knew but he came in like he was king or something. His Jeep raised a dust plume a mile long and he had the women and kids ducking for cover. He brought a bottle of Scotch, Dewars White Label, and we sat on the porch of my hooch and drank it and he told me what the score was.

"New billet, that was how he put it. People up top liked my stuff. Best field analysis they were getting from anywhere. Salvador was the new hot spot and that was where they needed me. No military role. Just get to know the people and let him know what was happening from time to time. I should've told him to go fuck himself but I went in the hooch and packed my duffle and got in the Jeep with him and took off."

Powell picked up his coffee cup and raised it to his mouth, found it empty, set it down again, turned to the window and then back to Hernandez, who was hugging her knees and watching his face.

"It was the doctor, wasn't it? She was there."

A guess? Or did she somehow know? Powell searched her face, impassive now above her knees, and wondered. Did she understand what it was like to watch a muddy river flowing? To find a child's thin, naked corpse beside a trail, a neat red hole in the back of its head? To walk and eat and sleep in a grey rain that never ended? And then a woman, bottle in hand, on the narrow porch outside the door. "May I come in? I have something for you." The voice as simple and wonderful as salt.

"She wasn't there. Near, though. Near enough. I don't remember how Kinlock worked it in. There was no reason for him to know her. Maybe he asked if there hadn't been a doctor there, a woman. And said that he'd heard she was in Haiti now, I don't know.

"Whatever he said, it was enough. I went to Costa Rica to learn Spanish and then to Salvador as a teacher. I had a one-room school on a farm cooperative in the highlands. At planting and harvest times, the kids were in the fields and I went to Miami or Port au Prince to see Nicole. Every three months, I left a report for Kinlock with the deskman at a cheap hotel in San Salvador.

"The guerillas were going to win, I told him that. The peasants had nothing, even less than in Cambodia or Laos, and so they had nothing to lose and when they figured that out, nothing would beat them. Almost everyone sympathized with the liberation front and in time you knew they'd support them actively. I didn't give him names but no one ever asked for any, and things seemed pretty quiet there anyway."

Now, watching a cab pass on an empty city street, Powell knew that it had not been true. On the surface nothing much had happened. No firefights or bombs, no landmines on the mountain paths. The families worked the fields and the children came to the schoolyard, hunkering down in groups of five or six or chasing each other barefoot through the fine dust or kicking an ancient soccer ball back and forth until he rang the hand bell to call them in to lessons, and all of them scrubbed clean on Sundays, packed into the whitewashed church where the priest, Father Manny, told them that the Kingdom of God was among them.

But young men disappeared there - whether taken by the Army or gone to the guerillas you never knew, no one ever spoke of them again. And the Army swept through from time to time, sullen young men in trucks who herded all the people into the Plaza and searched the houses and barns and sheds, never saying what they were looking for and never finding anything. And Manny came and went, hiking up a narrow track path in the grey dawn straining under the weight of a green field pack, returning in the moonlight with it tucked under his arm.

"I liked him," he had said to Maria. "His family had money and he was smart, had studied in Barcelona, but he wanted to be with the people, the forgotten ones, he called them. I admired him.

"And I told Nicole about him. Because I couldn't tell anyone else." He had looked at Hernandez for approval but she hadn't understood until later. "Priests were all suspects and the Jesuits particularly.

"And then the kidnapping. '79. The daughter of one of the oligarchy.

Fifteen years old. Taken in an ambush in San Salvador on her way home from a birthday party." Powell heard himself reciting the facts like an attorney prepping a jury, that wanted a judgment, exoneration, innocence again; knew that it wasn't coming. "The car turned up on a road near my village, shot up and bloodstained.

"The Army came. Not the locals but one of the crack outfits from the capital, and the Treasury police with them. They sealed the town. Two or three of the young men got away but the rest, twenty or so, they put in the back of a truck and drove away. I saw them go. One, just a kid really, maybe thirteen or fourteen was crying. Had shit his pants. Another, just a little older, maybe a brother or a cousin, was holding him."

Powell wondered how this could sound from a distance of thousands of miles and a dozen years when the only link was the memory of a guy you'd met a midnight at a murder scene. No answer, though. Never. Only the sound of his own voice

"And Kinlock was there. With another American, a guy I didn't know, a fat guy with bad teeth. Who asked me point blank who the Commies were.

"I told him all of them or none of them, depending what he meant. Kinlock said it would go better for the people if the thing got settled while we were still there. I said it would have been settled a long time ago if we had never been there. The fat guy asked me about Father Manny, said `He's one of them, isn't he?' I told him that he took care of his people, that was all. Kinlock said it was time to go and I told him I was staying. He said I had to go, that he could not guarantee my safety. `No,' I said, `you can't, can you?'"

The room had gone quiet. Hernandez was sitting cross-legged, her dark eyes intent on his face in the failing afternoon light. She had not spoken. Powell had heard his own breath quickly coming and going like that of a runner beginning a long uphill stretch.

"I stayed and the Army stayed. On the first day nothing happened and on the second the Colonel sent for me. I recognized him. Viscarra was his name; he was high up in one of the right wing parties, married into one of the planting families. He and his men had taken over the church. When I came into the sacristy he was smiling, almost jovial. Told me they were making a movie. Like Hollywood, he said. And then he showed me.

"Manny was tied to the main altar which was fixed against the rear wall. Naked. Blood caked around his nose and mouth, eyes swollen almost shut, standing in a pool of his own piss. Near the altar rail was a video camera, a Sony, on a tripod. I started for him and Viscarra shot at me, two bursts from an Uzi that he had in his left hand. He said, 'We must have quiet on the set.'"

The sound, Powell remembered, had been like a living thing, swelling up in the sanctuary and sweeping back through the knave and returning, somehow almost louder, a black noise that pounded him back even as the dust from the bullet holes settled on the tile floor. Had Hernandez understood that? Now he left his perch by the window and walked to the kitchen door but the sight of her sleeping, hair and face and shoulder and arm outside the blanket, told him nothing, and he crossed the room past his own empty bed and stood by a another pane, now looking down into the seminary Close, seeing only shadows and hearing only memories.

"Sit, amigo."

That was all Viscarra had said, and he had done it, lowering himself into the carved mahogany chair against the whitewashed wall where the priest sat while the Bible lessons were read. At a gesture from the colonel a young soldier had covered him, leveling the poky barrel of an M-16 at him from just over a yard away. And then the nightmare, still vivid, almost blinding, even after so many years. How had he put it into words for Hernandez?

"Viscarra had a scalpel and he went to work, first cutting a straight line above Manny's chest about where your collarbones are and then two more going down just outside his nipples andanother across the middle of his belly. Blood was dripping down and Viscarra was whistling, and then he turned to me and said that Manny, the padre he called him, had admitted the trips into the mountains that they knew about from me. Had said he was taking medical supplies to refugees but had not said who or where. Yet.

"He turned and took hold of the skin at the bottom and tugged and it came up a little and Manny groaned. I had thought he was unconscious. And Viscarra asked him if he had anything to say to me, and he shook his head, and then Viscarra yanked hard and all of Manny's skin tore away and he screamed and passed out and you could see his raw meat and guts quivering and twitching and there was blood spattered up on the wall above the altar dripping down in lines and the guy watching me turned white and Viscarra went out and came back with a silver bucket and an aspergillum, you know, that thing with holes they use to sprinkle holy water only the guy behind him had a jerry can of gas.

"And they filled the bucket and it was hotter than hell in there and the fumes were . . . I was sweating . . . and then Viscarra shook the gas out on Manny he came to and screamed and again and . . . ."

And then he had been able to say no more and his head was down and Hernandez was kneeling beside him and her hands were on his arm. Now she was asleep but then she had been touching him and when he had looked up the tears were tracking down across her face. For whom? For him? Or Manny? Fucked up, Powell thought. Looking down at the night shadows on the close, he thought it was all fucked up, Viscarra and Manny and himself and Wolfson and Anna and Case. The whole world. But you were in it and you did what you could do. He had tried to tell Hernandez about that.

"The soldier guarding me threw up. A young guy, maybe nineteen or twenty, and Manny was screaming and his skin was on the altar and it was hot and the blood was dripping down and he

just puked. And I killed him.

"When the guard went down to vomit I kicked him and grabbed his gun and shot him. And the guy with the gas can, too. Two rounds. And Viscarra turned but he'd set his Uzi on the altar and there was no chance he'd reach it and he smiled and said I didn't have balls enough to shoot him. `No huevos,' he said and then I squeezed a short burst, three or four shots, into his thigh and he went down like a bag of cement and tipped the can on the way down and blood was gushing out and gas and the smell . . ..

"And no one came. There were more of his people outside but none of them came in - they must have heard it before, gunshots and screaming, and maybe the stone walls muffled it some. And I went up to Manny to cut him down, to tell him I hadn't put him there, but he was gasping and almost gone and he pulled his head up and said, `Gracias, amigo.'"

Thank you. Was that what it had been? In the night quiet it occurred to Powell that maybe the dying priest had been talking about grace. How had St. Paul put it? "Where sin increased, grace abounded all the more." A funny thing to think of, holed up with a cop, hiding from a killer. But it was a seminary kind of thought. Down the Close, the chapel's dark silhouette rose behind the trees above the walk where Hernandez and the Stickman, whoever that had been, had jumped him. Ninety feet, maybe less, from the fence where Wolfson had hung lifeless-like Manny on the altar. Where sin increased.

But where was the grace now? Three people dead - was that grace for them? You were supposed to believe it was. Powell shook his head in the darkness and thought that the only grace he'd felt lately was the soft cloth

WHITE ANGEL

of Hernandez's shirt against his face. But maybe that was enough.

"And I put the rifle muzzle up to his face," he heard himself saying, "and he nodded and tried to smile. And I shot him."

He had stopped then and Hernandez had slipped closer to him, next to him on the carpet. How long were they there before her right hand found the middle of his back, like a mother's steadying a dizzy child?

"Finish, Powell," she'd said. "You need to finish."

"Viscarra was trying to pull himself up. He got one hand on the top of the altar and then one on the handle of his gun and then I hit him with the M-16, sort of threw it at his bad leg and he went down again and the Uzi was flying and maybe it discharged or just struck a spark or something but the gas fumes exploded and I was on my back and the my hair was smoldering and the whole altar was on fire and Manny and Viscarra, too.

"And I knew I wouldn't get out, there'd be people at the exits so I took the tape out of the camera, I knew I needed to do that, and went to the back of the church and sat in the confessional. And I stayed there. At first there was smoke but when the first people came in they left the church doors open and the fire sucked it the other way like a chimney. And people were yelling and the church bell started to toll and there were more voices and then the sound of the trucks leaving and the shouts of the people fighting the fire and then the fire noise quieted and all I could hear was loud weeping and I wept, too, thinking of Manny and Nicole."

"Nicole?"

He had not answered but his silence had told her, and then Hernandez had held him while he cried. The cloth of her shirt had the faint lemon smell and beneath it her body was firm and strong, and now at the window it seemed to Powell that their embrace had gone on forever.

Not true, though. At some point she had pushed him away, straightened him up, wiped the tears from her own face and then reached to gently wipe them from his. At some point he had told her the rest.

How no one had found him in the confessional. How he'd left the charred church in the middle of the night and walked to the capital, three nights, moving only in darkness, how he'd gone to the university, to the Jesuit residence there and told the superior what had happened to Manny.

But not about the tape. He'd told no one there about the tape, managing instead to get it copied at the university A/V room, convincing one of the maids to deliver it to his drop at the hotel with a note that said "Don't look."

The Jebbies had kept him there for a month. Garbed in a cassock, he had followed the novices about, to meals, to meditation, to Mass, standing when they stood, kneeling when they knelt, sitting when they sat. But seeing his own vision. Each day when the chalice was raised and the priest spoke the words, "this is my blood," he saw Manny, tied and bleeding, heard the whispered syllables, "gracias." When they had finally smuggled him onto a shrimp boat at Jucuaran, he knew where the current was taking him.

"And Kinlock?" Hernandez had asked. "Did he ever find you?"

Powell remembered shaking his head. "He may have known where I was. But he never came."

"And Nicole?"

"I tried to call her once, to tell her exactly what she had done. But she was gone. Just then I believe I hated her. I don't know now."

Now there was no knowing, only a memory of kind brown eyes and lined, cracked hands, and nights clinging to each other in the face of a huge, black monster, a terrifying vacuum that sucked the light out of life. Who could say what it would make you do?

And now a sound, something new in the city's night hum to pull Powell's interest away from the question, something below him on the seminary Close. At first nothing to grab onto but then the solid thump of the door to the lobby swinging shut and from somewhere below the trees footsteps on the stone walk. No one in sight yet but the sound was moving away to the far side of the grounds toward the faculty townhouses. Powell found a sight line through the trees to a spot near the Chapel at the far end of the quadrangle where the walk was visible under the orange glow of a halogen light from the street.

And then a body hit the light and Powell heard his own voice speaking sharply. "Hernandez!" And the figure was gone again: a tall man in what appeared to be a long sleeveless cloak wearing an odd broad-brimmed hat with the edges turned slightly up.

Chapter 19

SUNDAY - 1:28 a.m.

Hernandez rolled over, half sat up, and curled back into her blankets. Moving quickly to the two-foot space between the twin beds, Powell snapped the switch of the lamp on the night table and pulled Hernandez's shoulder towards himself.

"Maria! Something's going down."

"Jesus, let go of me~~!"

Now she was sitting up, eyes squinted tight, her hair a wild black tangle framing her face, her white tee shirt clinging loosely to her breasts and nipples, a cold contrast to the warmth of her brown skin.

"Something's going on out there. Get some clothes on."

"What? What the hell you talking about?"

"Where're my shoes?" Fumbling under his bed, Powell found the left, then his right loafer, and sat to slip them on his bare feet. Hernandez was up, standing on the far side of a mass of rumpled sheets, hands on hips, and glaring.

"You gonna tell me what this is about?" The tee shirt stopped at the top of her thighs. Beneath it her legs were dark and slim and muscular.

"No," Powell said, "I'm not. And I'm not going to wait for you either if you don't get some pants on and get moving."

Hot. Almost boiling, Powell thought. She grabbed her slacks from the floor and started to step into them while Powell moved to the window again. Nothing there. Probably too late. Turning back, he headed for the door.

"The hell you goin'?" A challenge, not a question.

"Out. Meet you downstairs. Bring your light."

Powell didn't look back and didn't stop. His feet crashed loudly on the wooden steps, deafening in the night silence, sure to wake someone. But didn't. On the stone step in front of the door the cool darkness was as quiet as city air ever got - only the traffic hum and the whine of a jet engine way off somewhere, and the faintly palpable rumble of the IND train a block or two away. In a moment, though, footsteps behind him coming closer, Hernandez in the stairwell, and the door swinging open, her hand on his left arm just below the shoulder pulling him sharply towards him, her voice a whispered hiss.

"What the fuck is this about?"

"Saw a gay john on the street paying his squeeze. Now he's in here."

"You got me out of bed for that?" Her face moving from anger to amusement and back again. "You could see that on any corner of the West Village."

"I tell you about Tony and Jamahl? The Roach Motel?"

"What? The what? What is it?"

"I don't know. But it disappears people. Now come on."

He pulled free and loped off down the walk, listening for her to follow. When he stopped at the corner of the chapel just at the edge of a pool of yellow lucency from a spotlight high up on the façade, she was at his elbow, sucking wind in hard, controlled breaths. He watched her eyes scan the scene, darting from point to point and back again, lingering for an instant on one stretch of the wrought iron fence that ran along 20th Street where, Powell guessed, Wolfson had been hanging two mornings before.

"What're we looking for?"

"Tall guy. Funny coat like a long cape or a cloak. Flat wide-brimmed hat, brim kind of curls at the edges."

"See his face?"

"Nope. Not with the hat."

"Well he's not here. C'mon."

Following her across the light's misshapen circle, Powell heard her question again: "What're we looking for?" A good one. What was it? Some poor queen of a seminarian, in from a furtive night on the town? Whose bishop would pull the plug if the scandal of police contact ever reached the halls of the diocesan house? Or something else? Something darker and harder to know? Unless you'd been there and had seen the blood dripping down. Hernandez moved off the curving walk and followed the right-angled lines of the buildings moving across grass and flower beds and brushing past shrubs. Ahead of them, another reservoir of fluorescence welled up from a gap in the row of buildings that lined the north side of the Close.

"What's down there?" Powell's voice surprised him with a quaver in its treble line.

"A gate to 21st Street. Deadbolt lock on it, I think." Hernandez sounded fine, as calm as a woman window-shopping on a bright-lit avenue. "If I remember right, there's a big bin there, too, where they stack the garbage."

Two watchmen making the rounds, that's all they were. A quiet night, a cab passing on 20th Street, faint stars in the sky above the city glow and wispy clouds. And then the screech of metal on metal and shuffling footsteps close and indistinct voices.

Hernandez moved first, running in a crouch to the corner of the brick building closest to the gap. Watching her, then following, Powell found himself smiling at the picture of a cop in a white tee shirt and loose linen pants holding a flashlight. And no gun. No smile now. Problem if this was the guy. He reached for her shoulder but her left arm shoved him off and the flashlight beam snapped on.

"Right there!" Her voice a solid shout. "Hold it right there!"

And she was around the corner and down a flight of cement steps and the flashlight's beam was bouncing off walls and cutting through a chain link fence where the street was and Hernandez was tugging at a doorknob of a metal and glass door in the base of the building on the far side of the gap.

"Goddam it. In there!" Another hard, rattling pull. "She's in there."

"The key. Try it. The M key."

Powell had the plastic rectangle that held their suite keys out; two coppery tabs hung from it. Hernandez snatched it and fumbled, a light came on in a window two floors above them and another in a building across the narrow greensward, and the key turned and the door swung towards them and Hernandez was through it and running.

First, a long cinderblock hall and then a laundry room, chipped tile floor, a half dozen each of washers and dryers lit by the red glow of an exit sign. The beam of Hernandez's flashlight was beyond it far down another passage. Powell followed, stumbling on a three-step staircase, falling forward onto the concrete floor of a narrow tunnel. Pulling himself up, he felt his way forward, right hand on rough brick, no light now, and Maria's footsteps faint ahead of him beyond some sort of divide that he could not see. Until it hit him.

Or he hit it, nose and mouth and chin smashing into a metal wall invisible in the blackness, teeth tearing lips and blood welling into his mouth. Fire door. Shouldn't be shut but it was. His hands found the metal handle, down and to the right, and pulled and the light was ahead again, sweeping walls and floor and ceiling, and a voice, too, not faint now but loud and echoing in the cramped space.

"JESUS FUCKING CHRIST!"

And then the light was on him and footsteps were rushing at him and he was spitting blood and the voice was close and quiet and a hand was on his arm.

"What the hell happened to you?" The light swept the passage where they stood. "Did she hit you?"

"Found a door with my face. And what `she' are you talking about?"

"The woman. The woman in white."

Powell shook his head. "Must've hit harder than I thought. What woman? I thought we were looking for a man."

"You didn't see her? In the doorway there? A tall woman, blonde, some kind of a white dress? Just like she said."

"Slow down, Maria. Like who said?"

Hernandez chuckled and Powell felt her right hand slide up across his back to his shoulder as she sidled up close to him. "Don't know what the hell I'm talking about, do you, Padre? Not a clue?"

"Not even an inkling," Powell said, "whatever an inkling is. A young inkle, I guess." Her hand squeezed the top of his shoulder gently and dropped off of him and she eased back down the passageway, talking over her shoulder.

"Remember the other night? At Duggan's?" Powell remembered, remembered wanting her then before this had gotten complicated, when Case and Anna were still alive. Now her light's beam was playing slowly over the passage walls and he wished it was still then and not now, and her voice was drifting lazily back to him through the cool damp air that was somehow unsettling and familiar. "I had to leave to come up here, to brief el Dino and to talk to a possible witness. Remember?"

"El Dino?" His voice but none of his attention with it. The damp air was important and he searched backwards for a reason but didn't find one.

"The Dean. Wanted to know how it was going. Was already hearing from trustees. Shaken up, too. Nothing surprising there."

"The witness?"

"Coming to her." Hernandez had climbed the short flight up to the laundry room where Powell had stumbled coming down. Now she waited and played the light on the grey cement risers. The space smelled of detergent and fabric softener and from somewhere there was the high-pitched beep of a truck backing up. "She's an old Cuban nun who lives in the convent across the street. You religious types are everywhere, aren't you?"

"Our boss is, anyway." Powell smiled. "What'd she say?"

"Couldn't get it all. She was almost hysterical. The bottom line was she was looking out her window in the middle of the night and saw a woman in white in the seminary grounds, very pale, like a ghost. And that's what I saw, right down there in that window by the gate.

"A ghost?"

"A woman. A pale, blonde woman."

"What time did the Sister see her?"

"Couldn't tell. If I was getting it right, she had got up to pee. Late, though. No one around. And before we got there."

"She didn't see a body on the fence?"

Hernandez shook her head. "She didn't and I don't think she could have. Showed me the window. There's a tree that maybe you could see around if you were trying but not if you weren't."

"You believe her?"

"Tell you the truth? No." She looked down into the circle of light on the floor and back up at him again, chewing her lip and searching for something. "I thought she was crazy. Talking about Los Angeles the whole time like she was hoping to go there. You gotta say that's odd for an eighty-year-old sister."

Powell chuckled. "Hey, maybe she wants to try Hollywood. You would, too, you spend a lifetime in a convent."

"Yeah. But now I've seen it, too."

"Somebody who lives here?"

"Could be. But I checked out the Sister's story with the housing director; she didn't think so."

"Visitor?"

"That runs around in a white dress after midnight? You ever have guests that do that?"

Now she crossed the room to the doorway they'd sprinted through, stepped over its metal threshold back into the cinderblock hallway, stood with her light playing on a steel and cement staircas by a small elevator door.

"I guess she could have got up there before I got the door open."

"Where's it go?"

"We're under the faculty building. Wolfson lived upstairs. Top floor."

Powell could picture the building from the outside, a nondescript red brick pile that was completely out of character with the rest of the seminary's Victorian architecture, like a fragment of Co-op City that had slid back a hundred years. He reached to catch Hernandez's arm as she started up the steps.

"Someone comes out, be tough to explain."

"She's here, I'm gonna find her." She tugged to pull away but he tightened his grip.

"She's not here. There's a door at the top of that flight, goes right out onto the walk. She's scared enough to run, she'd be long gone now." Hot eyes again, a glitter visible even in the semi-darkness. "Anyway, we're supposed to be secluding ourselves. That's not a real good way to do it."

"You're a prick, Powell." A barb in her tone, but agreement, too.

"Nice of you to notice." The pain around his mouth was turning dull, and his swollen lip was muckling up against his teeth. "I don't say 'you, too,' do I? Don't guess that'd be appropriate."

She laughed. "No, man. You're s'posed to call me a bitch. Or 'beach' if you wanna do it in Rican."

He was still holding her arm and she had edged a half step closer to him so her face was just below his, now.

"Okay, beach. You wanna go to bed?"

"Smooth, Padre." Big smile, a smell of sleep and sweat. "Muy smooth. You must be a city guy, from San Juan, no?"

"San Juan and I are old friends. Went to seminary together."

And then closer, her breasts brushing up across his rib cage, their nipples firm enough to be felt through two layers of cotton, and then her lips light on his, then hard, hot and pressing hard. And a sharp stab of pain up through his gums and behind his nose and the taste of blood fresh in his mouth.

"Aaarh!" Holding her arms at the biceps, he pushed back, did not let go, watched successive looks, first of anger, the of amusement, sweep over her face.

"You say that to all the girls?"

Powell ran his tongue over his swollen lips and tried to smile. "Only the vampires."

Her hands rose to the sides of his face, fingers landing lightly on his cheeks.

"Open." Now her face was close again, her eyes as intent as a dental hygienist's on the inside of his mouth, her body still supple against his. "Bad one, Mick. You gonna need some stitches?"

"Maybe. Think it stopped for a while, though."

"'Till I planted one on you?"

"Mighta had something to do with it. Why d'you do that, anyway?"

"I wanted to. You wanted me to." Her dark eyes were searching his. "Didn't you?"

"Yep." A stab of pain again as his smile formed and pulled at the edges of the cut, and within a twinge of disquietude over some older, deeper scar. "I did."

Her hands slid from his face and grasped his fingertips, and she eased a fraction of an inch, a space as big as a mile, away from him.

"What now?" Was it his voice asking?

"I could use a drink." Definitely hers now. And what emotion was there beneath the matter-of-factness of her tone? "Any of that Dewars left?"

"Must be some. We couldn't have finished it."

Hernandez dropped his hands and moved into the dark passageway towards the door they'd first come in. "We finished plenty," she said over her shoulder, "and you should be happy about it. 'Cause now it's gonna burn like hell goin' down."

And what would hell burn like? At the core, Powell thought, Dante had it right. No fire at all but an endless lake of ice and only you in it. He had Ciardi's elegant translation in his office, could picture it there just recently on the corner of the desk just in front of the window from which Anna had flown. Or was it recently? More like a million years ago.

Now they were outside again in the narrow interstice between buildings where the door and gate were, the chilly air - or something - raising gooseflesh on his bare arms while the detective's flashlight played quickly over the scene. A bin of green plastic trash bags, all right, the high chain link fence whose razor-ribboned top and dead-bolted gate testified that even places nominally of God were subject to the all too temporal fears of the city, the flight of concrete steps they'd hurried down, and two facing doors: the steel and glass one they had just exited opposite a pointed arch in which double wooden panels were set, inset really, back six inches from the plane of the wall and harder to see, all of it lit by single shaded bulb projected from the far wall perhaps a quarter of the way across the gap.

"Didn't we hear voices?" Hernandez asked. "More than one?"

"Coming down here? I thought so. Why?"

"Only saw one person. Maybe the dude you saw was down here, too?"

"Could be, I guess." He didn't care. And knew it. She was the pro, let her think about; he was caught between the feel of her body pressed close to his and the promise of a drink to come.

"But you saw him with a guy. Odd that there'd be a woman now."

"This is New York, Detective. Is anything really odd?"

She grinned. "Maybe not. Except maybe you. You're pretty strange even for the Apple."

"Yeah, right. And what about you?"

Hernandez' smile wavered for an instant and she looked away, then back again.

"Yeah," she said. Touched his arm, pushed him away towards the steps. "C'mon, let's go get that drink."

And then silence. On the walk, no words. On the steps back up to the suite nothing. But in the stillness, something. As in all quiet, he thought. A voice there. Silence always saying something. Something between them now. He searched the evening for a clue, a key to its translation.

Nothing, though. Nothing clear. After his confession she had waited, had sat lightly resting her fingertips on his knee, as if that light touch was the ballast that could keep him from spinning off into a void. When he was settled again, the jagged burden of his history still aching but submerged again, she had somehow known, had taken charge then. "We need to get something to eat," she'd said. Thinking back, Powell reflected that it was what Jesus might have done. He was always good about food.

And then it was details: Maria giving the orders and he himself running the errands so that she would not be noticed; first to the phone in the lobby to call the Szechuan place up the avenue, then to the car to pick up the bags, then to Felippe's, a liquor store by the subway stop where one aisle was winos getting Night Train and the other was yuppies after chilled champagne, and finally back to the suite with White Label in a grey plastic sack slung from one hand and a sweet-and-pungent-smelling, grease-spotted, paper bag clutched in the other.

Eating and drinking and conversation, that was how the evening had gone. Moo shu and plum sauce and spring rolls and fried dumplings and scotch without ice and baseball - a Mets fan - and restaurants and recipes. And, odd for a cop, Powell thought, foreign films - she knew them all for the past two or three years and none before that. And then, "I'm beat. Disappear yourself." From the kitchenette, buzzing with the whiskey, he had listened to the rustle of her clothes and blankets and then, with no interval it seemed, the even breathing of her sleep.

And now they were on the steps again and at the suite door and through it, and silence trailed from her in lines that spread like the wake of a boat in still water. In the suite, she moved straight to the kitchen, to the bottle on the table and the smudged glasses on the sideboard by the sink. Four inches left in the bottle and she poured it all, picking up one glass, leaving one, brushing past him, past the beds and the desk, leaning against the back of a chair by the windows, kicking shoes off her sockless feet, sipping scotch and staring out at the glowing darkness.

"Something on your mind, Maria?"

"Nothing." No slack in the sound; syllables tight as twisted cable. "So you think I'm strange, is that it?"

"Marie, what's the story here? I jus-"

"You want a story?" A shrill, crazy question. "Is that it, Father? An odd one? A good one to tell your friends? 'I met this lady cop once; boy, was she a piece of work.' Or will it just make you feel better about your stinking self?"

Thinking, from nowhere. She's coming from nowhere. Saying, "Maria, what's wrong with you? I don't-"

"Wrong with me?" A liquid hiss at the edge of tears. "Is that what you want to know? You fucking priests always think that something's wrong."

The glass slipped from her hand, hit the floor, and shattered, scattering shards and whiskey in a wide arc. Hernandez, crying now, paid it no mind. Her turn in the confessional.

"How's this: I was married to a guy, a good Catholic guy, Knights of Columbus, everything, who." Sobbing now her breath coming hard. "Beat the shit out of me twice a week. And then finally once. He raped me while. My daughter. Four years old. Was watching."

The tears were running down and Powell smelled sweat and scotch and lemons while Hernandez fumbled with something at her waist.

And then the linen slacks had dropped to the floor and before Powell could move, her arms crossed and rose towards the ceiling, pulling the tee shirt with them revealing blue cotton bikini briefs and a slim waist, firm round breasts and small dark nipples. And she was moving still. In a smooth bend and step motion, as graceful as a dancer's, the panties disappeared and then she stood, arms down, eyes hot and shining, bright tear tracks on her cheeks.

"You want it, Powell? Is this what you want?"

He did. The stiffening between his legs answered that. Moving quickly, he pulled the spread from the nearest bed, his bed, wrapped it round her, threw an arm over her slumping shoulders, pulled her gently forward.

"There's glass. Watch where you step."

"I couldn't tell anyone. I couldn't." She seemed to be talking to herself as to him as he eased her down onto the sheets. And then she told him why.

"I couldn't tell. He was a cop."

Chapter 20

SUNDAY - 7:14 a.m.

Maria had been sleeping when he awoke, sleeping through his shave, shower, and dressing, and still asleep when he'd left. And the whole city was sleeping when he hit the avenue, the wide pavement empty, not a car, not even a cab out there until your line of vision stretched up towards 24th or 25th where a downtown bus lumbered towards the shelter at 23rd, dwarfed beneath the hulk of the London Terrace apartments.

The sidewalks, too, were empty as he headed towards the diner in the crisp morning air, only a fat woman with two tiny dogs in knitted sweaters, a wino passed out in a pool of piss by the doorway of the hardware store, and a Korean woman squeezing oranges by the fruit market at the corner of 22nd, sitting on a wooden crate, apparently oblivious to the flattened condoms at curbside near her feet.

Fun City. Powell remembered that a former mayor had called it that, couldn't think of his name but bet that the next election hadn't been kind to him. Fun City - it made him think of Lethe and Tony, of Jamal and the wino in the doorway. So much fun, using people up and throwing them away. Somewhere something called the Roach Motel, where people were insects, stuck and rotting.

Maybe what Maria's marriage had been like. A sweet-smelling trap with no way out. But somehow she *was* out and Powell wondered what had happened to set her free. Or maybe not free, but out and walking around and still caught in the shit. That was the nowhere she'd been coming from.

Freedom hadn't happened yet but something had and that's where the grace would be. If there was such a thing. Always the thought that there was nothing. Powell smiled. Doubt. Just what it meant to be human. Could you look at a body on a fence and or crisped in an oven and not wonder? The blood in the sanctuary was on the wall - but that was what the promise was. 'Pick up your cross.' Doubt. Heavy almost beyond belief. But life was on the other side.

At the corner of 23rd, Powell crossed the avenue and went into the diner on the opposite side. Windows on Chelsea, the seminarians called it. Ok food, big portions, and decent prices, fast and somewhat surly service. No one there now except a man in shades with a seeing-eye dog staring intently out the window. At what? He sat at the counter, two stools from the near end and watched the waitress swipe her way up the formica towards him with a damp cloth.

"What can I get ya?" A big-boned blonde woman, 45, maybe older, in a too-tight, black and white waitress dress, white sneakers, and a name tag that said Kate.

"Two large OJ's and a couple of cinnamon danish to go."

"Your mother never taught you to say please?"

"Please."

"Please, what?" Now she was smiling, standing with her left hand on her hip, enjoying his discomfiture.

"Please, ma'am, may I have two large OJ's and two cinnamon danish? To go." A return grin forming with the words.

"Good. VERY good." An appreciative shake of the head. "Most folks come in here woulda said 'fuck you' right away. You from outta town? Indiana or somewhere?"

"Illinois, originally. Cairo, Illinois." The waitress pivoted to grab two blue cardboard cups from under the stainless steel counter behind her and

Powell knew that he liked her. "But then no one's from here. It's like purgatory in that respect."

Turning back, the woman set the cups down. No smile now, eyed him quizzically, said, "I'll be goddammed. A priest, right?"

"Wrong. Actually, I'm a nun. How'd you guess?"

"Who the hell else talks about purgatory?"

The waitress' eyes fell and she busied herself with pouring the juice, finding white plastic lids and snapping them on, shaking out a brown paper bag, turning, then moving down the counter to a clear dome covering a precarious pile of sweet rolls. Coming back, standing in front of him again holding two cinnamon danish in a sheet of waxed paper in her left hand, she leveled a look at him and moved her head almost invisibly from side to side.

"First guy to smile at me in a week and he's a priest in civvies. Tell me - you think I'm gonna have a good day?"

"You're already having one."

"How do you know?" Wanting to believe it, not quite making it.

"You like people." A barely perceptible nod. "As they used to say in the beer commercials, it doesn't get any better than that."

She smiled but her eyes said disappointment; she was wanting something more. Who wasn't? Taking the bag, Powell headed for the cashier wondering when something more was coming. When he looked back, the waitress was standing by a skinny black man, talking and laughing. Having a good day. Maybe that was all there was.

But the day wasn't good at the suite. Hernandez was up, waiting at a half open door in new jeans and an old Hard Rock Cafe tee shirt, lips tightened to a pink line, glowering at him.

"The hell you been?"

Powell stopped two steps below the landing. "Good morning to you, too, Detective."

"Cut the shit, Powell. Where were you?"

"The Russian Tea Room. I called for delivery but they don't do that anymore."

Gone. Head tossed and then gone from the doorway. Pushing the door open, he stepped over the threshold, pushed it shut behind him, and stopped. She was standing over the desk, her back to him, checking the cartridges in her revolver, its tan leather shoulder holster hanging on the back of the wooden chair.

"You gonna start playing with that now?"

"I don't play with it," she snapped. "I use it. And right now I'm wondering what would be wrong with using it on you."

"Maria." She didn't turn. Snapped the cylinder back into the pistol. "I'm not the enemy, Maria."

"No, you're not." Now she was facing him, jaw squared and skin lightly flushed, the gun held loosely at her side. "But just what are you?"

Don't turn, Powell told himself. Don't turn away now. Even if you want to, don't. He held the white paper bag in front of his thighs, both hands gripping the folded top, keeping his gaze leveled at her face, letting the silence build around them like warm water rising, rising in a pool.

"What am I?" The pistol on the desk now, her fingers lightly resting on its grip. "Right now, I'm reality and you're in it and you don't like it."

"What kind of shit is that?" Something different about her eyes now, still dark with anger but some uncertainty there, too; still a fixed stare, but the possibility of a blink as well.

"Shit's right, Maria. Shit's what I'm talking about. You told me about it and you hoped it would go away and it didn't and now you're mad at me."

"Fuck you, Powell."

"That kinda proves my point, doesn't it?" Now look away, create some space. When he turned back she wasn't facing him, had turned toward the desk, was examining the revolver as if it was an object that she had never seen. He spoke softly now. "Or do you always jump on guys who go out to pick up breakfast?"

"There aren't any guys doing that." Still looking at the gun, something important not said.

"Well then I'm the first." Into the kitchen then, out of her sightline, calling back to her, "Want coffee?"

"Yeah."

No conviction in the tone. Powell rattled plates and cups busily and waited before speaking. "Whatta we do today? Stay put and read the Times?"

"Don't know." Hernandez in the kitchen doorway. No pistol. "Guess we check in with Kelsey. See if he's got anything."

"Makes sense. Then what?"

Hernandez shook her head. "You like crosswords?"

"No time like the present to find out. O.J.?"

"Yeah." She pulled back a chair and slid into it, tucking her left ankle under her right knee. Powell lifted a cup out of the bag, set it in front of her, put the other one at the place across the table.

"Hey, Powell?" Hesitant voice, but her eyes steady on his face.

"Yeah?"

"Sorry. About this morning . . . and last night, too."

"Don't be. You listened to me, I listened to you. Pretty fair deal, wouldn't you say?" "Yeah." A faint trace of smile and now a glance away, down, towards the paper cup and the table. "I mean, I shouldn't have kissed you and . . . you know . . . I don't know why."

"Maybe because you needed someone not to take advantage of you. I know I did." Powell turned to the cabinet, found the coffee jar, pulled down the mugs, thought of her breasts and of the dark triangle of hair, spoke over his shoulder, "Can I ask you something?"

"What?"

Grinning now. "You'll tell me the truth?"

"Sure, I guess." Her smile starting to form, too. "What?"

"Am I an okay kisser?"

A chuckled answer: "Out of practice but not bad. The blood was a nice touch, though."

It wasn't much, Powell thought, but it was enough. Enough lightness to get them started, enough of a push to get them moving out of a wheelspinning, mudstuck mess. Hernandez shifted in her chair at the scuffed formica table and watched while he doled coffee into mugs and poured steaming water in on top. Dropping spoons in like markers, Powell lifted the danish onto a chipped plate, moved it first and then the coffees, sat and stared and said nothing and let Maria fidget.

"What? What're you looking at?"

"Nothing. Just thinking." True enough, he thought. Might as well tell her. "Just thinking that you're a really lovely woman."

Hernandez ducked her head down and to the left, studied her coffee, smiled, didn't answer. And this, Powell knew, would be the moment to remember later, the best part of this or any day: dark hair framing dark skin, dark oval eyes shy, warm pink lips holding on to a trace of smile.

It didn't last. Sipping her coffee, Hernandez broke the spell. Then it was conversation of no consequence, danish and orange juice, more coffee, a final long look at a wristwatch.

"Time to get a move on."

"What's first?"

"Calls. Check in with Kelsey. And with vice."

"Vice?"

"Look, you want this Roach Motel thing checked out or not? Maybe they know something."

She slid back from the table, rose, and turned in one smooth motion, leaving Powell to watch her back framed by the doorway and moving out. She tucked the .38 into the waistband of her jeans, zipped into a cop blue windbreaker, stepped around the unmade beds to the suite door, and paused to shoot him a peremptory grin.

"Back in a few."

"Take care."

It was an automatic answer and then she was gone. Good advice, though, Powell thought. There wasn't enough care out there; always best to take some. Too few caregivers. Anna had been one. And Kate the waitress looked like a good bet. And he himself, sometimes. And Jimmy and Ellen. And Hernandez? He saw the girl in the yard in Queens and knew that she must be, too. Crossing the room to the windows from which he'd seen the cloaked man in the darkness, he watched Maria crossing the Close in the clear light of the autumn day, watched her disappear through the glass doors into the lobby, whispered again, "Take care."

There was a space of time the - ten minutes? twenty? - that Powell was never able to account for in memory. Housekeeping time, bed making, dishwashing time. And then fast foot-steps on the wooden stairs and the door busting open in front of Hernandez.

"Something's up." She was flushed and out of breath. "With Kelsey. I'm going."

He caught her by the arm, his right hand firm just above her left elbow.

"Tell me about it."

"No time, Powell." She tried to shake his grip but he tightened it and pulled her closer.

"Make time. If you go down, I need to know what I'm up against."

She pulled again and then relaxed. "Okay. Okay, you're right." A deep breath, looking down, and then her right hand on his forearm.

"There were two messages. One last night just said, `Stay put.' But there was one this morning, just a little while ago. From someone called Ann Gelban or something. Gave a time and a place. 8:38; Irving Place at Grammercy Park. Said that Kelsey would be looking but he wouldn't see me. Only twenty five minutes from now."

"For you by name?"

"The first one was. The other they guessed was for me, said it was for Kelsey's partner." Hernandez clearly puzzled, mouth open, working, then shut. "Whaddaya getting at?"

"Set up. Maybe they want to see who else knows what he knows. Said to give it to his partner. You go down there, they got you."

"I'll get some back up."

"Same thing except nothing'll happen. If they got someone inside, they're gonna know."

"Maybe." She took a step backward toward the door. "But what else can I do?"

"Nothing. You do nothing. I'll go."

"No way. What good would that do?" Flat dismissal but she didn't move. At least, Powell thought, she was interested.

"Look, they may already know who Kelsey works with, what you look like. But even if they know my name, chances are they don't have a picture. And anyway, I've got an idea."

"Nope. No sale." Now she was moving again and he had to reach to catch her hand.

"Maria, if something happens to you, who the hell's gonna listen to me?"

Hernandez stopped, smiled briefly, shook her hand free. "Good point, Father. Not everyone's as dumb as I am. Tell me about it in a cab."

The scheme was simple. He'd come at the corner along the south side of the park from the east; she'd hold the cab to the northwest, at Park and 20th, where they'd found a pay phone. To set up a distraction, she'd call in a fire; he'd see who or what was to be seen and get the hell out. All this commencing at 8:36, watches synchronized just like in the movies.

The scene was benign enough. Powell surveyed it from the front step of a synagogue at the southeast corner. People bundled against a stiff cool breeze, jogging, walking dogs, strolling under falling autumn leaves along the wrought iron fence that surrounded the last private green space in New York City. If you had money and lived on the park you jogged inside where the homeless people couldn't even sit, much less beg for change. But no one in there now.

At 8:35, he crossed the street. Up at Irving, a streetlight and a trash basket and a huge grey dog leashed to a youngish red-haired woman who was leaning idly against the fence looking at a magazine. Further down a black man with a grocery cart full of bulky black plastic bags, and closer to him, a spectacled Yuppie in designer sweats and Reeboks, walking, not running, adjusting neon green headphones over her long dark hair.

At 8:37, the sound of a distant siren, then another. Powell started walking along the fence. The red-head turned her magazine arm, lowered it, reached into a pocket with her leash hand, and stepped up to drop something into the trash. She headed towards Powell as the distant sirens came closer and flashing light bounced off buildings down past Park Avenue.

The black man pushed his cart to the curb and stepped between two parked cars, peering westward as the first red truck lumbered across the Avenue towards them, horn blaring so loudly that even the dark-haired

Yuppie, still headphoned, turned back to see what was coming. The truck, a hook and ladder screeched to a stop, literally screeched, an ear grating sound, and a pumper roared up behind it, both blocking the street in front of the National Arts Club's ornate facade.

Powell passed the red-head, who now was tugging the jumbo canine behind her. And then knew what was wrong. Whirling, he snatched her magazine hand, twisted the arm up tight behind her, forcing a sharp, frightened groan. The dog stared placidly at the two of them.

"Drop the leash."

"Aaaah!" The woman pulled to get away and Powell twisted harder.

"Drop the leash."

The leash dropped and the dog trotted back up the street towards the trucks where face-masked men were dashing towards the double glass doors.

"Let's go see what you put in the trash."

"Let go of me. What do you want?"

Powell pushed her along in front of him and didn't answer. Nothing but paper visible in the basket as they approached. Paper and something shining.

"Take it out."

The woman wasn't struggling now. She bent forward and put her right hand on the trash basket's metal rim. One of the fireman, perhaps thirty yards away, was staring at them. A cab was coming up Irving towards the corner. The woman had a black case now, like a wallet but with something shining. The fireman pulled his mask off and moved a step closer. Not much time now. The cab was almost at the corner. NOT RIGHT! something screamed in Powell's brain. Something not right. The cab's back window down, too cold for that, something like an umbrella showing. He yanked the woman up and towards him at the instant that the cab stopped and the umbrella became a gun barrel.

Now something warm splashed up across his cheek and there was a poppoppoppoppop sound and they were falling backwards, the woman coming down hard on top of him. The cab door swung open and someone all in black with a black ski mask rose out of it, began to raise a rifle, crumpling backwards before it was leveled as two louder pops sounded behind Powell and to his left. A hand caught the man in black and the cab rolled and its back window splintered and disappeared and Powell turned to see Hernandez's hand and gun stretching through the wrought iron fence.

"Get the hell out of there! Church corner!" she yelled and was gone, sprinting diagonally across the park.

Powell rolled the woman off him onto the stone sidewalk. Oozing red pulp filled the space where her face had been, and two huge scarlet circles widened across her chest. He grabbed the wallet from her hand and ran. Rounding the corner at 19th and Park, he saw Hernandez scrambling into a yellow Checker a block up in front of a brownstone church. Sprinting, he caught the light and he dove in. Someone was yelling in Spanish and the tires squealed and they were in the traffic stream and speeding north.

"Great plan, Mick." Anger, hot as oil, spitting and sizzling next to him. Hernandez reached over and took the wallet from his hand. "Any other good ideas?"

Panting, Powell shook his head. "What the hell is that, anyway?"

"Kelsey's shield and I.D." She showed him the ornate gold badge. "But what's this crap hooked on here?

Stapled below the shield was a small clear plastic sandwich bag of something that looked like blue and red and white preserves. Beneath that a white card and neat script: 'Time to stop looking. Angail Ban.'

Powell took the wallet and poked at the baggie and knew what it was. He felt the danish and orange juice and coffee rising, and swallowed hard.

"Oh, Jesus. Oh, God."

"Mick? Mick, what is it?"

He felt tears coming and had to force the words. "Those are eyes. Kelsey's eyes."

Chapter 21

SUNDAY - 9:16 a.m.

The atrium was beginning to fill up. The black wire chairs and round stone tables collected signs of occupancy; first jackets and caps, newspapers, then tall paper coffee cups, some plain, some with the cinnamon-sprinkled foam heads, then small paper plates stacked with croissants and pain au chocolat. The people that went with them were an odd lot. Mostly white, with a black or brown face here and there as out of place as a raisin in a sugar cookie, running up the age spectrum from well-togged 20's in shades pretending to read GQ and Vanity Fair to sweat-suited 40's and 50's, hands greying with the ink of the Sunday Times, to slightly shabby 70's shuffling a bit and working stacks of newsprint in Yiddish and Italian and German, all of them there to get out of apartments the size of margarine sticks that smelled of bug spray and last night's dinner.

Hernandez was at the phone, one of four in a huge round granite and metal kiosk a dozen yards from the table Powell sat at. The white noise of sliding chairs and rustling papers and footsteps and coughing covered her voice but her gestures and expression spoke of vehemence. Powell was not surprised.

In the cab, she'd been as agitated as a bug in a spotlight, turning to the back window, cursing in English and Spanish, at one point trying to grab Kelsey's badge and the baggie with the eyes. Powell had gripped her arm and pushed it deliberately back towards her lap.

"What were you going to do with that?"

"Throw it out the fucking window!"

"Can't do it. Evidence."

She'd lunged again and he had again caught her arm and fired words before she could again make a try. "Did you reload?"

The question had surprised her. Weakly shaking her head, she'd slumped down in the cab's battered black seat.

"Might be a good idea." He'd tried to keep his voice low and had watched only out of the corner of his eyes as she'd fumbled in her bag for a leather case the size of a cigarette pack, which opened along the long side. Two rows of cartridges there, maybe a dozen in all. Hernandez had slid the revolver out of its shoulder holster and had held it down in front of the seat well out of the driver's line of vision. Pushing the three spent rounds out into her hand, she'd jammed three new ones into the cylinders, pocketed the empties and holstered the piece. Ninety seconds, Powell thought. Not more.

"Hey! Amigo!" Powell had rapped on the glass shield between at the top of the front seat. A nervous brown face glanced his way in response. "Once around the block and then up to 53rd and 3rd. Okay?"

"You think someone's following us?" A quick jerk to look over her shoulder back into the sparse Sunday traffic.

"Don't know. If they are and they're good at it, we're not gonna see 'em. But maybe they don't have much practice."

"Why not back to the room? No one knew we were there."

"We let someone know last night. Better not try it yet."

"Yet?" Hernandez had half turned to him; her lips were slightly parted, her eyes perhaps a millimeter wider than usual.

"Gonna have to go back some time. It IS the crime scene."

She'd nodded and turned away. "What's at 53rd and 3rd?"

"Citicorp Center. People. Phones."

"Who you calling?"

"I'm not. You are."

"The fuck's that mean?"

Still tight as a wire, Powell had thought. And this wasn't going to help. He'd looked away and drawn a deep breath before speaking.

"I don't know if that was your daughter I saw the other day, Maria. But if it was, you need to have someone get her out of there."

Her color had changed in waves, first to a doughy light brown - jaw slack and mouth open - then to a deep red-brown, lips snapped in a tight line and face squared in anger. She hadn't waited for him when the cab had pulled to the curb by St Peter's, the jazz church in the shadow of the slant-topped skyscraper. Before he had reached his wallet, she was out on the traffic side, around the back of the hack and racing for the revolving door.

No point trying to keep up. Powell collected his change and followed at a brisk walk. When he'd spotted her at the phone stand, he had staked out a table, dropped his jacket on a chair, sat in the one opposite and waited, watching her alternately snap at and caress the receiver. Finishing, she stared at the phone for a moment finally turning to scan the space, nodding briskly when she spotted his wave then weaving her way towards him.

"What now?" She stood across the table, hands flat on its surface. Tired, Powell thought. Just fucking weary. Too much for anyone.

"Your girl's okay?"

No answer, only two quick nods.

"Who's she with?"

"Marypat. She's a - " Hernandez glanced quickly at him " - a friend."

"Sit then. Sit a minute. I'll get coffee."

She draped his coat over the back of the chair and sat down heavily as he stood and turned toward the cafe. He was a step and a half away before she spoke.

"Mick." Powell turned back and stopped. "Thanks."

He liked it, wanted it, wanted the connection that gratitude brings. Nodding an acknowledgement to her, he wondered what else he wanted, felt an answer rising to consciousness as he turned again, and whammed it back down quickly. Just coffee, he told himself. Just settle for coffee.

Coming back with a capped cup in each hand, he found her sitting straight and staring vacantly, more adrift than the bag ladies who grew roots on chairs like these.

"Just regular, right?"

She met his glance and nodded and took the cup and looked away. Powell sat and waited and watched but she did not look back.

"Maria," he said softly after the silence stretched on. "I don't know what you're thinking or where you are right now but you have to come back. We're in trouble if you don't."

Her eyes seemed surprised when they scanned his face, as if it were something strange, a sight they'd never beheld before.

"We're already in trouble, Padre," she said at last, "unless you think God's getting ready to intervene."

Powell smiled and hoped to hook her. "No point worrying 'bout what God's gonna do. It's almost always a surprise. Just ask Moses."

No dice. Her eyes moved away again - but then looked back curiously. "Tell me something, Powell. Why'd you grab that girl on the sidewalk? Didn't look like she said anything. She do something?"

"Nope." Powell saw her again; tallish, freckled, green eyes, pretty red hair, jeans and a chic teal sweater, high black boots. And then again; a wet sticky circle edging wider just below her breasts, intestines with shredded ends pushing out beneath her beaded belt, a pot of red and grey-green preserves where her face had been. The effects of hollow point bullets on the human organism. "I think it was something she didn't do."

"And what - " Hernandez's eyes were focused on his, interested, a good sign - "was that?"

Until now he hadn't had to work it out. Something'd been wrong and now he replayed the scene and saw it fresh. "She didn't turn around. There's a fire truck coming up the block and she doesn't turn around."

The words were helping. Saying it was making it real, still horrible but somehow not random or accidental but a part of something purposeful that had a beginning and an end. It had to have an end somewhere. Hernandez was watching and he heard his own voice seeming to come from someone else.

"The jogger turned around. The street guy with his shopping cart turned. Even the damned dog she was walking wanted to see what was happening. But she didn't turn around."

And now Powell was gone. Following the Beast. Always there, always moving. In the highlands, along the Mekong, at the bloodstained, whitewashed chapel. Not just this time, though. In the catacombs and on the Crusades, on the battlefields and in the death camps. Moving with us always. The woman dead on top of him was only the most recent victim of its appetite. Across the table, Maria was speaking and he worked hard to catch her words, which seemed too quick, passing in bursts, as if the air was too thin to hold them.

" . . . Over," she was saying, "It's over now."

She was holding her cup with her left hand, her right thumb fumbling with its lid, not quite able to pop it loose. The tip of her tongue was resting on the middle of her lower lip, each hand slip on the cup rim pushed it closer to her mouth's left corner. An almost ordinary moment.

"Allow me," Powell said, feeling a smile forcing its way to his face. He found the lid tab on his own cup and, snapping the top off, slid it across the table to her. "I hate to see someone lose a wrestling match with a coffee cup."

She beamed an almost shy grin at him and pushed the recalcitrant container his way.

"Thanks."

"No problem." Opening the second cup, now his, he took a long, hot sip and set it back down. "Can I ask you something?"

"Sure." Eyes nervous, almost demure, looking away, then meeting his gaze, now clear and hard as stone.

"You were just talking, weren't you? When you said it was over?"

"What?"

"Because it isn't. It's just getting started." It was not good news. Powell could see that she didn't want to hear it.

"What are you talking about?" A little heat in her voice and no smile now, only a tight line tightening more.

"We had Kelsey helping us." Here Hernandez's glare broke off and fell to the table and Powell went on. "Who've we got now?"

No answer. No look. Her right hand, resting on the tabletop, trembled almost imperceptibly. Nothing else.

"Now they know we're out here. And we don't even know who *they* are except that some of them are in the P.D."

"*One* of 'em. Zang."

"He's not the only one. Remember that investigation at Jimmy's? You said Zang called that off. Only a lieutenant? You think so? Somebody higher up had to know."

No response. Her hand made a quick trip to the coffee cup, lifted it for a short sip, set it down again. Powell felt another pushy question rising in his throat, checked it, bit off the words, drew a deep breath, and exhaled slowly. Searching for a lower register, he spoke.

"So what do we do now, Detective?"

Hernandez shrugged, pursed her lips, and laughed. "Perhaps it's time to pay a call on the good looey. See if he's receiving visitors?"

"A bit hot for that wouldn't you say? Given the circumstances."

"Fuck the circumstances. They want some action? Let's give it to 'em. I'm not fucking scared."

Powell considered this and knew that it was true. Hate, like love, overcame fear. More easily, in fact. And that was what it meant to be fallen. Exactly what let Cain kill Abel. He didn't speak, and hoped that his silence would quiet her in this space of a thousand voices. Her eyes stayed hard on his, smoldering, glowing, finally dropping to the table. He sipped his coffee, reached across the table, and touched her hand briefly, just a tap to pull her eyes up again.

"Okay, let's go. Least they won't be looking for us there."

A smile, albeit weak, and then a determined nod. She leaned forward and was almost on her feet before he could push his next question out.

"Do we know where he lives?"

"Lincoln Center. New place near there. Remember Kelsey saying that?"

"Not exactly pinpoint accuracy, Officer," Powell said, the words coming up gritty and dry as sand.

"Someone'll know. Guy like that, he buys a fancy new place, he wants people to know where it is."

Someone knew. The desk man at the 6th precinct, Hernandez's fifth call. Zang had yakked him up right after he'd moved. 68th Street just east of Broadway. The building was a new midrise, a glass and chrome Kleenex box standing on its end. The doorman, a pale white guy in forest green, shoulders rounded under miles of gold braid, wasn't surprised to see them.

"You're here about the music last night, right?" he said when

Hernandez showed him her shield.

"Yeah." She didn't miss a beat. Pro quality lying, Powell thought. "What time was that, anyway?"

"Don't know. The night guy didn't say. Just said that the whole fucking floor called down and he couldn't raise the guy on the squawk box."

"What finally happened?"

"Guess he musta turned it off."

"Name's Zang, right? Or is that the gentleman who called us?"

The doorman shuffled papers on his podium. "Yeah, Zang. 11F. That's the one."

"He do this a lot?" Completely unruffled. Might've been talking baseball to the guy on the next stool at the neighborhood diner. Powell kept his hands in his jacket pocket and waited.

"Never had a complaint before. But I'm only here on weekends."

"You kidding?"

The pale man shook his head.

"Man, the presence you got, you oughta be the main guy. You mind if we go up?"

The doorman, beaming, shoulders a bit straighter, waved them through to the elevator. Just a question of making him feel some worth, Powell reflected. Same as what the Church was about. Or should be. Only she didn't really mean it. But what was a priest saying when he said, "Jesus loves you?" Something he meant? Does any of us even know what it means? A horrible kind of love, he thought. Hernandez pressed eleven and the car doors slid closed with an almost noiseless bump.

"Pretty smooth work, Detective."

She narrow-eyed him coolly. "That s'posed to signify something?"

"Just what it said, Maria." Signify. Powell thought it was a funny word for her to pick. All speech `signified.' The reality was behind the squeaking and grunting sounds we made. Just signs pointing the way. To what? Powell saw a wooden cross and Manny tied to a stone altar and shook his head. There was that good Jesuit training. Bring an image to mind. Become one with it. They didn't tell you that you could never let go.

A quiet bell rang and the elevator car jerked to a stop. Hernandez slipped her revolver and eased into the hall without looking back at him, stopping to glance at the doorplates as she worked her way down the corridor. 11F was the third apartment on the right.

Hernandez flattened herself against the wall on the far side, the knob side, and gestured to Powell to take up the opposite position. When his spine was flat against the painted sheetrock, her left hand rapped hard on the door panel. It swung open a half inch. Not locked? No one answered the knock.

Powell put his right palm flat on the door and glanced at Hernandez. She slid down into a crouch holding the .38 in front of her with both hands, its snubbed barrel pointed upward. When she was settled there, she nodded and Powell pushed hard. The door yawed open silently.

No sound. Nothing moving. Powell stood on tiptoe and peered around the doorframe. A long, empty passage; three doors on the left facing bookshelves on the right; light at the end from a window wall where the hall opened into a wider space.

The closest door would be a closet, Powell reasoned. Then probably a bedroom, then a bathroom last sharing a wall with the kitchen. That'd be where the space opened up. From any of them, a person entering the passage would be silhouetted by the hall lights. Down low, though, and against the wall where the doors were would require whoever waited to step all the way out to get a shot. Hernandez might have a play before he bought it.

She was peering around doorpost, piece still at the ready. Powell didn't wait to catch her eye. He whirled and dove into the corridor, sliding on the polished parquet past the first door, hooking himself into the second doorway, and rolling to a crouch. No sound anywhere except Hernandez's muttered curses from outside.

His guess was right. A bedroom. Light from a window, maybe to a courtyard or airshaft. Teak desk and dresser. A platform bed with a blue down comforter neatly made. Clothes hanging in the closet, four pairs of shoes in a row beneath them. A shoulder holster draped over the desk chair. The gun still there. Powell eased it out of the leather, a chrome-plated .45 automatic with ebony grips. He slipped the safety off, smiling grimly at the fact that he still knew how to do it, then jerked the slide back to chamber a round, catching his breath and listening.

Nothing. Hernandez's breathing from the hall. A faint drip of water from somewhere. Nothing else. He shifted the automatic to his left hand and dove out.

Hitting the bookshelves low, he pushed off with his right palm, tucked his frame into a tight ball, and rolled for the bathroom door. Hernandez popped into view, gun extended, and then disappeared quick as a shooting gallery rabbit. Powell's shoulder and elbow crashed the bathroom door, sending it back in a fast arc to a banging stop on something hard behind it as Powell skidded onto the tile in its wake.

The dripping was in back of him now, where the sink loomed in grey light or perhaps behind the glass doors of the shower. The room smelled of soap and dampness and something dull and musky like black dirt or composted manure or old meat.

Still no movement down the hall. No sound of a foot shifting or a shirt rustling. No breathing. No one there? But Zang was there, Powell knew. The guys at Jimmy's were looking for him - he wouldn't have left without the gun. He turned and shouted down the corridor.

"Maria?"

"Here." Her voice was firm and calm and Powell found himself grinning. No reason, he knew; just a kind of tense delirium.

"I've got his .45." Long pause to let that sink in. "I'm going on in. Three count, please."

"Okay." He heard her feet shifting on the hall carpet.

"ONE."

Powell didn't wait. Holding the weapon with both hands he belly-slid into the corridor, using knees and elbows to propel himself.

"TWO."

Easier in basic, he thought. There it was mud, you could get a purchase. No one ever suggested he'd be doing it on oak parquet. He cleared a closet and a wall and the kitchen slid into view. No one there. Oak cabinets, butcher block counters, a stainless steel faucet, copper pots hanging above a pass through. He pulled himself into a crouch and rolled into the open space beyond the kitchen.

"THREE."

He was in a dining area; a living room opened up from it to the windows. Hernandez was in the hall now, revolver up, walking fast. A man with a spotted face, a red-brown goatee and a red-brown bib sat at a nicely crafted maple table, not moving. Hernandez closed on Powell and he rose slowly, .45 square on the seated man's chest. On the table a book of matches and an ashtray of stubbed out butts and next to them, two knives, a large one laying flat, a smaller one stuck through a thick piece of cardboard. The seated man's eyes were blue. The face spots were round burns. The bib was blood. The man's throat had been cut. Zang.

"Jesus."

Powell lowered the automatic and stood stock-still. Hernandez brushed by and recoiled at the sight of the corpse. But didn't stop. She moved past the table to a pair of louvered doors in the far wall, snapped them open to reveal a closet full of stacked packing boxes, moved back across a nice rug through a living room area to a final doorway, which opened when Hernandez shoved onto a small den that shared the window wall with the living room. Nothing and no one there.

Powell looked back to the table and wondered why there was blood near the cardboard. And then glanced at the Zang's chin and knew.

"GODDAMN IT!"

The voice was his, Powell knew, but the shout seemed to be coming from somewhere else. In the corner of his eye he saw Hernandez wheel out of the den.

"What?"

He pointed limply, let his hand fall back to his side.

"They cut his tongue out."

The blood on his chin said he'd still been alive, Powell knew. It was the Colonel. Viscarra might have died but there was always a Colonel, someone who'd kill for a cause. And enjoy it. Hernandez stared, took a wobbly half step toward the table, and headed for the hallway. Powell pulled his eyes away and made them look for something, anything, else. The matchbook grabbed them. A familiar gold on brown design. Duggan's.

The light changed in the hallway and Powell turned to see Hernandez back slowly out of the bathroom, its light, now on, casting her shadow on the hall wall behind her. The revolver slipped from her hand and banged onto the floor. She collided with the wall, skewing a hanging frame, chrome around a sports print. But didn't notice, turning toward him, brown skin going ashen.

"Maria?"

No response. She grabbed his shoulders when he came close, buried her head in his chest, the sweet smell of her black hair keen under his face. When he turned, she clung, pulled him back off balance away from the bathroom door so that he had to brace his left arm on the wall in order to see what the doorway framed: Three feet from where he'd crouched in darkness, eyeless Kelsey staring at them from a seat in the bathtub, wearing the same red-brown bib that Zang had on.

Chapter 22

SUNDAY - 1:06 p.m.

Angels. Powell woke thinking about angels. Angels of mercy. Angel food cake. Archangels. Angelfish. California Angels. Snow angels. Angels of death.

Ann Gelban. Angail Ban. White Angel.

Jimmy'd found that out. Hadn't known what it meant but knew it was Gaelic and had called one of his regulars, a bricklayer, so Duggan said, from County Clare. The words meant white angel, but beyond that it didn't say anything to anybody. Not to Jimmy or to Ellen or to the bricklayer or to any of the ten Sunday afternoon patrons of Duggan's.

A start, though. Hernandez'd called in the stiffs while he had been slipping Zang's holster on, and they had followed the matches to Duggan's, and Jimmy'd gotten them a translation. White Angel. A piece of the puzzle. Once you had the first piece, you could find one to fit it and then another and then you'd have a cluster, enough of the picture to get some idea of what it was. That was, Powell thought, how it was supposed to work.

And now Kelsey's eyes were in the suite's refrigerator with the card still attached and Hernandez was gone and he couldn't keep the gun, Zang's automatic, out of his hand and at least one piece fit.

Los Angeles.

The old nun had seen an angel, or angels maybe, near Wolfson's hanging body and Hernandez herself had seen a woman in white, blonde like angels were supposed to be, in a doorway after midnight. A political angel, too. That was Zang's bag. What had Maria called it? Polsec. And an Irish one at that - that's what the Gaelic and the connection to Jimmy's said; guns involved because the BATF guys were in until they were called off. Hadn't Kelsey said that? Big time, too, or no one would risk killing cops. But what the hell did Wolfson have to do with it? Protesting a parade wasn't the kind of thing that'd get your throat cut. But what would? And how deep in it would you have to be? Maria had gone looking for answers. Or angels.

"Not a good idea." Powell heard himself saying it, leaning towards her across the rough wooden top of one of Jimmy's tables.

"No choice."

"You'll be a sitting duck. Someone inside is looking for you and you don't know who it is."

"Someone inside helped take Kelsey down and I need to get some names so I can start asking some questions."

Her dark eyes were flashing and her face was as square and firm as a wood block. No backing down.

"Go to the F.B.I. Isn't this stuff in their bailiwick?"

"First thing they'd do, they'd call the department. Protocol. Then someone'd really be looking for me."

"They already *are*, Maria. They set you up this morning."

"They set someone up. The message wasn't for me, remember? It was for 'Kelsey's partner.' They didn't know who that was. You show up, they think they're looking for a man."

"You don't think your whacking that guy in the cab gave 'em a clue?"

"Once the action starts, no one's takin' snapshots. I'd be surprised if anyone noticed anything about me."

"You don't know what Kelsey told them."

A glare for that. Heat like lightening in her eyes but something soft, maybe trembling, in her lips and a hard swallow before the words.

"Kelsey didn't tell 'em shit. If he had, they coulda hit me in my front yard and no one woulda known the difference. He didn't say shit."

Asshole. Hernandez hadn't used the word but the thought was there, between them, crackling and stinking with spleen like a third rail in a dank, dark subway tunnel. Leaning on the table, Powell had smelled old smoke behind the taproom dampness and had seen blood dripping on a white-washed wall and had known then where the anger was from.

"You're right," he'd said. Which didn't mend a thing. But nothing would and there was no way to say it. "Sorry."

A leaning back then; a long level stare. And then to him again, elbows finding the table and face gliding close, the voice low, almost a whisper.

"We're getting pretty deep in this now, Father, and I haven't seen your God guy in a while. Where do you suppose he is?"

No answer could be good enough. Too much death. Wolfson and Case in handcuffs; Kelsey eyeless; Zang's tongue. But all of that was part of it, part of where you were to look. Folly, Paul had written. The cross.

"I don't know where he is, Maria," Powell had said. With a balled right fist, he'd struck his own chest just below the left clavicle. "Maybe right here.

"Or maybe-" and now he'd reached across the table to grasp her arm, feeling it tense at his touch and then relax while her eyes stayed hard on his "-maybe right here."

For a long moment, he'd held on. And then she had lifted her right hand and put it on his, guiding it gently to the tabletop, clasping her fingers on it there.

"I'm going," she'd said.

Powell recalled that he'd nodded and that her hand had remained on his.

"Take care." He'd meant it not as an admonition but as an offering. Had she understood? Had he, himself? He hadn't then, he knew. But now, remembering, he understood. It was a gift he wanted to give. Care. Caritas. Love.

And then she had gone. A squeeze of her hand and she was up and out the door and he was alone at a scuffed wooden table in an Irish bar and then Ellen was there setting two pints of Harp on the tabletop and sitting, not across from him where Maria had been, but closer, at an adjacent side of the square, elbow to elbow.

"Looks like you got it, Mick," she'd said.

"Got what?"

"Don't be cute. You like her."

Ellen with her long hair in waves on her shoulders, light brown going blonde, Ellen now all in black cotton, loose drawstring pants and a looser open-necked blouse, an edge of black lace showing below her throat tight over the swell of her breasts.

"I do like her."

"I'm jealous, you know that."

"C'mon. I like you, too."

"Me, you left." Ellen had picked up her glass and tipped it high, hiding her eyes. Setting it down, she leaned back in her chair and stared at him levelly. "For God."

"She just said she hadn't seen him lately. Wondered where he was."

"And what'd you say?"

Shrugging, looking away. "I guess that I didn't know."

"You knew when I asked that."

"I knew a lot of things then. You get older, it's not quite so clear."

Ellen's green eyes had narrowed as she'd considered him, weighing, he felt, whether or not to tell him what'd come next. "That one, Mick, is gonna break your heart if you let her. And it's not gonna be her fault."

"Whose fault will it be, then?"

Ellen had laughed, a surprising sound, clear and light in the dusky room.

"You don't get it." A slight shake of her head and a big, winning grin. "No one's fault. God's maybe. Yeah, I like that. Maybe she would, too."

Standing then, still grinning, a hand on his shoulder moving up, fingertips light on his ear, her hand stroking his hair. "What a looney conversation - I mean I'm hanging in a bar on a Sunday afternoon tryin' to tell a priest about heartbreak."

But that, he'd known, was not the text. If there had been a page, there'd be notes in the margins. Between the lines. The stuff she hadn't said.

But then did say: "I'm scared for you, Mickey. I love you."

Catching her hand, feeling a nervous squeeze across his palm. "You love Jim."

"Of course I do. And you, too."

Jimmy moving then, around the bar and towards them, a pint glass of dark, creamy-headed stout in his left hand.

"Well now, Father, what would you be doin' in a saloon with a hussy like this?" He had stood next to Ellen, his right arm encircling her narrow waist.

Powell had felt his grin forming, an involuntary pull around the mouth and all the way up his jaw line. Jimmy. Just the way it was with him. "I'd tell you that I was trying to save her, Mr. Duggan, but actually she was just telling me that she loved me."

"Was she?" Mock surprise, bushy eyebrows raised, lips loosely pursed. "Well," he'd said, "it's good for business, anyway."

"Say, Jimmy?" Where had the question come from? "Who was that guy the other night?"

"What guy?" Not a dodge, Powell decided, just not something Jimmy needed to remember.

"The old guy. White haired. Buddy had a limp. And a gun."

A change of face then, curved lines going straight. Duggan had lifted his glass and swilled stout, clearing to a countenance as blank as a novitiate wall. "Don't think I know the one you mean."

"Jim, think about it. You said he was a regular. Daffy something."

Ellen had abruptly picked up her glass and walked, leaving Jimmy standing, watching, stiff and tight-lipped. Powell had seen it then, an almost translucent patina of stubborn suspicion glazing Duggan's face like the shine on fine china.

"You know who I'm talking about. I need your help. So, tell me what's the problem."

A slight, slow shake of his head, and a whisper, almost a hiss. "You shouldn't be running with those fuckin' cops."

He hadn't planned on laughing. The sound had been convulsive, pushing up from his gut in a heave, coming out as a loud, chortling howl. Pissed Duggan off. Rounded belly pulling in, a twitch of movement just below his ear, his color, already high, jumping up a notch on the scarlet scale. As he'd turned abruptly toward the bar, Powell had reached up and grabbed his forearm, spilling Guinness down over the pint's rim, across Duggan's hand, onto the floor in sloppy splats.

"Duggan," he'd said, "sit your pseudo-Irish ass down in a chair before I lose my temper and call your mother."

Jimmy had yanked free, spilling most of the rest of the stout, had glared at him for a long moment, had kicked back a chair and seated himself, still glaring.

"Can I tell you about my weekend, Jim?"

"Fuck you."

"I take it that's a yes." Spoken evenly, leaning then, both elbows on the wooden tabletop and all his weight on them.

"Night before last, someone stuck an old Jew I'd met in an oven and blew him up. Yesterday, someone pushed my housekeeper out a window."

The words were just words, sounds like other sounds, not sinister in themselves, as innocent as air. But voiced in this array, there, at that moment at Jimmy's, they had beaded sweat on his face and brought bile up from his gut into his throat.

"And this morning I find a cop's eyes in a baggie and some masked man with an assault rifle tries to do me and splashes a girl's brains all over my jacket and then I find the eyeless cop, Irish no less, in a bathtub with his throat cut and another one with his tongue nailed to a tabletop. And your friend, the old regular, knows him. And now you're gonna tell me where to find him."

Duggan looking at the floor, Powell remembers. Looking out the window, at his glass, at Ellen behind the bar, watching for a moment while she poured brandy into a wineglass for a white-haired crone in a bright paisley housedress. Finally, he had touched Jim's arm lightly, just above a blue broadcloth shirt cuff.

"Jimmy," he had said, "tell me."

"Fitzgerald. Runs the lighting company. Across the street." And then Jimmy Duggan, who liked to laugh, had risen and disappeared into the kitchen without even the faintest of smiles.

Things exist that laughter cannot cope with, Powell had thought. Evil exists. And what in counterpoint to it? Something? There is something. Yes. But always the tickling question mark.

Powell's pint, still almost full but no head now, had peered at him like the business end of some amber-tinted telescope. Seeing what?

An aging, confused priest? A living target? A sex-starved American male in crisis? Powell had chuckled then and grabbed the glass. A maudlin moron, he'd thought, taking a dip in a deep pool of self-pity. Draining the ale, he'd waved at Ellen behind the polished bar and left.

The Derry Lighting Company lived in a long, low, orange brick building just up Greenwich. Two stories, glass brick windows, frosted front doors locked up tight. At the back, a boxy Mercedes delivery truck on a short driveway in front of a loading dock. A ten-foot chain link gate in front, razor ribbon at the top, the blank wall of a neighboring brownstone to the right. Nothing special, Powell had thought, but now it would not leave alone, sitting stolidly in his consciousness all the way back to the seminary up the stairs into the empty.

Nothing to catch your eye, he thought – and the thought recalled for him the baggie in the icebox. Two gobs of jelly staring vacantly at an orange juice carton. Something to do with a banal brick building at the corner of Greenwich and Barrow. Guns and money, too. Guns to have had the feds involved, bag money for someone to have called them off. And somehow a pompous professor of world religions had wandered into the midst of it and had ended up hanging on a fence. Powell closed his eyes and tried to imagine a connection.

The Ignation method. For a moment he heard Father Aland, his novitiate's retreat master. "Put yourself in the picture. Smell Jerusalem, rank with dung and smoke. See the stark blue sky, the kaleidoscope of the crowd, the whitewashed brick of the buildings, hear the shouts and the jeering, the merchants' calling, the soldiers' weapons rattling. Taste the dust, feel the dry heat, the sweat rolling down your forehead."

It could work. You could be there - watching the bloody execution but at the more quiet moments as well. Hearing the voice, the teaching, the call, "Come, follow me."

And now it took him back to Jimmy's. Wolfson was there at a crowded table, holding court as he often did in the seminary's refectory, the young men at his table laughing appreciatively and sipping wine. And how does he learn of the lighting company and its secrets? An argument overheard? Possible, but not likely. Hot words at another table in a crowded noisy room - how much could filter through?

A careless slip from someone he knew, someone inside? Carelessness was not their mark, though. Loose ends were wrapped up tight. In shrouds.

A document. That would be it. A piece of paper, probably innocuous on its surface but containing some scrap of information that would raise a question in an eclectic scholar's mind. And that question, when pursued, would lead to another and then to another and another until finally the weight of the questions themselves suggested to someone that the person asking knew too much.

About what?

Guns or money, Powell mused again in answer to his own unspoken question. What else did Ireland have to do with anything that anyone in America would want to kill for?

The suite's air was warming now; Powell's shirt, pressed into the vinyl of the easy chair, clung damply to his skin. Out the window, past the golden leaves that quivered on a branch of an unseen tree, the sky above the low warehouses where the river ran was as blue as a mountain lake. Powell peered into its distant depth, looking again for the paper that told Wolfson - and would tell him - the answer to some poisonous riddle.

He saw nothing there and then saw that which was not there. The street again. Greenwich Street, sun on the east side, shadow on the west, leaves and trash along the curbs, the long blank wall of the lighting company, the green awning over the door at Jimmy's, the old woman in the paisley dress shuffling towards him, watching, her face pale in spite of the brandy. Across Greenwich a thin man walking a fat dog, a round shame-faced beagle in a pink dog sweater. Light like gold, a gentle breeze, a smell of fall and bus fumes. And somewhere there, out of sight and memory a clue to a riddle.

How to get in? No warrant, Powell thought, unless Hernandez came back and even then not likely. Best to wait, though. And waiting had brought him back to the seminary suite and weariness had pushed him into the realm of sleep. And angels.

And a man in a white dress.

Who had said it? Something clutched at Powell's intestines and tugged them hard. Awake again. Jamahl's voice. "Dude was wearin' a white dress."

White angel.

Angail Ban.

Not a woman in white but a man in an angel's white robe or a priest's surplice. A priest. That made the seminary connection. A priest in a long black cloak that covered some white vestment beneath. Powell felt a sudden dizziness seize him and spin him like a falling leaf caught in a quick, unseen whirlwind. He sat at the kitchenette's chipped formica table and caught his head in both hands. How many men could it be?

Counting under his breath, but audibly as if someone else were with him to hear his whisper, Powell came up with twentysome faculty. Three women. All of the men ordained. Maybe a half-dozen graduate students who were also priests. For that matter, any of the hundred or so divinity students, priestlings as their teachers had it, would also have cassock and surplice for chapel duty, working the sacristy or officiating at the Offices. Any of them Irish?

None right off a boat but beyond that what the hell did the question mean? His own great-grandfather had been born in County Clare but nothing much was left of Irishness except the name and some of the brogueing regulars at Jimmy's allowed as how even that wasn't authentic. And anyway, half of New York's eight million souls were Irish on St. Patrick's Day. But how many of them felt strongly enough about it to try to shoot someone on a sidewalk?

There was no answer and nausea now rose in Powell's guts like a tide, doubling, it seemed, the weight of his hands and arms and legs and head. His still swollen lips throbbed and he found his thoughts crazily alternating between Maria Hernandez and a hot greasy piece of pizza from Famous Ray's up the avenue. Where was she? Would there be any left with eggplant? Would she find him here? Sausage, mushroom, and pepperoni? And finally, Father Aland interrupting the disconnected monologues. Brother Powell, he had often said, do what you are doing?

Do what you are doing. Powell smiled. In the moment. Do what you can do in the moment and expend no energy on what you can't do. Slice of pizza for you, Father? Wherever you are? Powell pushed himself up from the table, exited the kitchen, crossed the suite's main room, pulled open its door.

And found himself facing the short cylinder of a handgun silencer. Behind it, a light-looking automatic, perhaps a nine-millimeter. Behind that a hand and an extended arm, a grey plaid sport jacket absolutely unwrinkled, and a pale, thick-lipped face with watery blue eyes framed by neatly coiffed silvery grey hair.

Kinlock.

Chapter 23

THE ANGEL

THE LIGHT HAD NOT FOUND HIM; THE ANGEL KNEW THAT. ITS BEAM HAD MERELY SLAMMED ONTO THE WINDOW OF THE DOOR OPPOSITE THE ALCOVE WHERE HE HAD STOOD AND BEEN DEFLECTED HARMLESSLY DOWN ONTO THE CONCRETE. CLOSE, THOUGH. TOO CLOSE. AND NOT GOOD. NOT GOOD THAT A LIGHT SHOULD PENETRATE THAT PART OF THE NIGHT THAT HAD BEEN GIVEN TO HIM.

THERE WOULD BE RETRIBUTION. ONE OF THE PROPHETS HAD DESCRIBED IT. "WOE TO THOSE WHO PUT DARKNESS FOR LIGHT AND LIGHT FOR DARK-NESS." BUT TO WHOM? THE ANGEL WONDERED WHEN THE TRANSGRESSORS WOULD BE REVEALED. HE HAD SEEN TWO FIGURES AFTER THE RIDICULOUS COPS AND ROBBERS SHOUT OF 'FREEZE' BUT HAD NOT STOPPED TO WATCH - HE AND THE YOUNG MAN WERE ALREADY MOVING DEEPER INTO THE DARK.

THE YOUNG MAN HAD BEEN LAUGHING THEN, HOLDING HIS HAND LIGHTLY AND LAUGHING AS HE LED HIM FROM ROOM TO ROOM IN BLACKNESS, THROUGH THE KITCHEN OF THE STUDENT LOUNGE AND THROUGH THE LOUNGE ITSELF, INTO THE CLOAK HALL, DOWN THE UNEVEN STEPS TO THE TUNNEL. THERE HIS LAUGHTER HAD BECOME NERVOUS, A HIGH-PITCHED, UNEVEN CHUCKLE THAT ECHOED UNDER THE STONE ARCHES FINALLY LAPSING INTO A BREATHY SILENCE

When they'd stopped before the narrow door at the head of the crypt's staircase.

His guests were often silent then. The angel pondered this, tapping his fingertips lightly together as he thought. Perhaps it was the dankness of the tunnel air that quieted them. Or the odor that rose from the crypt as the door swung open. Or a glimmer of something else. Perhaps just then they were able to peek beyond the veil at the glory that was to come, when they would beg and plead for fulfillment, for delivery from the finitude of time and space.

But this one had not pled. Turning, raising his face, he had spoken flatly. "I'm not going down there." And had insisted. The effrontery of this memory made the angel seethe. He had insisted until at last the rod had been necessary. `You shall break them with a rod of iron' was how the psalmist put it. And so it had happened. Vindication. Vindication in the taste of the young man's blood on his lips and tongue. Now the crypt held him, would hold him, shamed, until his time had become all time and the earth opened to receive him.

Which might have happened if not for the light. Light where darkness belonged, a voice where stillness should have reigned. And now, suddenly, the angel knew whose was the light and whose the voice. A woman's. Hernandez.

Chapter 24

SUNDAY - 2:18 p.m.

"Hello, Michael. May we come in?"

Before Kinlock's raspy voice asked the question that was not a question, Powell had not noticed the others. Two men in dark suits, both dark-haired, both in sunglasses, standing on the staircase below the landing, one noticeably taller than the other, the shorter one holding a fat briefcase.

Hello, Kinlock." Powell stepped back into the suite and let the three of them pass. "You found me again."

Kinlock's laugh was wheezy and quiet. The gun stayed up, still only inches from Powell's face. "You aren't hard to find, Mick. We hadn't been trying. But now you seem to be an asset."

"An asset? How's that?"

The taller of the two dark suits moved to the bedroom's windows, peered out, and stood then in a corner. The shorter man set the briefcase down, checked the kitchenette and the bathroom, closed the suite door, and leaned against it. Kinlock sat down heavily on the nearer bed.

"You may know something we need."

"And what makes you think I'd tell you?"

Both of the dark suits straightened, hands loose at their sides. The shorter man was just to Powell's left, about two feet away.

"These guys agency?"

Kinlock shook his head. "Associates. Just associates."

"What's with the glasses? You have 'em watch reruns of `I Spy' or something?"

The short man edged nearer, almost imperceptibly.

"Don't get too close to him, John. He broke a police detective's jaw just yesterday morning and that guy was drawing down on him."

"But I'm not a dumb cop." John's voice was smooth and slightly foreign, perhaps tinged with an accent of Eastern Europe. `Cop,' came out, `cope.'

"Ah. Well."

Kinlock lowered the gun and without waiting, Powell flung his right hand into the empty air in front of him, taking John's gaze with it for an instant. Long enough, though, Powell thought. Long enough to make the turn, cock his right leg high, and drive it home hard into the short man's midsection. The dark suit doubled but did not drop. Powell grabbed his hair and pulled him close, swinging his left forearm in under the man's chin, wrapping his right hand around his own left wrist, yanking the gasping man up, up past standing to a dangle. His sunglasses jerked loose and clattered to the floor and Powell hefted him around to face Kinlock once again.

Who sat unperturbed, gun still in hand. The other dark suit moved quietly towards Powell until Kinlock waved him back.

"Slide the gun over here or I kill him," Powell heard his own voice saying, serious as a B movie heavy. The short man was still struggling but now his movement was weak.

"Then he'll be dead."

Kinlock spoke without affect in the flat, colorless tones of an idiot. Or, Powell thought, a madman. He released his grip and the short man, John, Kinlock had called him, tumbled forward gasping, first to his knees and then forward again, catching the bed with his chest and slithering to the floor like a movie queen in a dead faint.

"Kenny, take care of John."

The tall man moved around the beds and tugged John up into a sit, slapping him hard twice. Kinlock watched idly for a moment and turned to Powell.

"Not becoming for a man of the cloth, Father," he said dryly, "but very much the way I remember you. Good to see you haven't changed."

"And what about you, Kinlock?" Powell felt blood and anger rising from someplace deep and old. "Is your devotion to the clergy still what it was?"

"You're talking about Viscarra and our young Jesuit friend? What was his name?"

No answer. No way to answer. No way to pronounce Manny's name for his destroyer.

"Do you think I could have stopped that? He was helping the rebels, everyone knew that. You knew it yourself."

"He was helping his people."

Kinlock sighed and nodded. "Yes. Yes, he was. In that one I think we were on the wrong side."

"Is that what you think? And does that make it better?"

"Nothing makes it better, Michael. Time has made it history. Why don't we leave it at that and get on with today?"

John was coughing now and holding his throat with both hands. The man Kinlock called Kenny stood and moved back to the window. Beyond it, a tree's branches moved in the sunlight and yellow leaves drifted on the breeze. History, Powell thought. That which was and is and is to come. The past always present. Kinlock drifting in on a tide from somewhere years ago.

"And what, exactly, is today's problem?"

"I believe you already know, Michael."

Powell met Kinlock's liquid eyes. "Angail Ban?"

"Precisely."

The short man pushed himself to his feet, breathing hard still, and red-faced, but otherwise all right. Before he could move, Kinlock caught his arm.

"A bit tougher than he looks, eh, John?"

"He zookered me." Without the shades, the short man's face looked pasty; sallow skin surrounding red-tinged, dark eyes.

"Suckered? Yes, he did, didn't he? Now, watch the door."

Something short, almost curt in Kinlock's voice. John rolled his shoulders and moved back to the door trailing a sweet scent of some familiar aftershave. Aqua Velva, maybe, or English Leather. Kinlock's gaze followed him and then swung back to Powell.

"So, what can you tell me?"

"What makes you think I know anything?"

Kinlock's lips pulled back in the briefest of smiles, showing yellowing teeth and a pink tongue that darted to the corners of his mouth before he spoke.

"Michael, there are not fifty men in North America who have ever heard of Angail Ban. But you have. That's one thing. Then there's the fact that yesterday a police detective named Kelsey began asking questions about an investigation at a gin mill called Jimmy D's and about a lieutenant named Zang. Just before that, he was talking to you. Not long after that he and Zang were killed in Zang's apartment. And then this morning a girl named Mahoney was shot by a man in a ski mask firing an assault rifle. Someone who looks a lot like you was on the scene. And lastly, you were photographed this afternoon outside Jimmy D's - about a half hour before a Molotov cocktail went through the front window."

The final sentence snapped into Powell's mind like an arrow just off a bow. Stepping back a half step, he blinked and refocused on Kinlock.

"That end part surprised you, didn't it? But none of the rest of it."

"Was. . . was anyone hurt?"

"Two dead – one of them the owner. Maybe a half dozen hospitalized."

The owner. Jimmy Duggan gone. His voice in seminary saying, `Pay no attention to that man behind the curtain.' Jim, like Dorothy, sucked up in someone else's hate. Powell felt anger and nausea in equal parts rise tightly through his guts. And then thought of Ellen. She had been there. Two dead. But too much interest now would work against him. That was how they got you. He swallowed hard and met Kinlock's calm blue gaze.

"You know all this stuff," he spat, "why d'ya need me?"

"There's someone I'm looking for." Kinlock shifted the automatic from his right hand to his left, reached into his jacket pocket, fished out a photograph, and proffered it to Powell. "I want you to help me find him."

It was not Fitzgerald. The photo depicted a heavyset, white-haired man with a florid complexion and no smile standing in front of a blue car, a big Chrysler, '60's vintage. Pistol. Fitzgerald's partner. The man whose gun had climbed Zang's crotch in a narrow booth at Jimmy's.

"Who is he?"

"The name he uses now is Eamonn Flynn. We believe his real name is Rossa."

Powell studied the picture. This man was not tall enough to be the cloaked figure on the seminary Close.

"What's it about, Kinlock?"

The two dark suits, Kenny and John, watched in apparent disinterest while the silver-haired man studied Powell closely. From outside, perhaps on 21st Street, came the sound of a truck laboring past.

"You used to have pretty good instincts, Father. What's your guess?"

"Guns or money. Maybe both."

Kinlock grinned, showing his teeth again and pale pink gums as well. "Quick answer. You've been thinking about it. And almost right, too."

"Almost?"

"Not guns. Symtex-5."

"Which is?"

"An explosive." Kinlock paused, then waved the automatic from side to side, as if crossing out what he'd just said. "THE explosive – no one will even acknowledge that there is such a thing. Army just developed it. Eight ounces of it goes off here, we're sitting in a smoking pile of bricks, what's left of us. No detection for it yet. Very stable, too. All this is classified, of course."

Powell felt himself nodding, speaking without wanting to. "And this guy Rossa has it?"

"We don't know that." Kinlock glanced down, slightly forlorn, Powell thought, then brought his watery eyes back up. "We do know that a truckload of it is gone from the Aberdeen Proving Ground and an M.P. sergeant with it. We think he's hooked into Rossa. Let's say it'd be worth talking to him if we could find him."

"Looks like kind of a domestic affair. Or army, maybe. Not really your turf." Of course it wasn't. Which was what made it interesting.

Kinlock shrugged. "You're probably right. All I know is this guy's an international terrorist and the Agency wants me to find him. Maybe the Bureau and defense intelligence are looking for him, too."

"No K.G.B. to spar with now?"

A thin smile then, almost tired. "Something like that."

True, Powell thought, but not the truth. The truth was that something else was happening. And the truth was something that Kinlock, if he knew, wasn't going to tell. What was it? What was the truth? Powell found himself smiling. Pontius Pilate's question.

"And what if I don't play along?"

"I get to split open-" John's voice, quick to hiss his interjection, "-your foogin' 'ead."

Powell turned to him and caught the glittering hate in his eyes, eager to find its object. Violence, his own, begetting violence. Another piece of the truth. Still smiling, feeling almost stupid with a weird glee, he turned back to Kinlock, heard himself speaking:

"Then I'll be dead, John."

Kinlock, rasping like sandpaper, laughed. The short man glared, his sweet scent still rising around him.

"He's different, John. I tried to tell you that." The taller man, Kenny, idly shifted his feet as if the occasion had no more significance than a random encounter on a bus. "We need," Kinlock wheezed on, "to think of something in which he has an interest."

"I can't imagine that you know anything that would be of interest to me."

Kinlock tilted his head slyly. Behind him, out the window, the gold-laden branches of a tree shifted suddenly in a gust of wind.

"What about Nicole?"

Shock waves. Something seismic - a sharp spasm rolling up Powell's spine from somewhere unknown deep within him, snapping his head up involuntarily.

"There, you see." The silver-haired agent wheezed, chuckled, gasped for a breath. "You ARE interested."

"She was one of yours, wasn't she?" Heat, searing heat rising now from his chest, along his throat, prickling across his scalp toward his eyes. "She sold me out."

"Didn't you mean one of OURS?" A look of phony incredulity and a brief punctuating pause, then the same low raspy voice. "And, no, she wasn't. Worked for the French, actually. I think they made her believe she was somehow protecting you. In Salvador, anyway. I don't really know what she was up to in Indochina."

"Fuck you, Kinlock. If that's really your name." He did know. Knew everything. Had known from the start. Powell glared at him and felt familiar pieces jumble themselves. `As it was in the beginning, is now...'

"Actually, it is my name. First name George... I wonder if you knew that?"

Powell did not speak. Neither of the dark suits moved but the short one's cheap cologne and sweat tickled Powell's nostrils like the sweet, rank smell of something dead.

"You know, another thing worth wondering..."

Kinlock, at first, seemed to be speaking to no one in particular, not even to himself, simply releasing words to hear the harmonics of their juxtaposed sounds like a composer humming tunelessly. Then an even stare and slight tension in the voice, a tightening that pulled the notes to order.

"... you know what that is? I'm wondering whether you could have known that she had a baby? About six months after you took a powder."

"You're a liar!" The words surged up and out under their own power, like something vomited.

And were met by a quiet chortle in response. "Of course I am. Sometimes. But not this time."

Kinlock raised his eyes to the suite's white ceiling as if to read something written there. "Anne Dubois. Born in Paris, 1976."

For a sliver of an instant Powell was gone, somewhere else, in a bed on a steamy tropical day while the faintest of breezes touched a gauzy curtain at a long window looking out on a lushly overgrown courtyard.

Nicole was asleep beside him and the room smelled of sweat and flowers and sex. Haiti. On leave - how many times? Telling her about Manny and the village, the soldiers in the city and the rebels in the hazy blue mountains. Somehow protecting him.

"Where is she?"

"Nicole? Dead. Beirut, 1982." Kinlock looked as sad as a circus clown. "A car bombing, I think."

Powell felt a twinge and, strangely, no more. Dead already, was that it? Had she died for him long before? Wondering, he watched the tall man, Kenny, straighten, shift his weight, and turn towards the window, towards the golden light behind the autumn leaves. A daughter. Or a lie.

"Where's the girl?"

Now Kinlock chuckled again. "That's exactly what I want to tell you. But I need some help from you first."

Of course. And what difference did it make? Kelsey dead, Duggan dead, maybe Ellen. And Maria?

"All right, I'll tell you what I know. Which isn't much. Now, where's the girl?"

Kinlock looked at the two dark suits, first turning to Kenny, then glancing to John, showing them each a brief, toothy grin, saying, "This isn't the way we're supposed to do it, gentlemen, but then you two don't know Michael. If he says he'll tell us, he will."

To Powell: "She's in school in New Hampshire. Town called Bethlehem. Don't you love that name? I knew you'd appreciate it. Some kind of boarding school exchange. I have the address somewhere."

It rang true. Too odd and too specific to be a lie. A lie would have to be more believable. And what did it matter? Two minutes earlier the girl had not existed, not for him at least. If Kinlock was lying, she still did not exist. And if it was true? If it was true, it meant something. It meant that something he'd thought dead was still, somehow, alive. Again, the resurrection. Always life, that was the promise.

"Well, Father?" Kinlock was smirking. "A nice irony in that title now, don't you think?"

A surge of hate so pure it might have been distilled coursed up along Powell's spine and wrapped tightly around his ribs and then he knew who he'd been talking to. The Evil One again. He lived, too; death had a life of its own. In Cambodia, in Salvador, here in New York. In me, Powell thought. Was there any overcoming it? No answer. But there was a sound, syllables, words, a sentence.

"Let me ask you something else, George." Powell knew that the voice was his own but it seemed far off, as if someone had taped it and was now transmitting from a distant hillside. "What did Wolfson and Case have to do with this?"

The smirk gone. All the lines of Kinlock's face gone straight in surprise. He didn't know. Had never heard of them. And now, Powell recognized with a tiny speck of gathering joy, he has something new to worry about. Answering, Kinlock spoke a trifle too loudly.

"Those names, Michael, signify nothing to me. Who are they?"

"Wolfson was a professor here at the seminary. If you read the papers, you'd know he was murdered on Friday. He hung out at that bar, Duggan's, and he knew Zang." Here a twitch, a faint flicker of something across Kinlock's face. Zang was significant. "That's what Kelsey and the homicide people were looking into."

Powell paused and watched Kinlock's lower lip move out and to one side as if he were adjusting a cud.

"And Case, was that his name?"

"Seymour Case. A Jewish bookseller. Wolfson seems to have known him."

"Seems to?" Kinlock's lips pursed themselves and his eyebrows moved a millimeter closer to his silver hairline.

"He claimed not to have met Wolfson."

"What makes anyone think he did? Know him, I mean."

"Just that he got blown up. The night after the cops talked to him."

Now the brow knotted downwards and John, watching, shifted uneasily. Kinlock concentrated on the tip of his automatic as if he expected it to whisper something to him.

Finally, he glanced to the dark suits, first to Kenny behind him and then over to John, shook his head, and rasped hoarsely, "Complications. Always so many."

Then, flatly, looking to Powell: "And what about Rossa?"

"I don't know much. Only saw him once."

"Where?"

"Jimmy D's." Duggan laying dead there on a charred wooden floor. And Ellen? "Probably not much point in looking there now."

Silver-haired Kinlock eyed him wearily, coughed, let the .45 sag down toward the floor, ran the pink tip of a tongue over thick, dry lips. To his left, John shifted his weight and the cloying odor of his cologne mounted a fresh assault on Powell's nostrils.

"That it?" Kinlock said.

Better to tell or not? Powell leaned back against the kitchen doorframe. Hard to figure. They leave, they'd probably have him watched, already were. No chance to check out the lighting company. And he needed them and their watchers out of here before Hernandez showed up. Tying her in would make it more dangerous for everyone.

"He was with a guy."

Instant interest. Kinlock leaning forward, eyebrows up a bit. Even slouching Kenny standing straighter. No one speaking, not a word, not even the sound of a breath.

"Named Fitzgerald, I think. Runs a lighting company across from Duggan's. Derry Lighting."

A wet hiss as Kinlock inhaled. His mouth produced a decidedly nervous smile.

"I believe that is new data-" turns to the dark suits in quick succession "-and I'm grateful for it, Michael. John, if you please."

The short man bent, gripped the briefcase handle, and swung it easily up onto the bed next to Kinlock. Snapping the clasps crisply, he eased the case open, took the agent's automatic, and stepped back toward the door, as obsequious as a rented butler. Inside the case: electronics. A small grey tape recorder whose spools were silently turning, a half dozen green cylinders with wires protruding, short, the size of cocktail weenies, and a sleek black laptop that Kinlock now removed and set carefully on his knees. Tucked in slots on the case lid were an airline ticket envelope and a plastic card, both narrower and longer than a credit card, perforated by irregularly placed circles and bearing the letters ST.MOR along the visible edge before it disappeared into the lid flap.

The computers keys clicked almost noiselessly under Kinlock's pink, square fingers. As he worked, he hummed bars of something familiar. Watching him, Powell worked on the tune. Not recent. Way back, in fact. Beatles - something about love. `All You Need Is Love.' Crazy, but that was it.

"Nothing," Kinlock said, smiling. "Nothing under Fitzgerald, nothing under Derry Lighting. I knew it. You see?" The dark suits did not return his grin. "I knew as soon as I realized that you were part of the scene that you'd have something useful for me."

From behind Powell, through the kitchenette window came the sound of another truck on 21st Street laboring through its gear progression, headed for the avenue, Powell thought, and then uptown for the tunnel and Jersey. An image formed of it emerging, winding up the hill on the far shore, and then the song's tune and words, bitter now, no sweetness at all, crowded up behind and pushed it out. All you need is love. In front of him, Kinlock was talking.

"-know about this company anyway?"

"Nothing," Powell answered. "The sign says importers. That's all."

"That's quite enough. No question. Yes. We'd better pay a visit." He gently folded down the laptop's screen and returned it to the case. "John."

The short man stepped up, handed him the gun, left hand to right, closed the case, and secured it, leaving it flat on the bed. Kinlock stood and moved a half step towards the door, the automatic's ugly squarish barrel still trained on Powell. Now it was coming, Powell knew. The thin veil, the mystics called it. Now it was close. Even before Kinlock spoke, he knew it was close.

"-question is what to do about you? Can't just leave you - no telling what you'd do." The raspy voice was smoother now, almost unctuous. The gun came up an inch and leveled. "Perhaps disposal is the best option."

Chapter 25

THE ANGEL

Now it was only a question of time, the Angel knew. He had found their nest. Empty, true, but they would return and that which was intended would be accomplished. It had been foreseen. The son of Peor spoke of it, who always spoke the truth: "Your nest is in the rock, nevertheless shall it be wasted."

The room itself was revolting, suffocating with the presence of the transgressors. The woman's panties, found at the top of her bag and now moist in his hand, reeked of fecundity. She had been the first to leave, bustling across the close, as brazen in front of his window as any seaport slut.

And then Powell and his pathetic entourage, the slick, silver-haired man with the briefcase, looking like a televangelist or a political bimbo, and the two with sunglasses and cheapish black suits, imitation hoods or pseudocops. Whoever they were, it was unlikely that they would return when the blasphemous papist returned to clean up his dirty laundry. And when that happened, the Angel would be waiting.

IT WOULD DOUBLY SATISFY HIM TO TAKE THEM NOW THAT HE HAD DISCOVERED THEIR FOUL TRACES HERE, SO CLOSE TO HIS OWN SACRED CHAMBERS. HOW COULD SUCH POLLUTION HAVE BEEN PERMITTED? THE ANGEL CONSIDERED THIS WITHOUT RESOLUTION. NOT ALL WAS GIVEN TO KNOW, NOT EVEN TO THE SERAPHIM. IF THEY WERE HERE, IT WAS TO THE DIVINE PURPOSE, EVEN AS THEIR ELIMINATION WOULD BE. SURELY THIS WAS THE LESSON OF THE FOOL WOLFSON AS WELL WITH HIS SANCTIMONIOUS THREATS.

NOW ONLY A QUESTION OF TIME - A PLEASING POINT TO CONSIDER. WAS IT NOT THE PREACHER, EVEN ECCLESIASTES HIMSELF, WHO HAD CLAIMED THIS REALM FOR THE ALMIGHTY? A TIME TO BE BORN, A TIME TO PLANT, A TIME TO SEW. YES, AND MORE. A TIME DIE, A TIME TO PLUCK UP, A TIME TO REND. YES, YES. A TIME TO BREAK DOWN, TO WEEP, TO MOURN, TO CAST AWAY. A TIME TO KILL. IT WAS CLEARLY SO ORDAINED AND WOULD COME TO THOSE WHO WAITED. THERE COULD BE NO DOUBT. "FOR THE LORD IS A GOD OF JUSTICE, BLESSED ARE ALL THOSE WHO WAIT."

ONLY A QUESTION OF TIME.

Chapter 26

SUNDAY - 3:09 p.m.

Complete blackness. Blind. On his back. Hands stuck, won't reach his face, caught on something, tied probably. Foggy. No pain in blinking, though. Sightless maybe, but eyes still there. Not like Kelsey. Pieces coming back now. Kelsey in the bathtub, Zang's blood-soaked shirt. Jimmy dead. Kinlock.

Who had not pulled the trigger. The gun steady, the black cylinder of its silencer looming like a primed cannon, Kinlock's eyes glittering like shards of broken glass, and then his voice, taut, cold. "In spite of your fucking videotape, Powell, I like you."

"Not my tape, Kinlock." They had found it, then. Knew what was in it. Viscarra and Manny and the ripping skin and the blood on the whitewashed wall. "Your guy was making it."

"No. *You* were my guy."

"I suppose I was." The sides of the stairwell were closing in on him. Behind Kinlock, out the landing window, a flagstone walk and no one on it.

"Looking for someone there, Michael?" Kinlock had asked with a grin that spread from his face to those of his two suited partners. "In case, you're wondering, she won't be coming back up here."

Maria. They had her, too. Alive? No point in asking. They couldn't want her to live long. And, in any event, nothing he could have done. Kinlock had been a step or two beyond his reach and both suits, John and Kenny or whatever their names were, had eased hands into their jackets.

He was in the charred church again, could almost smell the acrid smoke across the years there in the darkness of the confessional. Nowhere and no one to go to. The past never left you alone.

Something here, though. Here in whatever black hole he was in was something from the light, something he had seen before he stopped seeing. No memory. Shifting slightly, Powell searched his mind for pictures to push himself into.

On the stairs, the gun was the main feature. Light from the windows above and below silhouetting the men, the empty walk, a very faint scent of pine disinfectant and the gun. Then Kinlock's odd question.

"Do you have a passport, Michael?"

"No."

"Good." A brief, taut smile. "That could be useful later."

And back to business: "You will be with us for a while longer. We need to take a short jaunt. You will walk with Kenny; John and I will be a few steps behind you. You understand you must not try any heroics, don't you Powell?"

He had nodded. Except for the company, the stroll could have been any of a thousand like it. Footsteps ringing hollowly on the stone floor of the seminary's entrance hall, Sunday traffic, on 22nd Street a demented street lady howling on a grate, the air warm but crisp enough to let the sour subterranean fumes rise, a quickened pace as the light changed crossing Eighth. Halfway to Seventh, Kenny's nonchalant shove and the detour into the grey rectangular mouth of an anonymous parking garage. Red letters - Special Weekend Rates. Short John at the booth ahead of them; the attendant handing over the keys. Down a ramp in the half light, two levels, was it? Kinlock ahead then, at the back of a large black or dark blue sedan, the trunk lid coming up, Maria lying face up, and then the dull thud at the base of his skull that brought down blackness like a curtain of ebony glue.

Maria. In the car trunk, where he must be now.

"Shit!" Rolling left brought Powell face first into a hard, carpet-covered wall. Twisting right and leaning: a sharp pain in his elbow, shooting up toward his shoulder; under his face: hard lumps, moving under nudges, cool and rigid along his nose, then close ridges of something softer, loose strands, something known. Shoelaces. Feet!

"Maria?" No answer to his urgent hiss. Rocking his head over the shoes: loose movement, no stiffness. Sliding his face up to the soft, bunched cloth of what had to be her sweatpants, catching it between his teeth and tugging, feeling a patch of skin along his cheek, smooth and, thank God, warm. Thank God. Was there someone to thank for being trussed unconscious and stuffed in a car trunk? Powell rolled back onto his back, arms pinned painfully under his weight, and considered this. The ghosts of Manny and Viscarra wandered through his mind, both closer than they had been in years. Manny, he knew, would have said yes. `It is simple, my friend,' his shade whispered across time, `as long as you are alive, and perhaps longer, you have the potential to love. For that, give thanks.' Viscarra had known nothing of that. And yet in refusing it, Powell knew, even he had been shaped by it, twisted into a cruel caricature of a person. And now Maria Hernandez was beside him in the dark, not dead but not moving, and Kinlock was not far away. Again, the quandary.

And again, the helplessness. As in the whitewashed chapel, sour with the smell of fear and gasoline.

"Fuck this!" Powell yanked his wrists up as his shout fell back on him and died, sending a streak of pain like lightening up along his left arm from elbow to shoulder. Wincing then, sinking back, feeling tears well and roll. Losing focus, grasping for something in the darkness, some thought, some image to hold onto. Feeling the thorns, the lash, the dead weight of the splintery wood. Then hearing again the voice, finally the voice again: ~`Yet not my will, but your will be done.'

Powell's shoulder socket throbbed and the bindings, whatever they were, chafed at his wrists. Inside out, though, a ripple of calm was spreading starting at that invisible, ineffable, precise point at which the voice had touched him. Around him, blackness closed in like cotton. But he knew the words now. From John, the prologue, he spoke aloud: "The darkness has not overcome."

A statement, a conviction. He rolled onto his side, facing the space where Maria was, and spoke it again: "The darkness has not overcome."

And again, pulling his knees up to his chest, sliding them along the softness of her body: again: "The darkness has not overcome."

Now, he jerked his bound hands down and under his rump, gasping at the sharp stabs that coursed upward from his shoulder. Next, the simultaneous push and pull: left knee up to touch his chin; left hand even further down, straining to slide under the left heel.

"The. Darkness. Has not. Over . . aaiihh."

And he caught it, his shoe on the taut rope bridge between his hands. Another grunt, another pushpull - and it was over! Powell's right hand now rested almost comfortably between his thighs, a few inches below his crotch. "Has not overcome," he whispered, and laid his head on the trunk floor. Feeling the itch of the carpet tickle in his ear, he caught his breath and listened. First, only the sound of his own gasped respiration, then the muffled thump of his heart beneath it, then: nothing. No sound from Maria. No voice.

Had there ever really been one? Or only his own projection? Powell felt a misplaced grin contort his lips and cheeks as the memory of his novicemaster, what was his name, stocky and florid, bulled his way into the present. "Pretend! Pretend, damn it! If you're not sure of it, then just act as if it is true. Who's ever sure of anything? Pretend and see what happens!"

What happened was they cut your throat. The grin was gone. What happened was they plucked your eyes out. Or nailed your tongue to a tabletop. Or yanked your skin off.

But even then, a thank you. And now the pieces, almost ancient pieces now, fell together and Powell knew that Manny's final gratitude had not been for him and his gun but for the One who had given so many opportunities to love his people.

"Thank you," Powell said softly, unsure of whom or what it was he addressed. The grin again. Who's ever sure of anything? With a sudden, almost fluid, motion he pulled his right knee tightly into his throat and slid his bound hands under his right heel, now bringing his fingers to his face, rubbing the bindings across his lips.

Fairly thin rope; nylon, though. Not much hope of fraying it even if there was something rough at hand. Knots in the middle, between the wrists - perhaps possible to tug at them with his teeth if he could see what he was doing.

Which meant: not now. Darkness pushed down on him like dirt in a grave. He raised his arms to test its limits, banging his knuckles on the trunk lid before his elbows could straighten. Eighteen inches, not more. To his left, only a few inches; to his right, beyond where Maria lay, two, maybe two and a half feet. Not a lot of room to maneuver.

Pulling his feet up behind his thighs, Powell pushed and swung right, over Maria's legs, easing himself down across her thighs, scootching his feet along the trunk wall, repeating, easing down this time across her chest, feet swinging clear now, and back down next to her, reaching out left then to where she had to be.

And was. Face about where his was, head turning limply in his hands, arms tied behind her as his had been, breath faint but regular on the back of his hand. Out, but not a coma. Grabbing her shirt, bunching it, Powell shook her. And was rewarded with a low sigh. A bucket of water, Powell thought, was all that it'd take. A pissed-off snort at this. Not something that'd be easy to come by. But what would?

And then an answer, an odd one. Could he use it? Cats did, he told himself. Dogs did. What choice was there? Rolling again, leaning across Maria's prone body, Powell began to lick her face, working up across her cheek, her nose, her eye, to the base of her forehead and down the other side again. A taste of salt and something else underneath it, something sweeter, soap, maybe, or lotion. Her face stirred a bit as he licked her chin and started the cycle again, this time tonguing her lips and gliding all the way up to her hairline, the lemony smell still faintly there, and a nascent awareness of the sweet stiffness growing between his legs.

"Jesus. Mary." Maria muttered and turned her head and Powell moved down her throat and started up again.

"JESUS!" Her head came up fast, clocking him hard on the right temple just above the cheekbone. His reflex jerked him up even faster, smashing the back of his head into the trunk lid. Red streaks in the darkness and a door inside closing, almost shut tight, and falling down on something soft, something moving, and a voice, words, hold onto the words.

Which were: "Motherfucker! Get the fuck off me! Fucking asshole!"

Maria, he knew through hot throbbing behind his eyes, was awake.

Rolling back now, away from her, against the trunk wall, Powell, no control now, began to laugh. Which first intensified the epithets spewing up out of the perfect darkness, then slowed them, then stopped them altogether. His crazy shriek finally faded to a wheezing chortle and he heard her quiet question.

"It's you, isn't it, Powell?"

It struck him funny. A kind of `Doctor Livingston, I presume,' thing.

A laugh started to rise again in his belly, but he forced himself to swallow it.

"It's me, Hernandez."

Long moment without sound, not even breath.

"What were you just doing to me?"

"Waking you up. Trying to."

"You were licking me? Were you?"

No laughter now. Nowhere near.

"You like it?"

"It worked."

"Did you like it, Powell?"

"No. Yes. I guess I did."

"And you thought it was funny?"

"No."

"What was then?"

"Nothing. Everything."

"Which?"

"It's the same."

Stillness. No light, no sound, no movement. An empty point in the pit of Powell's gut seemed to contain all the stillness in the world.

"Powell?" A tense quavering at the back of the word.

"Yeah?"

"Fuck you."

"Yeah."

Back in the void. But something different now. Now the empty point was filling, expanding, ready to burst again with laughter. Stupid laughter. Loony laughter. Coming from somewhere else, not from him. From someone else. Grace, Powell thought, choking it back long enough to speak. "Maria?"

"The fuck you want?"

"You forgot to say thanks."

"GODDAM YOU!" He heard her roll toward him and fall back snorting and then he was laughing and holding her down with his tied hands and she struggled against his pressure, cursing, and then her laughter came as well, peals of it, wailed like grief and he pulled his arms back and rolled slightly toward her, still laughing, guts hurting with it, and felt her hair along his cheek, coming closer through the peals and then her lips found his nose and kissed it.

"Hey?" Still a chuckle at the back of the word, but something else, too. Concern? Anxiety? Maybe fear.

"Hey, what?"

"Whadda we do now? Any great ideas?"

"Just one - we get out of here."

"How?"

Just a touch of irritation there. Which was good, Powell thought. Or if not good, at least better than despair. "Don't know," he said, "but if we're still here when they come back, we'll need to be way more than lucky."

He heard Hernandez shift, wince, then shift again. "Where's `here', anyhow?"

"Car trunk. Big black car. Chevy Caprice, I think. Was in a garage on 22nd. Don't know where we're parked now. They turned my lights out just when the lid came up. Saw you and then nothing else."

"Who's `they?'

"Remember my telling you about Kinlock? Him. And some hired hands."

"C.I.A.?"

"Could be." The darkness was friendlier now. Was it like this in marriage? Powell wondered. Just relaxed and talking in the dark.

Sometimes it had been with Nicole. He remembered Haiti, the heavy tropical air and the sheets cool on top of them and her warmth palpable. "Or maybe he's freelancing this one."

"What makes you say that?"

"I don't know. Something he said. I don't remember but something wasn't right."

"Tell me. Tell me what you do remember."

Powell told her. He spoke quickly and quietly and in some strange way the darkness seemed cozy with Hernandez in it. Speaking of Nicole brought back the salty sweet taste of Maria's skin and with it a cock twinge that passed when he whispered Kinlock's annunciation of the girl, Anne. The slightest pause then but no response. In a hurried flood of words, he finished.

"You don't think he knew about Wolfson? Or Case?"

The detective at work. Something hard about it. Necessary, perhaps, but cold and somehow wicked. "I don't think so. He could've been acting but why would he? If he knew what this guy Rossa was up to, he wouldn't have had to put out the feelers that finally felt me."

"Someone in the department's talkin' to him."

"Apparently." Strictly business now. "Who'd know enough to tell him all that?"

"Polsec, maybe. Even if it's deep cover, they woulda had to set up some files. When Zang went down, maybe someone decided to sing."

"Or maybe Kinlock's been in since the beginning."

Hernandez grunted acknowledgement and Powell heard her struggle to move, wince, fall back heavily. "How'd they find you, anyway?"

"My car. Someone was in it. I got it in and the lights went out. Head hurts like hell now."

"You had the room key, didn't you?"

"I guess so. Why?"

"That's how they found me."

"Sorry."

"Hey, no problem. I missed you." Powell pushed himself up and peered blindly into the darkness where her voice was. "Gotta get your hands in front of yourself, Maria."

"Great advice, Padre." Hacked off sarcasm. "Any bright ideas as to how?"

"Decrepit old geezer like me did it; ought to be that you can, too."

Silence first, then a half-amused snuffle from her part of the darkness. "Ok, Houdini. Talk to me."

Powell described the maneuver and listened to the thumps and breathing - gasped intakes and blowy harsh exhalations - that marked her progress. To what end? If this was Agency, it was a dirty op, and if Kinlock was on his own, they were gone anyway. The Roach Motel, Jamal'd said. Once you checked in, you didn't check out.

"Got it!" Triumph and panting and hands reaching over invisibly to give his arm a long squeeze. Which ended abruptly as though she'd been yanked away. Knows, Powell thought. She knows. Not a pretty place to be. All that stuff she wasn't going back to. The little girl in the yard. The guy, whoever he was. Hot coffee in the morning and cold beer on Sunday afternoon. Reaching up to the trunk lid, he patted his way his right and then left, until he found the latch, searched it with numbing fingertips, dropped his hands back to his chest.

"Hernandez?" His voice, but where was the calm coming from? "Hey?"

"What." A tone as flat as Kansas.

"You ever drink wine on Sunday afternoon?"

"The fuck kind of-"

"Do you?"

A rustle of movement, her edged voice a bit closer: "Yeah, sometimes. So what?"

"So let's go get some now."

Acid in the air. "Better idea - I'll call the waitress over. Maybe she's got a key."

Let it go, he thought. Just let it go and keep moving. To Hernandez: "Move your butt down and swing your legs over mine."

"What good's that-"

"Look, Maria, a car trunk is made to keep people out, not to keep 'em in. So just shut your yap and do it, will you?"

"Hey, Powell. Fu-"

"NOW, goddam it!"

No words. The sound of cloth on cloth and quick pants of breath, the weight of her bound legs dropping across his thighs.

"Ok, I'm coming around." Powell eased his legs out from under hers and pivoted on his lower back into the space where her voice had been, thumped his head into the trunk's wall, slid his fanny down a bit more, pivoted again, found the top of her head with his shoulder.

"Jesus, Powell!"

"Sorry. Can you pull your knees up and turn more?"

"Yeah, maybe." A grunt and more movement in the darkness next to him. "Yeah."

And then he was around, hands on the latch again and head wedged underneath, knees on his chest and curled toes set on the lid above, breath coming quicker. Next to him, Hernandez farted loudly.

"Oh, God!" The laughter was welling up and she was laughing, too. "What charm school'd you go to?"

"Man, don't make me laugh." The smell rose warm and rich around them. "You make me laugh, I'm gonna shit my pants."

"You sure. You didn't. Already?" Laughing now 'til it hurt, wheezing, laughing more, tears streaming. "This doesn't. Work the first time. We're in trouble."

"Madre Dios."

"Yeah." Calming a bit, still gasping but less reach for air. "Yeah, that too."

Powell's fingers exploring again now, sizing, testing, trying to see what his eyes couldn't.

"Ok, I've got a couple of pieces that move. I'll push 'em as far as I can and I need you to get your feet on this end of the lid and give a helluva kick up. You ready?"

I need you. His words. That, Powell knew and didn't want to know, was what it was coming down to.

"Ready."

"On three then. One."

Has to work. God, let it work.

"Two."

Chilled wine on a Sunday afternoon. Maria Hernandez.

"THREE!"

Chapter 27

SUNDAY - 4:04 p.m.

The answer was in the room, a two-story shipping space by the loading dock. All the data available for inspection. Now it was just a question of interpretation.

The man Kinlock had called Rossa was there, the Crotch Gun man from Jimmy D's, tied to a chair, mouth taped. Kinlock was sitting just above him on a long metal table, humming tunelessly, legs crossed, right toe keeping a very slow time in the air, black briefcase flat behind him. The dark suits, Kenny and John, guns drawn, silencers on, stood slackly at opposite ends of the chamber.

Two pieces missing, Powell thought, but what's missing is data, too. One piece was Fitzgerald. If the stage was his and he knew the cast, he had to be somewhere in the theater.

Given Rossa's trussing, though, it was possible that the curtain had already come down on him.

The other piece more problematic. Powell did not know who it was. A cop, though. There had to be a cop. Kinlock knew too much. About Zang and Kelsey. About the girl on the square, Mahoney or whatever her name really was. About Jimmy D's. Even about Maria's car. Possible to have a network in place that would know all that but not likely. A much better bet that someone inside was funneling information out.

The rest was predictable, though, based on bits of intelligence they already had. Kinlock was looking for Rossa or Flynn - or whomever he was

– who had worked the explosive heist, possibly with the help of the missing sergeant, possibly as part of a sting gone wrong. Then Rossa and his thugs had done Wolfson and Case who must have been too close, though they might not have known it. Would have done him, too, if he'd been home when Anna'd been pushed. Because of the Wolfson connection, NYPD had put Kinlock onto him, and he had located Rossa. But not the explosive. The Symtex-5 was not there. Fitzgerald and whoever the cop was had gone to get it. When that happened, Kinlock would disappear and the rest of them could sort out the loose ends. The Agency was in because you couldn't put a man on trial for stealing something that didn't exist. That was the whole ugly package.

And all in the name of freedom, Powell thought, watching from the balcony where he and Hernandez lay behind a stack of long, thin cardboard boxes. Killing for freedom, the innocent with the guilty. And yet it was a strong impulse. Tied up and locked in a car trunk, would he have been willing to kill for his freedom? Perhaps. He had certainly been willing to come close.

The lid coming up had flooded the trunk with light, blinding him even as he pushed himself up towards it. Blinking, he saw the parking lot and the back of the building, Derry Lighting, no surprise, the chain link fence and the street beyond it, a smell of putrid garbage and diesel fumes. Then Maria was sitting next to him and he was tugging urgently at the nylon knots at her wrists, which stubbornly fell away. When she had pulled his loose, he had seen the woman, a white-haired crone in a flowered housedress, staring at them through the fence near the unchained gate. At the bar at Jimmy's, Powell thought. And then on the street outside. Coincidence not possible. Never a coincidence for the paranoid.

"Ma'am?" Powell had pushed himself up and out of the car, and had staggered he few steps to the fence. The woman's eyes were wide and blue and her shoulders were surprisingly square. "Ma'am, could you help us?"

The woman had opened her mouth and closed it without speaking, had turned and begun to shuffle away. Powell had eased through the gate, almost running now, had caught her, dropping his left hand on her left arm before she'd gone five yards. Something was coming. The tension in her bicep had given just warning enough for him to dance backward as she had whirled. The glinting blade in her right hand had missed by less than a centimeter.

The woman's nose had fallen off. His kick had landed square on her mouth and the putty construction above it had detached and arced over her falling body, landing a foot beyond the square of sidewalk where her head had cracked hard onto concrete. Leaving it, Powell had pocketed the knife, had caught the woman's arm and leg and slung her up over his shoulder in a fireman's carry. Back through the gate, back across the lot, back to where Maria stood aghast, then dumping the body, mouth bleeding, thick make-up mask coming off in chunks, into the just vacated car trunk.

"What if someone saw that?"

"Are you kidding? This is New York. And even if there is a good citizen around, what do they do? They call the cops. C'mon."

"Is she gonna live?"

"I don't give a shit."

Powell had slammed the trunk lid down and headed for the building and now, watching, realized that he had meant it. The woman had gotten Jimmy killed, probably had, and had tried to kill him. No ear for the voice now. No way to hear: `Do good to those who hate you.' Running, another scuffle came to mind, another swinging blade: the high priest's servant losing an ear. Would have done that, too, he thought. That, too.

The building's rear door appeared to be open, out a quarter inch from its frame, but they had avoided it and opted for a small window to the right of the loading dock. Powell dug his fingertips under its lip and tugged. And it swung out - a surprising bit of serendipity. The window opened from a small bathroom, one stall, one urinal, one stained sink. Cracking its door, Powell saw boxes and a metal stairway further to the right; voices came from somewhere back to the left. The two of them had slithered up the steps to an open storage loft.

Nothing was happening in the room below. Kinlock stopped humming but his toe continued to mark time in the air. Above the tape, Rossa's eyes were glittery and hateful. Kenny and John were as calm as morticians. Kinlock bent and glanced at Rossa's face, straightened and smiled.

"Still hoping, aren't you, Rossa?"

The gagged face moved slightly but did not turn towards Kinlock. Watching, Powell felt a searing impulse to walk down and tear the tape off Rossa, to hear him talk, to make him explain. Wolfson, Case, Anna, Jimmy D's, Kelsey, even Zang - all of them were him. His doing. Real lives, lives webbed to others, to children and parents, to friends and colleagues, lives stamped out as easily as one might step on a spider on a basement floor. Barabbas. Or Viscarra again. The Colonel come back. And this time Kinlock on the other side, Kinlock and whatever he represented.

Democracy? Liberty? Hardly, Powell thought. Finally, Kinlock was just about power and this time power had put the Colonel in fetters instead of giving him the key. In a decade, in a year, even next week, some subtle balance in some closed room halfway around the world could shift and reverse the situation and only half a score of men, all men, all white men, would ever know the reason. Manny and his comrades, the Cambodians along the Mekong, all just pawns. The power was never with them.

Hernandez touched his elbow. Something changing downstairs. Sounds offstage, bodies stiffening a bit, heads, even Rossa's, turning.

Fitzgerald came in, red-faced and swaggering, followed by a tall, well-tanned, bald man in creased khakis and a navy blue polo shirt carrying a thick blue suitcase.

Maria's fingers on his arm again, clutching this time. "Polsec," she mouthed without breaking silence. The missing cop.

"Welcome back, Commander," Kinlock said. "I see you found the package. Is it all there?"

"See for yourself." The voice was smooth and unaccented. He hefted the case onto the shipping table and fumbled briefly with the clasps. Kinlock was standing now, leaning forward. The lid came up.

Revealing money. Not explosives. Neat tight rows of green bills, too far away for Powell to see the denomination. What could be the urgency of getting it? If all the principals were accounted for, if the substance itself was in hand, and it must be, why not just get this with a simple search warrant?

Stupid question.

It was about greed.

Kinlock was part of the taking, not an agent of retrieval. Rossa and company had tried to stiff him on the payment. And had almost pulled it off, Powell thought. With Zang dead, no one had known how to get to Rossa. His own information, not much more than an educated guess, had been the only link.

"What do we do with them now?" the commander was asking.

"A very good question." Kinlock's torso was still bent across the money. His hand was on his briefcase. "But before we discuss it, I feel a tremendous need to defecate." He grinned briefly. "Now that the pressure's off, so to say. Where's the can, Fitzgerald?"

Fitzgerald pointed mutely.

"Commander, bring the cash. No need to subject Fitz to any

unnecessary temptation. John, come along."

The trio disappeared under the loft and Powell pondered the oddly out-of-place scene. Not the way it happened in the movies. No one ever had to shit. Which made it, perhaps, more likely to be true.

A long moment passed. Nothing happened below and the dissonance increased. At the seminary, too, Powell thought. Something quirky there as well. What?

And then pieces were coming together as if some unseen electric field had suddenly switched poles. The passport question. The open bathroom window. The wires in the briefcase. He grabbed Hernandez arm and hissed, "Gotta get out of here!"

Kenny looking up. Maria's reply: "They'll see us!"

"Don't matter! Go!"

And he was running, Hernandez behind him; a long box slid off a stack and thumped hollowly to the floor, their footsteps clanged harshly on the metal steps. Powell barged past the bathroom door, down a narrow corridor towards the loading dock exit.

Kenny there first, off balance, gun coming up, Powell throwing his legs forward in a baseball slide, silencer coming down now, a flash, and a hornet whizzing by his left ear and his right leg coming up, foot jamming hard into the gunman's crotch. The two of them in a tangle, a glimpse of Hernandez with the gun, raising it, swinging hard down onto Kenny's skull, then leveling it to move into the room where Fitzgerald was working at Rossa's ropes.

Grabbing her then by the back of the shirt, throwing her towards the door, the gun dropping, moving to dive out behind her, and then the hand had him, lifted him high, higher than possible, a flash somewhere behind him, and sound, possibly sound, but before he could make it out black gelatin closed over him and there was nothing but dark again.

Chapter 28

TUESDAY - 3:12 p.m.

Images: Jimmy caught up in a cyclone and Margaret Hamilton in the costume of a witch bicycling by in the air. Ellen bending over him, holding his head while she arranged a pillow. The Grand Inquisitor, black-garbed and foreboding, standing in a doorway. Maria seated, crying, neat suit and creamy blouse, a bandage over her right eye; behind her a tall redhead with very short hair, her hands on Hernandez's shoulders. Anna exalted, rising on a sunbeam. Lethe lying peaceful in a dirty bed.

And now a scene reprised. Hospital room, strong anti-septic smell, Hernandez seated there, who DOES have a small bandage over her eye, wearing jeans, boots and a silky black tee shirt that says something about a dance company he can't quite make out. She is reading papers on a clipboard.

"Didn't we just do this, Officer?" A taste like clean cotton in his mouth. "What is it you want to know now?"

Head snapping up, big smile. "Mickey! You ok?"

"Obviously not. What's wrong with me, anyway?"

"What's wrong is you been in a coma. Seems like some of a brick wall fell on you."

"That explains why everything hurts. Why'd a wall wanna do that, anyway?"

"You don't remember?" Maria looking somehow anxious. Painful to shake his head. "The building it was part of blew up."

Now Powell remembered. Rossa and Fitzgerald. The commander and the gunmen. The money.

"Any trace of Kinlock?"

"He didn't get out. Found him buried in the bathroom."

Not possible. Not possible that he'd have laid it out so carefully and then got the timing wrong. To Hernandez: "You see the body?"

"No." Her voice uncertain.

"Who else would know what he looked like?"

"They got clean fingerprints. Feds had him on file. And you'll like this - they say he worked for the State Department. Never in intelligence. Also, no explosive missing anywhere."

"Of course not. Why'd they think the building blew? Goddam gas leak?"

"The big boys are `looking into it.' PD is out now."

"Where'd they send the stiff? Kinlock's?"

"Here probably, for the DOA pronouncement, at least." Hernandez looked confused or doubtful, like a child who may have done something wrong without knowing it. "Could've gone up to the M.E. at Bellevue by now."

Powell found himself grinning. "If I can ask without this seeming too philosophical, where is `here' and when is `now?'"

Maria smiled back, a warm and glorious movement of lips and teeth and eyes. "Here, Padre, is St. Vincent's. And now is Tuesday afternoon." She checked her watch. "'Bout three-fifteen."

"Carrumba." Powell gave a low phony whistle. "Thees ees some siesta, no?" Maria was still smiling. A sight, Powell thought, that you could get used to. "Anybody else make it out?"

Hernandez's smile faded as she shook her head. "No one inside. No bodies even except Kinlock and a big chunk of Commander Nelson. Just pieces. The girl you put in the trunk came through, though."

"Girl? That old—"

"That old hag without the makeup turned out to be a twenty-year-old body builder. I heard she's singing."

It hurt to sit up, stabs and aching all along his back. Needles of pain along the back of his legs, too, when he lifted them. Apparently, nothing broken, though. No casts anywhere. An IV tube in his right arm and incredible wooziness, like someone had set a spinning anvil in his skull. Still, Powell thought, some hangovers are worse. Maria was watching, eyes wide and anxious. You could get used to it.

"I got another question for you, Officer." She nodded, waited. "How come I'm in here and you're not? Weren't we together when that wall fell?"

Now she stood. Crossed the room, gently set an arm around his shoulders. Softly kissed the top of his head. "You covered me, Powell. I appreciate it."

You could definitely get used to it. He slipped his hand around her waist, squeezed softly. "Yeah. Well. We still have some work to do, no?"

"Like what?"

"Like right now you gonna help me get into that shower over there. And then when I'm dressed, we'll take a stroll down to the morgue and see who's in the drawer."

"Powell, they're not lettin' you out of here. You—"

"What do you think they can do? Arrest me?"

"We KNOW who it is. I told you, they got good prints."

Powell's neck cracked audibly as he shook his head. "An old spook like him, prints mean nothing. I want to see."

Slipping the IV feed out, Powell knotted the tube and dropped it on the bed behind him. Hernandez, he thought, was beginning to look desperate.

"Mick, he's probably not even there. Probably already outa here."

Another head shake, another crack. "You said the Fibbies were trying to push the PD out? Of a cop-killing case? Nothing is moving anywhere with that kind of turf thing. He's still here. I bet you dinner on it."

He was up now. A little wobbly, but ambulatory. Hernandez was standing, too, shaking her head but on board, opening a dresser drawer, handing him folded clothes.

Which were filthy, covered with a fine layer of dust with occasional smudges of heavier grime, pungent with sweat.

"Nice," Powell said. "You do my shopping for me?"

"I can't help it you don't take care of your things."

"Real nice."

Powell took the stack, stepped past her to the bathroom zigzagging a bit, and groaned pulling the light blue gown over his head. Propped in the shower, the hot water cascading over him, he felt for a moment that all was well. And heard a voice, a woman's: `All manner of things shall be well.' Julian. The mystic anchorite alone for years in her cell. One who knew. But `well' to her, he recalled, meant `wounded,' always and divinely wounded. Was that what it took? Almost there in any case. Toweling himself, he called loudly to Hernandez through the closed door: "Any publicity on this yet?"

"Publicity? What publicity?"

"News. You know - TV guys with bad hair and serious voices."

Powell heard her laughing, a melodious flow down a scale or two. "No-o-o-o. News? Building blows up in the Village, breaks windows for a half mile - why would that make the news?"

"Ok, I get the picture. Were we in it?"

"Oh yeah. You'd've looked great on TV. Limp as a dishrag."

"Not pictures. I mean names. Were our names on?"

"Mine was. Department released it. I don't know about yours. Is it important?"

"Probably not. Kinlock was interested that I didn't have a passport. Said it might come in handy or something. He thinks I'm dead, maybe he'll go apply for one on my behalf as it were."

"Man, Kinlock is DEAD."

"So you say." Powell dropped the hospital gown on the bed. "Let's go see."

Hernandez shrugged, opened the room door an inch, peered out at the corridor. "We ain't gonna make it past the nurse's station without all hell breaking loose."

Powell looked past her through the crack to where a white-starched woman of about fifty sat officiously at a desk. "Ok, here's the deal: walk past her to the first open room door, step inside and hit the call button. I'll meet you in the elevator."

"Wait a minute." Great eyes - brown and wide open and almost smiling. "What do I say when she shows up?"

"Nothing. You won't be there."

"You are crazy, Mick."

"Right. Now go."

The nurse only glanced up as Hernandez walked by. No, Powell thought, walked wasn't right. Sashayed. Wonderful figure, nice movement. Her motor really shaking. And stupid of you to notice, he told himself. Too old to blame it on hormones. Just longing - or lust.

Maria was past the station now, past the first door, nonchalantly slipping into the second. Powell tightened his grip on the doorknob, saw Hernandez re-emerge as the nurse's gaze moved from her file to a console in front of her, saw her push herself back and stand as Maria turned by the station towards the elevator core. In a moment the nurse was bustling away from him and he was out of the room and around the corner, feeling conspicuous and trying not to show it.

In the elevator, Hernandez was giggling. A schoolgirl who had just slipped something past the nuns. Powell felt himself catch the feeling, felt the grin coming, spreading itself across his face in spite of the woozy nausea that encircled him.

"Floor, please," she said, trying to get a nasal sound into her voice.

"I don't know. I'm looking for something in a dead body."

"That'd be retreads. All the way down."

He laughed. Not funny but what could you do? Only so much grieving possible until you had no capacity for it. Then you could only laugh or hate. Or both. Still smiling, he asked, "Why's the morgue always in the basement, anyway?"

"Where else they gonna put it? Can't be hauling stiffs up and down the elevators all the time, can they? Bad for business."

Two doctors in lab coats got on at two, eyed Powell quickly, stood away from him, got off at one.

"Something to be said for stink, anyhow. People don't crowd you."

"Man, anyone crowd you now, we'd be starting artificial respiration right here in the car."

"That bad?"

"Worse." She was still smiling like a kid.

At LL, the doors opened on an empty cinderblock hallway. Hernandez nudged him to the right and guided him around a corner to a pair of glass doors. Behind them, a uniformed cop, white guy, sat thumbing a magazine on a brown couch in a neat, well lit, reception area. A sliding window in the wall framed the attendant's head: a young, very black, woman with corn rows. A nod to the cop and the badge out and up before they'd reached the counter.

"Need to have a peek at a man named Kinlock."

"Can't do it." The cop's voice. "No one sees him."

Hernandez turned and considered the source. The policeman, chewing gum, had set the magazine carefully on the table, was now leaning towards them earnestly. "No one sees him," he repeated, "that's what the orders are."

"You didn't get a call about this, did you?" Maria sounding warm and sympathetic.

"Nope. No call."

"Situation normal." She laughed. "Look, what's your name, anyhow?"

"Loring. Rick Loring."

"Yeah, well, look Loring, this guy is the one who can put our buddy Kinlock at the scene. With one of his friends. We do that, we get the D.A. to take it to the grand jury tomorrow, it's a state thing and the Feds get pushed. We don't, they take it, Fernando here-" A thumb jerk towards Powell. "-disappears with the marshals. Who's your C.O.?"

"Howard. Jack Howard."

Another laugh. "You got Howard? What a dickhead!" Turning now. "Well, get him on the phone. I'm going to ream Howie's butt for you."

Not what Officer Loring wanted. Powell noted the new glisten across the cop's forehead and his lips, pursing and loosening like a fish's. "Hang on, hang on a second." Rick still sitting but coming their way now; the weathercock moving with the new wind. "Just looking, right? Not moving him or anything?"

"Just a peek. The stiff stays right on the tray."

"Ok. But make it quick."

The black woman at the desk opened a metal door for them; led them down a short hall to a bright, white-tiled space with a wall full of stainless steel doors, let them stand staring while she checked a chart on her clipboard.

"You really know Howard?"

Hernandez smiling. "Nope. All C.O.'s are dickheads."

"Right here," said the black woman with the neat corn rows. She stepped up to the drawer wall, pulled a handle in the second row up from the floor, slid out the long tray, pulled a sheet back. To reveal: a naked short body, short and pallid, with heavy features and dark hair, the upper right side of the face concave, caved in like a rotten pumpkin.

Not Kinlock. John, without his dark suit and sunglasses.

"Well, Detective," Powell said, "How 'bout that dinner you owe me?"

Chapter 29

TUESDAY - 7:12 p.m.

Dinner was too crowded. Too much haunting. Too many ghosts. And not just imaginary projections, either. They were real, Powell knew. Part of what it meant to say that life overcomes death. The spirits of the past could move you to act, to laugh, to cry. The communion of all saints and all sinners, always speaking in the present tense.

Anna's had been the first. Giddy and high when Maria had freed Powell from the hospital, guiding him out through the ambulance entrance to her car, parked in front of a hydrant on 10th, he'd come down fast and hard at the rectory, greeted in the vestibule by the round brown visage of an enormous, huge-busted woman where Anna's tiny, fine featured face had always dwelt.

"Yes, may I help you?" A faint trace of a West Indian accent.

Powell speechless, almost stunned. Feeling Maria step up, close, her voice over his shoulder. "This is Father Powell. He lives here."

"And you are?"

"Detective Hernandez. Police Department."

The badge had probably been out; Powell could not remember. There was too much of Anna's ghost there, loving him and all of them who lived there, tending them like flowers, needing their affection in return to ward off the ghosts of her own past.

"I don't know nothing about him." The big face completely impassive.

"Then I guess you'd better check."

"You must wait here." She had emphasized 'must' and eyed them suspiciously as if either or both might try to slip through that sliver of doorframe not filled by her ample frame. When she returned, Ottarski, the youngest resident, trailed in her wake.

"God, Michael. Where have you been?" Question to him, eyes on Maria.

"It would be difficult to say." Wanting then only to be moving, to be out of Anna's vestibule, now so crowded, somehow pushing her out of the space as never would have happened in life. "This, Mark, is my keeper. Detective Hernandez, meet Father Ottarski."

Ottarski had nodded gravely. Not taking his eyes from her face, said, "You heard about Anna?"

"I heard."

Still staring: "Everyone's been-"

"Mark, I need to get some clothes. Perhaps we'll talk later." Powell had shouldered him aside, squeezed past the immense gatekeeper, and headed for the staircase with Maria and, somehow, Anna close behind.

"The woman cannot go up there!" A shrill, urgent note.

"So call the police!"

Whose voice had that been? His, he knew, though it had seemed disembodied enough that it might have been anyone's.

"What was that guy looking at?" Hernandez's question.

"You. We don't see many like you here." At the time he hadn't known how true that was. Then, only a shave mattered. A shave, and clean clothes, and the prospect of an evening with Maria. Without fear. Nothing to be afraid of now. Except, he had thought, what would happen between them. And that was only fearful in the looking-ahead way of a roller coaster, the click, click, click of the ascent that would lead to some whirling, twisting climax.

Which had not happened. Though Anna's ghost had stepped back, there were others. The blast and its shades, Fitzgerald and Flynn or Rossa, whatever he was called. The Commander, what was his name? Kenny and John "zookered" once again. They were there. When he had stepped back into the hall, clean and almost crisp, slapped with aftershave, they were waiting with Hernandez.

"What's going down," he had found himself saying, "with Kinlock?"

"I just called and reported." She'd shrugged. "I'm not on it now. With a two-day jump, though, I'm guessing he ain't in the neighborhood."

"Unless his business isn't finished."

"He got the money. What else you think he'd want?"

No certain answer, only a vague shadow, something cold and rank. "You, maybe."

"Me? He had me, man. You been hit in the head one too many times."

"He had you, Maria. And me. And he didn't intend to let us get away since I'd know that the body he'd get planted in that drawer wasn't him. Some part of his plan didn't work and you got out, the papers would have told him that. Was I with you? He doesn't know. And he doesn't know what I might have told you even if I'm dead now. Maybe he ran. Maybe not."

And then a puzzle piece sliding into place. Kinlock's briefcase, the wires, letters on a plastic card tucked in the flap: S-T-M-O-R; a space between the second and third. "You're not on it, Hernandez, call whoever is. Kinlock was staying at the St. Moritz."

"What, man? Where's that coming from?"

"He had a key, one of those plastic kinds. In his case. I think that's where it was from."

"Why you remembering it now?"

Powell had shrugged. "You said it, Detective. Been hit in the head one too many times."

She had handled it from her car, a crisp radio call, details repeated back to her through the static, then a different voice, a man's, with a question: "Where's Powell now? St. V's doesn't have him."

"I have him. He doesn't like hospital food."

Nothing for a long moment, finally the man again: "Keep your head down, Hernandez." Nothing again for a two count, then simply, "Out."

Out. What, Powell had wondered, did it mean to be Out? No connections. Entirely on your own. A theological impossibility unless you chose it. But an easy choice to make. Too easy.

Hernandez then, sounding tense and jittery as if some edge of hers was being pulled across a whetstone: "Ok, Powell; where to?"

"Jim-" He'd caught himself and swallowed but not before the second ghost had come in. Jimmy's a boarded up storefront by now. Jimmy himself gone, caught in a game that was not a game, gone on a journey that was not his journey, trapped in a cause that glittered and shone only if your lenses had the right tint. Gone to Oz.

Maria, reaching across the car seat, had touched his arm. "I know a place."

A bistro in Chelsea, long polished bar, black and white tile floor, painted tin ceiling, plain tables with butcher paper covers and unmatched steel flatware. At the back an ornately carved Art Deco room divider rising in an arch toward the ceiling like a rood screen in some monarch's chapel. En route, they had not spoken; arriving, they'd been beckoned to a table by bone-thin waiter with an ear cuff, wan and fey, and Powell had felt the vacuum within him, the space near his heart where Jimmy had been, where Anna had been, swell inward like some antonymic balloon gone mad. Then fingertips, Hernandez's touch again, brushing across the back of his hand

and along his wrist.

"Sorry, Mick. I'm sorry."

"Oh. Don't . . it's . . it's not . . I . . ." And then the tears and his hand holding hers, holding tight, hanging on to a slender, smooth lifeline. And then somewhere in the acrid, billowing clouds of black hurt, her voice.

"A pair of scotches here, Dewars, water back."

The waiter, still possessed of a doomed air, had brought the drinks. Nodding at Hernandez, a long, slow, swallow, the mellow warmth of the whiskey calming, something steady taking hold like a hand extended after a fall. Not the drink, though. Her. Something about her had brought him back to firm ground.

"Thanks, Maria."

"Nothing, man." She'd raised her glass. "Good health."

Health, he had thought. A word meaning wholeness. Not about him, all in pieces, sharp-edged shards scraping and cutting. What would health be like? What would it be like with her? Coffee in the morning's clear light, a drink when the sun was falling down past the Hudson, watching the child cruise the shady street on her bicycle. Would that be wholeness? He had touched his glass to hers and said, "Good health."

"Are we ready to order?" The waiter's voice faint and low.

"We are not." Feeling the smile form, seeing its reflection on Hernandez's face. "We are to negotiate the release of another drink into our custody."

The waiter's pencil had scratched a note on a pad and he had disappeared, a spectral diplomat on an unending mission. Though Powell could not recall seeing him return, new drinks had appeared, and crusty bread, and a vegetable terrine that hinted tarragon and shouted garlic. Hernandez, leaning forward, had looked warm-eyed and wonderful, and pieces had seemed to be coming together in tight fits that promised wholeness and even good health.

"Ellen came to see you. Do you remember?"

The stinging sensation of a cut there, and a tightness somewhere just above his eyes. "Ellen? Where?"

"The hospital. She wasn't hurt bad."

"How the . . . how do . . . "

"I was there."

Flustered then, not about Ellen whom he could vaguely see now, pale and gentle in the white room. Something else. Or someone, someone unknown also there.

"-there a lot, got my own cut stitched first, then the department crap, then I got cleaned up and came back. And then yesterday, afternoon I think, whenever, Ellen came. Don't know how she heard you were there, but she came."

Hernandez stopping, watching him, sipping her drink, still watching, speaking again. "She, uh, I think . . . she really cares about you."

"I care about her." Seeing not Ellen but Maria now, in the hospital room, a white square bandage cold and bright against the brown warmth of her skin. "We were together once. A long time ago now."

In the restaurant, a change, something different in her look; in the hospital room, now coming into sharper focus, someone with her. "How's the eye?"

Her hand rising, touching an almost invisible line at apex of her right eyebrow. Exactly where his mind had painted the white rectangle. "This? It's nothing. Four stitches. Bled like hell, though."

"Maria?"

"Yeah?" Had she known the question was coming? Had he known the answer? Now it seemed that he always had but had wanted to find again the place before that always.

"At the hospital? Who was with you?"

"When?" Eyes dropping, rising steady then to meet his gaze.

"Weren't you waiting in my room? With someone else?"

A slight tightening along her jaw, her lips drawing a millimeter thinner. "That was Mary. My lover."

My lover. What he had wanted to hear; even his bones knew it. What he had wanted to hear - about himself. And then Ellen's voice. From when? `This one is gonna break your heart.' His stomach had fallen down a bottomless shaft but he believed that he had nodded, smiled, perhaps uttered a neutral `oh,' and reached for the menu. But Hernandez's reaction said that she had seen and heard something else.

"Can't take it can you?" A dark flash in her eyes, and a blood surge pushing her dark skin a shade darker; both hands grasping the table's edge and shoulders square. "Tell me something, Father; is it because the Pope says so or just because you're like every other man?"

His own anger had risen then, flowing hot up from his gut, tensing across his back, tightening in his arms, his hands, his fingers. And then grace. From somewhere, release. An ebb of emotion, the beginning of a smile, sweet sadness cooling the heat, a shake of his head easing his tension.

"Not like that, Hernandez. It's not like that."

"The fuck you smiling at, man? You think I'm funny?"

Other diners looking then, peeking unobtrusively around the corners of wine lists.

"No. It's me."

"You?" Angry still, but doubt too. A possibility, an opening. "What the fuck about you?"

"I think I'm jealous."

Dumbfounded. Literally.

"You put the black shirt on, sometimes it's like you really ARE different. Sometimes you don't think about it, maybe for a long time. Women are people, men are people. Kind of beautiful space. And then sometimes you're just a guy with a funny shirt and you're so lonely that you ache all the time. And then once in a while there is someone."

Peace then, spreading in rings he could feel, firm and alive like a tree's, out from his soul across the table, across the room, out from there across the city. Hernandez simply staring, without anger, the fire banked.

"Does she love you?"

A silent nod.

"And your daughter."

Another.

"You're blessed, then."

"I am." Her voice quiet, almost a whisper.

And in that quiet, dinner had been ordered, eaten, cleared away; the ghosts joining them for duck with chutney sauce and Caesar salad, Anna chuckling over the matchstick carrots braised in champagne, Jim Duggan proudly pouring a respectable chardonnay, Nicole there, and Mary, a shade of the living, and Wolfson somewhere across the room, eloquent and pompous, holding forth on some abstruse bit of doctrine, all of them glowing like seraphim. And with them a greater presence, an archangel of sorts, Powell had thought, some powerful emanation of connectedness, throbbing and suffused with life.

In the midst of this intimate host, their own conversation had been soft and disjointed, starting and stopping and turning down side lanes whenever they presented themselves, moving from vacations past and future to high school dating, newspaper columnists to movies, occasionally sailing into silence and out of it again like a boat moving through a grotto. And then a question that took them deep again, beneath the surface, into the invisible cold currents. "Why," he'd asked, "did you become a cop?"

Head down, an instinctive duck, then up, meeting his eyes head on. "I don't know. Didn't seem like much of a choice at the time."

"Aren't there always choices?"

"No, Padre, there aren't." Voice as steady and firm as an oak beam. "When you're twenty and scared and the man you hate is a dead hero and you don't know how you'll take care of your kid - there aren't many choices then."

"Your husband was killed?"

A curt nod. "In a drug raid. That's what they said, anyway. He was a user himself, though, so I was never really sure. Anyway, the department said it'd always be there for me. Which was complete bullshit. When was it ever there for me before? But I said fuck it, send me to the academy. It's a job, right? And you know what? The papers loved it! Slain cop's widow vows to pick up the fight! What a load of crap!"

Powell met her flashing eyes and smiled. "You're still doing it."

"Yeah." A big return grin. "You know what? I found out that there are some good guys."

And then, above the rich vapor of espresso, the sound of his own laughter, tinged, it had seemed to him, with sadness.

"Man, you're strange." Hernandez's voice, bemused, somehow lovely. "What's funny now?"

No way to say without just saying it and, anyway, nothing to lose. "Hey, I love you, you know that?"

Her gaze on his then, even, no anger and no joy. "I do know. Not funny, though."

"Jimmy used to say, `You can laugh or you can cry.'"

The faintest trace of a smile. "Well then maybe Jimmy wasn't an idiot."

"No. Not an idiot." Only a Scarecrow, Powell thought, who had caught the fireball at the wrong moment.

Hernandez smiling wider, eyes as gentle as flowers. "So how does this act end, Mickey?"

"You put on your ruby slippers and tap your heels together. Say, `I wanna go home.' Right?"

"I guess."

A gentle spin in his gut turning faster now. The hole forming. "I won't see you then, will I?"

"I guess not. Not once the loose ends are tied up."

"Which are?"

Hernandez shrugged. "'Bout a million statements. More maybe.

"Speaking of which," she went on, "I could go make one now."

"Where?" An automatic response. Nothing more to hear. Only nothing.

"The seminary; since we're close. Update the Dean. You come along, I'll drop you off after."

Saying: "Might as well. Still got stuff there anyway. You do, too."

Thinking: Drop me off. Off the edge of the world into the whirling vacuum.

Hearing: Jimmy's voice, alarmed through a gathering interior darkness. "It's a twister!"

Chapter 30

TUESDAY - 7:55 p.m.

The seminary's lobby was as quiet as the short walk over had been. Sitting on a polished wooden bench, an old pew actually, the relic of some now gone piece of urban ecclesiastical real estate, Powell worked the stroll over, kneading it in his mind like a potter prepping clay, hoping to find something beautiful in smooth, dense mud.

Not much there. A half embrace at the bottom of the bistro's short stairway, his right hand resting comfortably on the small of her back, her left laying gentle on his shoulder blade, fingertips just below the collar, her body a close but impossibly distant inch away, and her eyes cloudy with something that could have been joy or could have been sorrow.

"Nothing against men, Mick. Or you." The words low, not much above a whisper, almost inaudible against the dark white noise of the street. "She's just someone special."

Had he answered? Now he thought so but was not sure, now he wanted to have said, "You're very lucky, Maria."

Reply or not, she had kissed him then, her lips soft against his cheek, the familiar lemon scent of her hair rich around him. And then, abruptly, they were walking, down to the corner of 23rd, scurrying across the avenue at the end of the light and on down 10th past the garish glare of the Empire Diner and the park with the seal fountain where winos and old hookers and neurotic homeless folk clustered on the benches like pigeons roosting. Flying rats, Powell had reflected. That's what the city called the birds. Its opinion of the bench people wasn't a good deal higher. Passing them brought Jamal to mind, and Tony, and Lethe. Living and dying only a step above the benches and only able to stay there because sick men with money would still buy their bodies to fuck and discard like shat on toilet paper dropped without thought in a gutter. And sooner or later - mostly sooner, really - the money bought bad horse or a needle brought H.I.V. or there were no buyers anymore or they met the one buyer who wanted to fuck them over completely. All the numbered doors of the Roach Motel.

"Hey, Hernandez," Powell had said.

"Mmmm?" She'd turned, her face dreamy and distracted in the halogen light, thinking, he guessed of Mary or her daughter or someplace without needles or fixes or johns or benches full of dirty people.

"You ever hear anything from Vice? You know, on that Roach Motel thing?"

"Huh?" Hardness coming back then, eyes narrowing, muscle and flesh and bone tightening along her jaw, eyebrows pulling themselves in and down. "Yeah. Actually, I did. Nothing much, though."

"What'd they say?"

"Said there's always talk. Said the street always believes there's some snuffbox out there. Never any evidence, but always talk. Roach Motel is new, though. Maybe six months, less than a year. And, yeah, it is s'posed to be somewhere downtown; here in Chelsea maybe, West Village, Clinton. No one ever knows."

"Anyone missing? Anyone they're looking for?"

"Someone's always missing."

Someone always missing. That, Powell had thought, was the eternal truth. Always missing. And until you knew that, you could not be found. Maria's face faded into shadow as they had turned onto 21st Street. On the right, the high brick walls of the seminary's buildings loomed up towards an almost purple sky; to the left, a row of brownstones stretched to the middle of the block where one tall apartment building broke ranks and pushed high opposite the well-lit gate where he and Hernandez had chased shades. When? Two nights, three nights before? Trying to recall, Powell's head had throbbed. Too much memory. Eyes in a baggie, brains splashed on a sidewalk, throats slit, greed unbridled. The Evil One prowling.

Crossing the street near the middle of the block, they had passed the chain link topped with razor ribbon where the search had taken them. Powell eyes had scoured it. The fence gate locked, a green enclosure just inside stacked high with black plastic bags reeking of putrid garbage and beyond it facing doors before the steps down which they'd raced: the steel and glass one they'd taken, obvious under the light, and opposite it an arched wooden entrance recessed into the brick wall. Which suggested something, a thought that would not fully form. Powell struggled with it for a moment, tried to find something there to hold onto, finally sighed and let it go.

And then they were past. Without speaking, they'd made their way through the crisp night air along the street, brushing shoulders twice, touching hands where a piss-soaked drunk lay contorted and snoring in a stairwell leading down into some seminary undercroft, rounding the corner where the tall man in the dark cloak had bought his whore, waiting at the school's entrance while a stocky black man with three gold chains fumbled with the door's buzzer button.

At the reception desk, Hernandez had flashed her gold detective's shield. "Here to see the Dean if he's available."

"Office hours are nine to five." The black man worried and pensive. "Going on eight now."

"I realize it's not convenient but I think he'd want to see me." A big winning smile with this. "He does live here, doesn't he?"

"Yes'm." Genuine concern now, anxiety spreading on his face like a blush. "Not s'posed to call him, though."

"I see. So I should call him and tell him that you refused to call him. Would that be good?"

"No." Looking panicky, the deskman had turned to Powell in a mute appeal for assistance.

"She's got the badge, man," Powell had said with a smile and a shrug. "The Dean, he's just got God."

No way out. Just the way it went sometimes, Powell had thought. The deskman picked up the phone receiver and jabbed at buttons as if they had risen, snakelike, to strike him. His words were bitten off, perfunctory. Police detective. Here now. Says you'd want to see her.

"He's coming up." The man had sounded miserable.

"Hey, man," Hernandez had barely suppressed a grin, "don't worry about it. I'll cover for you. Say I pulled my piece."

No smile in return, not even a glare of acknowledgment. Easier to see him then. Hanging on, not even able to rise up angry. Night guy at a school, making nothing, just hanging on, couldn't even get pissed, and now the Boss'd beat on him for the interruption. No way out, and she's talking about her piece.

"May as well go get the stuff, Mickey," Maria's voice, talking about what? "Long as we're here."

"What's that?"

Now a laugh. "Man, you did get hit hard. I'm talking 'bout your clothes, man. Your bag. Had one, didn't you? Kinlock have the bellman bring it along?"

Almost over for her, Powell thought. That's what her ebullience had been about.

"-at it, get mine, too."

Hers, too. One more detail to nail down - like her chat with the Dean would be. That and some paperwork and it'd be over for her, all the nagging bits and pieces gone, a life rewoven into a seamless whole. Which would not include him.

"Can do, Detective," Powell had said, turning abruptly away from her, away from the sudden searing, cold that coursed through his gut like a streak of anti-lightening, away from the sterile light of the lobby and towards the door that led inward to the teeming darkness of the Close.

There, safe, invisible, his obvious pain hidden, he had looked back. For a moment, Hernandez, skittish, had paced: from the desk to the lobby bulletin board, from the board to a portrait of a fabulously rich donor of days long gone, from the portrait to a huge old oil depicting the burning of Savaranola, hung surely with irony intended at the foot of the steps leading up to the library. Then a green door had opened inward, a tall, grey-haired man in black clericals had beckoned, and Maria had disappeared.

Not safe, Powell had thought, though it felt that way. The darkness that let him peer into the now-empty lobby was not safe. Comfortable, yes. Perhaps too comfortable. But nothing of healing there. Darkness only a place to nurse pain; no avenues there to take you past it. Weary, he had turned to the building where, three nights before, he and Maria had drunk whisky and told each other some of what there was to tell.

The rooms were lifeless. The beds had been stripped, what dishes they'd used had been cleaned and hidden, and their clothes and bric-a-brac, toothbrushes, combs, clocks, and books, had been swept together and dumped into their bags which alone testified that anyone had been there. No signs left of their fear or their intimacy. It might never have happened. Dread had welled up in Powell like a fountain of nothingness and he had picked up the bags and fled.

Back to the lobby, back to the oily, blonde-paneled walls, and the waxy light, back to the aggrieved receptionist who studiously ignored him, back to the monotonous hiss of radiators and the too-clean smell of dusting spray. Back to the pew, hoping that some of whatever inner freight it had borne was there yet.

It was not. The seat was simply a bench, and the ghosts that sat there were only the ones, Powell knew, that he had brought with him. Wolfson, Anna, Lethe, Kelsey, Case, Zang, John and Kenny, the girl on the sidewalk, what was her name? All of them caught in a whirl of principalities and thrones that had finally proved greater than the life force that held them in the world.

Too many dead, he thought, and stood, hoping to leave them on the bench. Nowhere to go, though. He paced across the lobby to a bulletin board crammed with announcements and offers: "ST1 meets in Professor Carver's Apt." "NEC Desktop for Sale, Low $$", "Straight Student Support Group? Ask Me. x2197," and two score more. The dead read them over his shoulder and followed when he re-crossed the emptiness to stand in front of the painting at the foot of the staircase.

Savaranola again, surrounded by flames though as yet untouched by them, looking as serene as a yogi on a bed of coals. Powell could not read it, could not tell whether the artist had intended to glorify the monk or to vilify him, but while he watched the painting changed, the calm face above the flames was first Manny's and then Seymour Case's and the rest of the dead appeared among the solemn witnesses.

What could Case have had to do with anything? He'd said he didn't know Wolfson. What could he have had to do with Rossa? With Kinlock or with Zang? Not a fit, Powell thought. The gentle scholar was not part of it; the Jew above the Chinese market was out of place in this puzzle. Who would know? Who could make the connection that would draw him in? In the painting, books were scattered on the ground behind the fire and the crowd, presumably those that Savaranola would have cast into the flames had he himself not been put there first. The figure of an aged man knelt reverently to pick them up. And Powell knew then who to see.

"Is Verteau around?" he asked the night man. "Steve Verteau?"

The man's head swung up slowly, like a turtle's, Powell thought. The faintest trace of a grin appeared before he answered. "He's up there. He's always up there."

Which made a world of sense. Verteau was the seminary librarian, a bibliophile of abnormal proportions. Where the books were, he would be. Powell could imagine him appearing in the dead of night at the lobby desk to alert its occupant about some 19th century theological tome that he'd just uncovered from an obscure shelf in the library's dusty stacks. Stuff the author wouldn't even read again. If anyone would know a Hebrew bookseller, Stephen Verteau would.

Powell took the steps up two at a time, found the heavy steel door at the top unlocked and pulled it open to step into a cramped waiting room with two glass walls. The Smoke and Joke Cafe, the students called it, though smoking had long since been prohibited. The space where you could forget the Bible and its myriad interpreters, sit on a couch, have a cup of bad coffee, and laugh about the church.

Behind the glass on his right, the landmarks of the unlit reading room loomed dimly: the maple counter of the circulation desk, the upright and somewhat uptight shelves of the reference area, and beyond them the rows of polished tables which shone faintly in the red lucency of an exit sign. Behind the transparent wall to Powell's left were the cluttered grey metal desks of the library's cataloguing area and a rectangle of brightness outlining the door to Verteau's inner sanctum. Powell tried the door, found it locked, and rapped on its pane. First silence, then hollow bumping, then a widening swath of light as the inner door swung open, and a shadow emerging that turned into Steve Verteau.

Tall and thin, almost gangly, greying red hair, blue eyes with sharply etched crowfeet, and an easy wide smile that widened further when he saw Powell behind the glass.

"Padre Powell!" He pulled the door open and swung an inviting arm. "What turn of meditation hath sent you my way?"

"I ran into Savaranola in the lobby. He thought there might be some work for me here."

"Goddam Dominicans. One wants to watch out for them." Mock seriousness and a twinkling eye. "Nearly as bad as the Jebbies, would you say?"

"Nothing could be that bad." A pause to watch the librarian watching him. "How's things, Steve?"

"Things are fine. Except that the chapel stinks again."

"What?" Chapel was the center of seminary life, Powell knew, the one thing everyone agreed on. Alexander Neill, the Professor of Liturgics, had been there forever and `did' chapel better than anyone. "What's Alex up to?"

Verteau laughed. "It's not the liturgy! I meant it literally stinks."

"C'mon, you're kidding."

The librarian grinned and shook his head. "God knows what it is. Broken sewer line, maybe - but the funny thing is it came and went and now it's back. Other than that and this Wolfson thing, everything's just great."

"How're people taking that?"

"Shock. Nobody's said anything much and there's all kinds of whispering. S. and M. stuff. Talk that he was hanging naked on a fence. Drug stuff. Crucifixion. Even the goddam I.R.A." Powell watched Verteau laugh at this last theory, clearly unimaginable to him.

"What do you think?"

"Me? I don't think anything except that Wolfson was a brilliant and strange man. Lots of folks didn't like him but I can't think of one who'd've wanted to kill him. Exactly what I told the cops."

Pretty much, Powell recalled, what he himself had said. "You talked to the police?"

"Sure. I think everyone did. A couple of detectives spent the day here. Mine was a guy named Arnold something."

Arnie. Maria's partner, now with a jaw wired shut. Powell grimaced at his stupidity, set now against a stark background of death.

"What're you doin' up here anyway? Avoiding the Provincial? You're not on the visit schedule for a week or so."

Powell felt the smile spread from the corners of his mouth back and up towards his ears and eyes. No doubt the Provincial WAS looking for him. "I am," he said. "He'd never think to look for me around books."

Verteau chuckled, and Powell waited for the sound and feel of laughter to fade before he went on.

"Actually, I have a kind of reference question to check on." Verteau nodded and Powell continued. "You ever hear of a guy named Case? Seymour Case?"

The librarian nodded again, answered without a second's thought. "Not a guy actually. An incident. The Seymour Case."

"What?" A vise tightening behind his ribcage. "A what?"

"The Seymour Case. Seymour was the seminary's first Dean. Robert Seymour. Started 1868, something like that. Before him, the senior faculty member presided but it didn't work well.

"Anyway, after Seymour had been on board for a year or so, his brother came to live with him. A black sheep sort, apparently. And no charmer. His after-dinner habit, so the stories go, was to walk about the seminary grounds smoking a post-prandial cigar, looking for hobos to throw into the street. Or maybe hook-ups – if you read between the lines, you get the feeling he might have been closeted. 'Unnatural inclinations' was the phrase back then. Nice, huh?"

"Lovely." And still, Powell thought, a million like him today.

"July 4, 1870. Seymour the brother, George was his name I think, goes for his walk after supper. And doesn't return. Sometime early in the morning the Dean's wife realizes that he hasn't come back, rouses her husband, sends him out to look for the wayward sibling. Who finds him dead, a bullet in his head."

Verteau stopped there, watched Powell, and let silence feed suspense.

"So who did it?"

Verteau shrugged. "They never found out. The speculation got pretty lurid, though."

"Like what kind of lurid?"

A chuckle. "Nice word, lurid. Always a good hook. Exactly why otherwise reasonable folks put the Enquirer in their shopping carts."

Powell, the vise still tight and impatience rising, took a breath and played along. "I love the Enquirer. Never miss it. But I don't have the back issues. So, tell me what kind of lurid we're talking about."

"Well, first, the guns. Police did a search. Turns out that twenty nine followers of the Prince of Peace were packing heat."

"Seminarians?"

"Two of 'em were faculty, actually. Couldn't do sophisticated ballistics then but some of 'em were consistent with the wound that old George had."

"Mmmmm." Could guns be the connection, some kind of tie to Fitzgerald? Didn't seem likely. "Tell me something, Steve," he said. "Was Wolfson doing anything on this?"

A flicker of surprise across Verteau's eyes, just the slightest lift at the crest of the still red eyebrows. "He was, in fact. How I happen to know about the case at all was he dug the files out."

"What was he after?"

"Damned if I know. Never told anyone what he was working on, not this time, not any time. Only time I heard a squeak out of him, he was chuckling about the choir boy. Said something about how the best thing about history was that it just kept coming back."

"The choir boy?"

"Yep." The librarian grinned and shook his head. "Seems that one of our priests-in-the-making had a fourteen-year-old choir boy living with him. It's mentioned in the newspapers but the really good stuff is in the diary entries and between the lines in the faculty minutes. No one thought that the young man in question was just sheltering a lost soul."

"What happened to him?"

"Don't know what happened to the kid. The student was dismissed." Another grin, wider this time. "The letter to his bishop said that he 'wasn't happy at the seminary' but I'm guessing he was happier than a pig in shit."

Shit, Powell thought. What they were all wallowing in. Violence and greed. Even his own lust. Like the Prodigal Son: knee deep in pig shit and afraid to go home. And now the shitty revelation that his own mistake may have led someone with matches to a gentle Jewish bookseller whose innocence was beyond doubt.

The matches! Now the brown book with Jimmy's gold logo loomed up large again, and again Hernandez in the precinct house was trying to kill him in front of the now dead Kelsey. Who could have had the matches? Zang? Or some other cop? Or could there have been someone else?

"-was a woman, too." Verteau's words floating by him now, leaves on a rising stream. "Or someone dressed like one."

"Wait! Wait a minute." Thoughts tumbling, reaching for an off switch. "What about a woman?"

The words stopped, dammed in a sudden silence. Verteau stared at him wide-eyed; a slightly frightened look that did not make sense until Powell realized that his fist was clenched on a handful of the librarian's shirt. He opened it slowly and stepped back half a step.

"Sorry, Steve. I . . . I don't . . . I mean-"

"Mickey, what's it about? Wolfson, right?"

Powell nodded. "More than that, though. But what were you saying about a woman?"

"A woman? Oh, yeah, there was one. I mean when Seymour got shot there was. An old lady across the street said she saw him around midnight with a woman - but the language is funny. If you read the actual clipping it says she was `all dressed in white like an angel but her movement was a man's.' Let me show you the clippings."

Following Verteau, thought back in the spin cycle. All in white. An angel. A white angel. Angail Ban. The clippings in the file were yellow and brittle and Powell could not bring them into focus. Movement was a man's. A cloaked figure in the middle of the night, money passed on a street corner. Verteau was speaking again and the words were going by.

"Sorry, Steve, how's that again?"

"What? Oh, nothing much. I was saying that the Dean found it all fascinating."

"The Dean?" Powell felt an elevator dropping inside him from his throat to his bowels and nothing to stop it. "When did you talk to him about it?"

"The last time? Just this morning. He came up to see what Wolfson had been working on. Just wrapping up loose ends, he said."

The Dean. Hernandez was briefing the Dean. Had briefed him

before. Would have asked him about Powell. And about a bookseller named Seymour Case. Loose ends.

Chapter 31

THE ANGEL

AND NOW THE NET HAD CLOSED. THE ANGEL, FURY COLD AND STILL INSIDE HIM, LEANED ON THE COLD, STILL STONE AND REFLECTED. HOW EASY IT HAD BEEN, HOW EAGER THE WHORE HERNANDEZ HAD BEEN TO FOLLOW HIM. BUT THIS, TOO, WAS WRITTEN IN THE WISDOM OF THE ANCIENTS. "LET THEIR TABLE BECOME A SNARE BEFORE THEM AND THAT WHICH SHOULD HAVE BEEN FOR THEIR WELFARE, LET IT BECOME A TRAP." FIRST, FEIGNED PATIENCE AS SHE HAD EXPLAINED THAT THE RESPONSIBILITY FOR WOLFSON'S JUST EXECUTION WAS NOW BEING FIXED ON MORONIC THUGS RUNNING GUNS, MEN WHO KNEW NOTHING OF THE GREAT THRONE OR OF THE SEVEN LAMPS AND SEVEN SEALS. BUT THIS WAS, HE KNEW, RIGHTEOUSNESS OF THE HIGHER KIND. AND THEN THE BAIT: 'I'VE FOUND SOMETHING I THINK YOU SHOULD SEE. IN THE TUNNELS.'

THE TUNNELS. THE THOUGHT HAD EXCITED HER! SHE AND HER ROMAN BUFFOON HAD PURSUED HIM THROUGH THE TUNNELS, SO THEY SUPPOSED, AND AGAIN SHE DELUDED HERSELF THAT HE WAS THE HUNTED AND NOT THE HUNTER. WHAT FOOLS! THEY HAD CHASED ONLY A PHANTOM, THE FAINTEST SHADE OF HIS MAJESTY, AND THIS

HAD NOW EMBOLDENED THE HARLOT TO ENTER EVEN THE SANCTUARY ITSELF. THAT ENTRANCE HAD ALREADY HAD ITS PRICE - SHE COULD NOT FLY! - AND SOON THE FINAL ACCOUNTING, THE SACRIFICE, WOULD BEGIN.

THE WOMAN STIRRED, HER DANGLING HEAD ROLLED FROM SIDE TO SIDE, THE EYELIDS FLICKERED UP BRIEFLY AND DROPPED SHUT, A MUFFLED MOAN SOUNDED FROM BEHIND THE GAG. SHE WAS WAKING, AS HE KNEW SHE WOULD. THE SACRIFICE WOULD NOT BE ACCEPTABLE IF THE OFFERING WERE NOT AWAKE AND, CLEARLY, THIS OBLATION WAS MEANT TO BE. THE KNIFE COULD NOT HAVE BEEN RETURNED TO HIM FOR ANY OTHER PURPOSE. THE WOMAN MOANED AGAIN AND THE ANGEL, SMILING, CONSIDERED THE RIGHTNESS OF THE MOMENT. FIRST, THE WOMAN HER-SELF HAD ARRIVED, AS OBVIOUS AN INDICATOR AS A RAM CAUGHT IN A THICKET. AND THEN THE KNIFE.

IT WAS HERNANDEZ WHO HAD SEEN IT FIRST, A GLINT OUT OF BLACKNESS. WITHOUT SPEAKING THEY HAD WALKED ALONG THE NARROW PASSAGEWAY IN MURKY LIGHT, A WELTER OF PIPES AND CONDUITS ABOVE THEM AND BRICK CLOSING IN ON EITHER SIDE. THE BIN WAS UNDER THE RESIDENCE ABUTTING THE CHAPEL, BENNETT HALL, AND THE KNIFE WAS BURIED IN COAL THAT HAD BEEN UNDISTURBED FOR A QUARTER CENTURY OR MORE. PERHAPS, THE ANGEL THOUGHT, HE HAD LEANED IN ITS DOORWAY WHEN HE'D LUGGED WOLFSON'S DRAINED REMAINS UP TO BE DISPLAYED. PERHAPS THE KNIFE HAD SLIPPED OUT THEN. NOT THAT IT COULD HAVE BEEN AN

ACCIDENT. THE DIVINE PURPOSE WAS SERVED IN ALL THINGS.

AND NOW THE VICTIM HAD FOUND THE INSTRUMENT BY WHICH SHE WOULD HERSELF BE MADE PURE. SEEING THE FAINTEST GLIMMER, SHE HAD GONE INTO THE BLACKNESS OF THE BIN AND RETRIEVED THE KNIFE, ASKING: "WHAT ARE THESE FOR?"

HE TOOK IT SHE MEANT THE BIN ITSELF BUT THE IRONY WAS DELICIOUS. WITH HIDDEN GLEE, HE HAD EXPLAINED THE ORIGINAL SYSTEM; THE COAL FOR FIREPLACE HEAT THE DUMBWAITER WHICH TOOK IT UP AND BROUGHT DOWN CINDERS AND POTS OF SLOP. "BUT NOW," HE'D SAID, "LET ME SHOW YOU SOMETHING ELSE."

AND THEN THE PORTAL, THE ENTRY HIDDEN BEHIND THE PROPPED FIRE DOOR, THE ENTRANCE REVEALED TO HIM WHEN FIRST HE'D COME. WHEN THE HEAVY PANEL HAD SWUNG TOWARDS THEM, THE SWEET SMELL OF MORTALITY HAD SWEPT UP AND EVEN THE WHORE, WHO HAD NOT YET SEEN, HAD HAD THE SENSE TO CRY, "OH, MY GOD!"

Chapter 32

TUESDAY - 8:19 p.m.

Now he knew. Standing under the arch of brick, hard by the gate and the garbage, Powell remembered what he had not been able to bring back about the night of Wolfson's death, and knew too what the shape of his unformed thought on the walk was.

The first epiphany had occurred early, after his sprint down from the library, after his futile pounding on the Dean's door, after he had shaken down the shaking desk man for a key.

No one in the Dean's office, the door to his residence locked from the office side, and the desk man swearing that no one had come out. The only other door had taken him into a stairwell.

"Where's it go?"

"The stairway?" Verteau's voice. The librarian had followed after his abrupt, cursing departure. "Up to the rare book room and then further up to the guest rooms. No one uses it. The elevator goes to the same places and all the doors are alarmed."

"What about down?"

"Don't know. The basement and tunnels I guess."

The tunnels. The chase came back; Hernandez's shout and the scramble through pitch darkness, the collision with the door, the silence of failure.

"Do me a favor, Steve," Powell said.

Verteau nodded.

"Call the 10th precinct. Ask for a detective named Arnie and tell him Hernandez is in trouble. If he's not there, tell someone else but get as many people over here as you can."

Another nod. "Where will you be?"

"I don't know. Down there somewhere." To the deskman: "I need your flashlight."

"My keys, man-"

"I need them, too. When the cops come, show 'em how to get into the tunnels." He left them standing and clattered hollowly down the empty steps.

The basement corridor of the library building was as sterile as a hospital: flourescent light, tile floors, and a faint clean smell of wax. Not here, Powell had thought. Whatever he was looking for would not be here. No reason, but a strong conviction. Somewhere under the old buildings, in some quirky space. And if he was wrong, she'd be dead. He had jogged to the end of the corridor, fumbled with keys, pulled open a heavy metal door.

And remembered. The cool, musty, tunnel air was what he had forgotten. What his memory had not brought back to him from that first night was the tunnel smell. Somewhere near the oratory the last time he'd been there a door to the tunnels, one usually shut, had been open. His conviction was correct. Somewhere in the tunnels, he'd find what he was looking for.

But no telling its precise location. Powell had moved slowly, playing the light along the walls and floor and ceiling. To his right, damp stone rose ten, perhaps twelve, feet; broken at uneven intervals near the top by heavily meshed windows. Sidewalk level, Powell knew. Walking by on 21st, they would never catch your eye. To his left a series of wood slat storage bins, all locked and heavily cobwebbed. Two staircases reached up into buildings and one, granite glistening with humidity, towards the street.

The doors topping all three were padlocked. Electrical conduit and wrapped pipes hung from the ceiling; the latter steam lines from the boiler room which hissed out in jets at ancient seams and clanked with unnerving randomness. The odor was of mildew, and crunch bugs skittered across the light beam. Low doorways, no doubt cut through the yard-thick walls to satisfy fire inspectors, marked the lines that separated building from building. Their sliding metal doors were heavy as lead but they opened easily after the first prodigious tug.

Nothing. No sign of anyone. Only the mold smell, and the sounds of condensation dripping and cars passing above and insects passing below. And no voice, never a voice to tell him where to go or what to do or who he was. Only silence where the voice should be, only silence and fear.

Until he came to the chapel, Powell had not been able locate himself on his internal map of the seminary. He knew that there were four buildings along the north side of the East Quadrangle but the tunnel made little distinction. The stone and bins and stairs, the high windows, the sounds, the smells; all the same.

But at the chapel, even in the tunnel darkness, it had become clear that he was someplace different. The stone changed to brick and the brick bore the imprint of the One who had inspired the whole enterprise and all its faithful across two millennia: Paul and Polycarp, Augustine and Ambrose, Ignatius, yes, even Cranmer. Tutu and Teresa. Manny, Manny, too. And, Powell had thought, me. At five-foot intervals on the walls, in brick a shade darker than the rest: crosses. Empty crosses. The nexus of life and death. That could only be under the chapel.

Powell had stopped, stood, and played the light around the chamber. To the left, a staircase up and a locked door at the top, the door, he knew, that opened by the Oratory entrance. So many locked doors. But not unreasonable to guess that the Dean would have the keys. Another wooden bin, this one doorless, at the foot of the steps. Was something odd about it? It had seemed so, but the flashlight beam had revealed nothing but a heap of coal. Past the stairs, the tunnel narrowed again and approached an open doorway, its heavy door chained back open to a rusty hook on the wall.

For Commencement, Powell had guessed. If it rained on Commencement Day, the procession formed in the student lounge and on the steps leading up to the commons room and auditorium, all of which were in Hobart, the next building past the Chapel and the last one before the gate to 21st Street. No doubt someone had chained the door back to keep the faculty's academic finery from rubbing in the century's accumulated grime. Had to have been a while back, though, Powell thought. The rust said that, and in his eight years it had never been necessary to move the parade inside.

Not here, though. Powell had played the light around the walls again and wondered where Hernandez and the Dean could have gone. No answer here. Nothing from the crosses, nothing from the steps or from the bin or doorways. Only the harsh creak of a pipe somewhere and a faint but perceptible dead mouse smell, the chapel stink that Verteau had mentioned.

Perhaps he'd been wrong. Perhaps Maria had made her brief report and come back out while he was still clearing out the apartment and the nightman was in the can or something. Now she'd be on a bench and laughing as the blue and whites pulled up. `Chasing ghosts, Mickey?' she'd say.

But there *were* ghosts, as there had been at dinner. Seymour Case's gentle ghost with the light blue number on a bone-thin forearm. And Anna's - her death was not about spies or terrorists or money. And Wolfson's, still clinging to its tawdry research. Choir boys, and women in white. `But the movement was a man's.' Verteau's voice. `The Dean found it fascinating.' Who was this man? Where was he? Powell had snapped his light past the chained back door and moved on through the tunnel. Now was the time to find out.

And the brick arched doorway told him that he'd gone too far. Working his way carefully through the student lounge had brought him here, past the pool table and the booths, past the tables, and the counter, through the kitchen: to this doorway by the gate and the garbage bin. Nothing found in any of this but now the figure in the glass of the door opposite him - where the tunnel picked up again, where he and Hernandez had pursued a specter a few nights before - now the man standing there waved him back.

It was, he knew, himself. His reflection. And the white-gowned figure that Hernandez had seen was also a reflection. Of someone standing here where he was, of someone who had disappeared back into the shadows behind him at her shouted command to freeze. They had chased the reflection and not the person and along that false trail a half dozen people had died. Powell turned and ran back into the darkness.

Back through the lounge, back down to the tunnel, back to the cross-marked walls of the chapel. Here. The flashlight caught the narrow stairway up and the padlocked door at the top. Even with the key, it could not have been relocked from the other side. Something else to see, Powell thought. Some other way. The meshed windows, high in the wall behind him, were cobwebbed and undisturbed. The door he had come in and the door through which he'd returned provided the only other egress but neither of them, he knew, was the way. Wolfson's cruciform death pose spoke of the Church and a church killer spoke of the chapel. Here. Here, where the crosses marked the foundation brick. Here, there was nothing to look at but the coal bin and the coal bin promised nothing. Powell moved closer and shone his light in.

The beam lost itself in the low heap of blackness, the heap itself surrounded by blackened wall and a coal black ceiling. Nothing there to even hint at movement. Nothing but dust on the floor outside the bin. Either coal had been moved out and put back in or someone had stepped in and then back out. Kneeling, Powell examined the smudges.

Footprints of a sort. Not shoe-shaped but regular at least; first two sets in pairs, then alternating: left, right, left, pair, then alternating again and fading, making not for either doorway but for the hook on the wall where the far door's chain held it fast an inch from the wall. Powell held his light up to that inch and peered in.

Brick, brick, brick, then dark space, then brick and brick again. Pushing on the chained door, he lifted the rusty link off the hook, and let it swing away from the wall. Behind it, a low rounded arch and a knobless, riveted, metal door. Powell ducked under the arch and examined the hook. Possible, he thought. Difficult, but possible from where he stood to pull the outer door to the wall and loop the chain over the hook. This was the place.

Jammed hard by his shoulder, the door swung in with a speed that surprised him, seized his balance, pulled him stumbling inward. The door itself clanged hollowly against a wall and Powell found himself falling, steps down beneath him but no footing, a square of light below, and the door above, counter-weighted, now swinging closed. Pushing back, head landing sharply on stone or concrete, coming to a stop with the flashlight still in his right hand, seeing now that he was on a steep staircase along a brick wall and below him, where the dim light shone, an open space with a brick floor. No railing, only a rust-spotted line of conduit on the wall that ran from an ancient round switchbox, following the stairway before bending out along the chambers ceiling.

"Ah. That would be Father Powell."

A lugubrious voice echoing from below, clear enough, but the words and timbre and pitch of it were overwhelmed, nearly lost, in the sweetsick stench that rose like liquid around him.

Dead, rotting flesh. A smell that spoke of maggots and scavengers, and of Cambodia, and of Salvador. Nothing was past, Powell thought. Nothing.

"Come down, Father. Your friend is here."

No choice. Maria there and no one else to help. If Verteau had called, help would be coming soon, but not soon enough if he could not slow time down now. He eased down the steps, leaning on the damp brick wall, cleared the chamber's ceiling line, and bent to see . . . an angel.

Or what had passed for one. The Dean wore a long white surplice embroidered in gold, which trailed to the floor and a tight white headgear with long golden rays reaching up and out from it as from some demented tiara's. Funny, if not for the knife and the gun.

The gun, a revolver, probably Hernandez's .38, was levelled at him while the slim, silvery knife rested lightly on the fingertips of the Dean's right hand. Powell, still half bent, froze on the steps and looked past the apparition to the bodies, both hanging like meat in a cooler.

Maria, naked but for a bra and panties, was the nearer of the two. Her head hung limply and her hands were cuffed and chained to a steam pipe suspended from the ceiling. Clothes and shoes lay in a heap at her feet. The swollen corpse hanging next to her wore no clothes at all. Its skin, mottled brown and purple, was so distended as to make the face featureless. A huge bluish cock arched out from its pelvis.

"Remarkable, isn't it?" The voice was smooth and unctuous, pitched half a tone too high. "I'm going to ask the detective to ease his discomfort as soon as she wakes up." A low laugh and a slow shake of his crowned head from right to left and back again. "But first I believe I'll need to do something about you."

Powell pushed up and backward even before the last syllable had been spoken but the gun's explosion still surprised him. Two reports and the echoes swelling and the sharp pings of steel bullets on brick walls and acrid, heady odor of gunpowder over the rot stink. Still airborne, his right hand reached for the wall, found it, fumbled frantically for the switchbox. Unhit, he came down heavily on his hip as his fingers caught the switch. His head crunched solidly into the door and sharp hurt and darkness came together.

"Powell!"

The air was perfectly black, a sea of ink, and the voice was lower now, commanding and urgent, but with just a trace of doubt. Powell tucked the flashlight, miraculously not dropped, into the front of his pants. Easing his weight onto fingertips and toes, he began a silent crab walk down, each movement painful and ridiculously deliberate, a mime's routine in even slower motion.

"Powell, you're there." Matter of fact, as if he had peered through the empty dark and watched his odd silent dance down the staircase. "You're there and I want you to listen. It's time that the whore should die."

Powell eased himself to the steps. A bit more than halfway down, perhaps fifteen feet from where Warren, the Dean, had been standing. Too far to jump even assuming that he had not moved.

"How shall I begin? With her face? Would that suit you?"

Perhaps there was no choice. Missing could mean death for both of them, but what was the alternative? Powell felt fear seize him, felt a cold tightness clutch his chest.

"Or a breast perhaps? Did you suck them?"

Feet tight against his haunches now, leaning slightly forward, a wave of nausea rising from his gut to his throat. Dean Warren's laugh filling the room.

"How modest of you not to say. But I have no doubt that if you did not, someone else did. What the book says is, 'Woe to the breasts that gave suck.'"

The book. Did the book made a difference? And then the voice saying listen, listen to it, what does it say? And his own voice coming now, shaping air in his throat, words forming

between his teeth and lips. "The book says, 'Let he among you who is without sin cast the first stone.'"

The explosion's flash was immediate, the sound followed a millisecond later. The high whine of the riccochet just above and behind him came as Powell's hot pounding heart pushed its way towards his throat. Holding tight to the flashlight, he threw himself forward, tucking his shoulder, hitting brick hard, rolling, pulling himself to an abrupt stop, sucking his breath in and holding it, listening to the gunshot's dying reverberation.

"Fornicator!"

The Dean's choked scream seemed to swell up louder than the revolver's report had. Powell drew in another breath, pulled his knees up against his chest. He was closer, had to be, but the echo made it impossible to pinpoint anything in the lightless well.

"The book speaks to men, fornicator." Now the voice was a malevolent hiss, a little to his left he thought, but how far away? "It knows nothing about me or my kind."

Let the silence build, Powell thought. Let it work on his insanity, the crazy belief that he was not human, was, in fact, an angel. And what did the book say? Where were the angels and how were they described? He could not find the answer and needed it and finally let the question go and let the words come from some other place, not his, another voice speaking with his mouth.

"Revelation twelve nine."

Movement, the rustling of cloth, but no shot. The angel coming closer? Maybe - but how close? And where? The black air swallowed the sound and the stillness revealed nothing of direction. And where were the cops? Surely, there'd been time enough by now. "You think you know, do you? You know nothing." The whisper stopped his thought, stopped his breath. Stopped time. It seemed closer but nothing was certain. "You think I follow the Prince of Darkness?"

"Look where you are, War-"

The flash, the bang, the ricochet again, and something burning along the top of his left shoulder; the rustling again, and footsteps moving toward him, reaching up with the light now, switching the beam on, catching the Dean close, a yard away not more, pulling a shriek from him, and his right hand, the one with the knife coming up over his eyes. The nose of the .38 swung toward him, wavering, close, but close at this range would be enough, and Powell pushed himself forward in a lunge as he snapped the light off.

No shot. His right shoulder caught something solid, forced a grunt from someone, but his target had moved just enough and momentum carried him past and sprawled him wheezing on the damp brick, while something clattered behind him.

No. Not something, Powell realized. Some things. The flashlight was gone now, somewhere in front of him and off to his left. And the sharp metallic clangor behind him would be the gun banging and sliding on the brick floor; the knife was not heavy enough to make so much noise. The sounded faded almost to silence, only his own heart's pounding and the Dean's labored breath disturbed the stillness.

The knife was it, now. He might still have the knife and in the darkness there would be no defense if he got close enough to use it. The blood was still dripping on the white wall in the tropics and now it would flow here as well. Powell's thoughts raced and his hand, resting on his chest began to tremble. And then calm. From a point inside, spreading like a ripple on a pond, a sure knowledge that someone else was there. Be not afraid. The voice speaking. Be not afraid what you are to say.

"The light bothers you, doesn't it, Warren?"

No answer. The sound of rustling in the darkness.

"I know that it bothers you. Nothing you can do about it, though."

Closer now, perhaps a little to his right. Powell swung an arm out into the black air and touched nothing.

"The light, Warren. `The Light shines in the darkness and the darkness has not overcome it.'"

Movement once again, but no sense of location. Should have found me, Powell thought. Should have closed with me by now.

"Powell!" Something strange and powerful in the echoing shriek, a note of elation or triumph. "Powell, where's your fucking light now?"

What did the question mean? Had he found the revolver? Or was there something in the room that he had not seen? Powell sat rock still and waited.

"Listen closely, Powell!" Again the reverberation hid the voice's source. "Listen closely and you'll hear the whore dying."

Maria! Warren had stumbled into Maria's unconscious, hanging body. Powell felt cold rage surge up like ice exploding from a volcano. Instinctively he crouched, leaning forward, preparing to leap at that which he could not see.

"Did you hear me, Powell?" The voice now a lascivious whisper. "I'm going to kill her."

He did not jump; something held him in place. The Other spoke.

"Then she'll be alive."

Stillness and stink of a grave, not a molecule moving. Powell went on:

"You and I will still be dead."

Now sound, faint at first, then louder: footsteps, running footsteps, and shouts, indistinct but coming closer.

"They're coming, Warren. It would be best if you put the knife down before they take you."

A cackled, half-choked laugh. "Take me? What makes you think they'll be able to find me?"

And then the sick sound of a knife cutting meat and a rustle of cloth moving away and the door kicked open and light cascading down the stairs.

Chapter 33

WEDNESDAY - 11:32 a.m.

Even closed, Hernandez's eyes were lovely. Oval, almost almond-shaped, black lashes reaching towards high, fine cheekbones and the thin, straight nose, delicate, flaring eyebrows arched as if amused; all of this framed by smooth, dark skin, and all of it unmoving; perfectly, deathly still.

But she was not dead. The white sheets moved, fluttering almost imperceptibly below her nostrils, rising and falling gently over the soft curve of her breasts. A clear tube wound down from a bottle to her forearm where white tape held it neat and tight against brown skin. Reassured, Powell moved closer to the bed, leaning forward to look at her throat, knowing what he would find there.

Nothing. Not a bandage, not a mark, not a nick. Even knowing, he needed to look, needed to see, needed to convince himself again that the horror that he had heard and still heard, the wicked music of the knife, had not been played on her. Nothing there but a pulse marking the regular flow of blood in an uncut artery. Sighing relief, he closed his eyes and lowered his head and launched an unspoken thank you towards something or someone unknown but certain. It was there. It did speak, did listen, was always speaking and listening if only you could get the channel right.

A voice: "Father? Father Powell?"

A hand on his right arm, the unslung one. Turning to a woman, tall, short chestnut hair, wide face, full mouth, frank green eyes, beautiful blue-green dress cinched at a narrow waist with a wide black sash.

"Mary?" Who else would be there? "You must be Mary."

"Yes." Eyes widening slightly in surprise. "Mary Lambert. How did you know?"

"You were here once before. When I was in the bed. And Maria told me about you before . . . before . . . this."

"Ah." A tentative smile, almost shy. "She's told me a good deal about you, too."

A silence of ten seconds that passed like ten years. Why not, Powell thought. Why not go for broke? "Odd, aren't we?" he said. "Do you think we could go on Geraldo?"

"I beg your pardon?"

"You know: the priest and the lesbian both love the cop. Tune in tomorrow."

A laugh, unforced, lilting. Thank God.

"She told me you were goofy."

"Goofy? Not charming?" Feeling his own smile widen now, watching hers, the eyes crinkling, lips pulled back from even teeth.

"Goofy. Goofy and wise. Her exact words."

"Mmmm . . . a little better, anyway." And nice, he thought, to know that she talked about him. He turned to Hernandez, let the silence build again, turned back and asked, "How is she?"

"She'll be fine. Only a concussion and a lot of bruises. Amazing, when you think about it. And, well . . ." A faint blush spreading now across Mary's cheeks. " . . . and thanks."

Embarrassed, nodding. "I was . . . just . . .there. I'm glad the station house guys got there when they did."

There. There Maria, almost naked, was still hanging next to a bloated corpse. There, Warren's body was still jerking on the floor, a pool of hot blood steadily widening, fed by spurts from the dark, gaping crescent where his throat had been. There the lights came on and Arnie and three blues were scrambling down the steps.

Mary stepped closer, touched his left arm near the shoulder. "How are you doing, anyway?"

"You mean this?" Powell nodded left, pointing with his chin, shrugged slightly and winced. "Nothing really. Just stitches. They put it in a sling to keep me from moving it much."

Nothing more to say. Eyes meeting, searching for a moment, then her hand tightening on his arm and dropping as Maria stirred on the bed.

Eyelids opening, flickering closed, open again, head shaking gently and a soft smile forming.

"Powell." The voice a whisper. "You're here."

"Nowhere else to be, Hernandez. And anyway, it's my turn. Now you're in the bed."

She propped herself up on her elbows, wavered, fell back onto the pillow. "I'm tired."

"You will be for a couple of days." Or a couple of decades, Powell thought. Death just wore you out.

"He was going to kill me, wasn't he, Mick?"

"I think so. He was crazy and he thought you knew too much. Wolfson knew too much."

Hernandez's eyes narrowed, focused tightly on his face. "What did he know? And how do you know?"

"I found out what he was working on. Seems there was a seminary scandal once, a dean's family involved, some sexual overtones. 1870's. The Seymour Case. Wolfson must have heard about Warren's proclivities and thought he could use the case to frame up a parallel." Steve Verteau's voice saying, '*history just keeps coming back at you.*' "He didn't know that Warren was crazy and dangerous."

"The Seymour . . . you mean . . . he wasn't . . . " Now her eyelids slid closed and her face turned away.

"Mr. Case was just a name in the phone book. He had nothing to do with anything. But we didn't know that. And neither did Warren. And so, he killed him."

"We did." A single glistening tear flowed from the corner of her still closed eye down along the side of her nose. "I gave him those matches, didn't I? Why?"

"We did not kill him. I don't know why he's dead."

"Well, then fuck you, Father."

"Maria." Mary stepping up now, touching her hand. "I think-"

"Fuck you, too!" Shaking off the touch and rolling on to her side now, sobbing, shoulders moving, hiding her face in the pillow.

Powell, behind Mary Lambert, gripped her shoulder gently and eased her to her right, stepping up next to her at bedside. Hernandez still wept and Powell watched for a long moment before speaking.

"People can kill and be killed, Maria. That's the way it is." She turned half way towards him, her eyes dark and wet and glaring. "Do you think it would be better if that was not possible?"

No answer. Something flickering behind the stony stare and the feeling, too, that Lambert's eyes were on him.

"If life was not something we had a choice about, I don't think it'd be worth much."

"What choice did Case have?" The words angry, thrown, almost spit at him.

"He chose to go on living as long as he could in spite of what he'd been through. Why did he do that? I don't know."

Now she settled back into the pillow, her dark hair spreading like a black cloud on the white linen, the lines of her mouth and eyes easing into curves again.

"What are you going to choose, Maria?"

Her words, when they came, were not an answer. "I wanted to believe him, Mick. That's why I went. When he showed me where the door was, I thought, 'This is it.' The piece that'll make it all make sense. And then I saw something in the coal bin and went to pick it up, it was the knife and I knew I was close and I pulled the door open and the stink came up and then I think he pushed me and I was in the air and then I don't remember anything."

Hernandez paused and blinked and spoke again, softly now, looking away. "I didn't know it was the door to the Roach Motel. I wanted to be able to wrap it all up in a neat package."

Powell got it then, understood what she was trying to say, reached down and clasped her hand while Mary Lambert watched. "There are no neat packages, Hernandez. That's not one of the choices we get to make."

"They didn't get Kinlock, did they?"

"Apparently not. Don't think they'd tell us if they did, though."

"What did he have to do with Warren? Anything?"

"Nothing." Or maybe everything, he thought. In any moment lives could converge- all of them: his, Maria's, Jimmy's, Anna's, Kinlock's, even Warren's – parts of the greater whole.

"The agency come for you?"

"Nope. Probably won't if I don't talk to anyone. At this point I'm just an old sleeping dog."

Her hand tightened on his and she searched his eyes for a moment. He saw the question in her look and wondered if she saw an answer. Not him, though, he knew. He was not the answer for her. A clue at best. Goofy and wise. You could do worse.

"Time for me to go, Maria."

"Okay." Peace in the word, peace in the whisper.

"Call me sometime?"

"I will."

You won't, though, Powell thought. Too much that needed forgetting. He let go of her hand, turned to Mary Lambert, said, "See you on Geraldo."

A big smile and - surprise! - a tight hug. "See you."

And then gone. Through the sterile corridors, riding down an antiseptic elevator, out through a bustling, slightly panicky lobby. Outside, traffic pouring down the avenue, almost sparkling in the bright, clear autumn sunshine. Powell found his city pace and started up towards 13th Street carrying with him sadness, an amazing, light sadness; sadness as weightless and brittle as an eggshell. Walking, he wondered at its fantastic lack of density.

And concluded that it was to be expected. He knew, had known since the haunted dinner, what was coming. All night and all morning at the rectory he had known. The good-bye would have to be final. What luck had thrown together, time would put asunder. No forever in luck, good or bad. Love could last, but it flowed from somewhere deeper. Mary Lambert and Maria Hernandez had found that spring. Manny had as well, with his people. Lethe and Tony. And he, too, with Anna. And with Jimmy, whose ruby slippers had finally taken him home. What you knew was coming was never too hard to carry.

He let the sadness carry him up the avenue and around the corner onto 15th. Which looked as it had ten thousand times before. The trees, still red and gold but leaves now thinner, the cars jammed bumper to bumper, the stoops and their black iron railings reaching down to the walk, the tiny patches of color, red and orange mums, still bright, which residents had loved into life. Even the smell was familiar: the same sour mingling of exhaust and garbage and dog shit. Probably an epiphany in that, he mused, but sometimes better to let them lay.

At the rectory, the black housekeeper laid a baleful glare on him but let him pass. Doesn't trust you, he told himself. And why should she?

The house was dead silent - only the hollow sound of his footsteps on the stairs. Everyone else would be at their tasks now - nothing remarkable, teaching, counseling, visiting, planning; all the ordinary moments that comprised their lives. How to break back into it?

No answer to that. No answers to anything. He paused at his door, shook his head at the weight of his depression, tried the knob. Open. Shouldn't be. Ski would be on his case about it: he was responsible for the house. The door was almost closed behind him before he noticed the bare foot.

One pale bare foot, nicely shaped, black lace at the ankle, resting near the corner of his bed. Peering around the corner of his closet, his eyes followed a line up from the rounded heel, along a slender calf - tights above the lace, blue and yellow moons and stars - up the back of a thigh to a snug white leather miniskirt, smiling now, knowing, the same moons and stars above on a scoop-necked body stocking, pale skin and a mass of dark blonde hair. Ellen. Sound asleep.

Sitting next to her, Powell considered the curve of her hips, the almost imperceptible rise and fall of her back with each breath, the delicacy of her fingers on the bedspread, curved together as if to hold something fragile, a flower or a piece of crystal. He touched her shoulder and shook it gently.

"Ellen. Ellen, it's me."

Her body undulated and uncoiled like a serpent's, curled softly around his, tightened, and loosened as her left hand found his back.

"Jimmy?" Eyes still shut, breath warm and sour with sleep.

"No, Ellen. It's Mick."

Eyes flickering open, closed, then open again, and she was sitting up, both arms around him, hugging snugly, head on his shoulder. Powell returned the squeeze, felt her breasts tight against his chest, his slung left arm caught against the firmness of her belly, inhaled the scent of her hair; something musky and strong, no smell of lemons here. Good to be touched. Necessary. Human. Ellen kissed his cheek and loosened her grip, holding on lightly, first to his elbows and then to his hands.

"You okay?"

She nodded and smiled without meeting his look.

"How did you get in here?"

"That guy named Ottarski. I was crying. He didn't know what to do."

"I'll bet he didn't." Powell felt a grin come as he considered this. Ski was a solid citizen, a chem teacher at the Jesuit high school. No formula would have prepared him for Ellen.

Who was watching him now, searching his face for the answer to a question she hadn't asked yet - but then did: "You found out, didn't you?"

"Found out what?" Even asking Powell knew what she'd say.

"Found out about the cop. That she's a lesbian."

He nodded. "How did you know?"

"About her or about you?"

"Both."

"I knew at Jimmy's that day. Sometimes you can just tell. I knew you were falling for her, too. And now it's like some part of you's not here, isn't it?"

That, Powell thought, was exactly what it was like. Somewhere inside, in his ribcage, maybe, or hidden in the loops of his intestines, somewhere something was gone. How it had been with Manny and with Nicole, too - and Anna and Jimmy. And now Maria: gone like they were.

"I know how it feels." Ellen spoke quietly and looked toward the window. She was the pastor now. Shouldn't be, had her own grief as deep or deeper. But used it, rode it, made it work. God's work right here in the room.

"Thanks, Ellen. How are you doing?"

"Don't know. Okay." Now she turned to him, jaw taut, brow furrowed. "What was it all about? Will you tell me that? The cops won't say a thing."

What was the answer? Terrorism? Greed? Insanity? Trying to speak without emotion, Powell synopsized Rossa and Kinlock and Warren, finally concluded, "Take your pick. My guess is that Rossa had Jimmy's torched but Kinlock might've done it as a diversion. I don't guess we'll find out which one killed Jim."

"They didn't kill him. He killed himself."

"What? Ellen-"

"He went back in. He was out with me and remembered that old George was in the can. You know that wino that came in all the time? Neither one of them came back."

Now she let go of his hands, stood, moved to the window, bare feet making no sound, silence trailing behind her like fog.

"Ellen, I-"

"Mick, it's okay." She did not turn towards him. "I hate him. Hate both of them, Jimmy and old George. But I'd hate him more if he hadn't gone back."

Now Powell stood. From somewhere came the sound of footsteps. Still, Ellen did not turn.

"I hate you, too Mick." She was crying now, tears in silvery streaks on her cheeks, words coming between sobs. "For getting . . . into it the first place. For getting him in."

He moved closer and she turned, embraced him, buried her head in his shoulder.

"But I'd hate you more if you walked away."

That was the Voice. No walking away. Not for Jimmy and George, not for Manny and his people, not for Hernandez and Mary Lambert. The footsteps came close, stopped, someone knocked on the wooden door. No walking away. That was the message and Ellen was the messenger. The door swung slowly inward.

"Father?" Ski's voice, and then Ski himself stepping in, tall, thin, gawky. "The Prov-"

Father Ottarski gaped. Ellen still held him tightly. The Society's Provincial, ramrod straight with white hair combed straight back and blue eyes that might, just might, pierce stone, now stood in the doorway. Ellen did not look and did not let go.

"Father Powell." Powell had forgotten but now recalled the Provincial's oddly nasal voice. "Who is this?"

No walking away. Ellen, the barefoot messenger.

"This, Father . . ." A laugh there which he did not hold back. " . . this is an angel."

ACKNOWLEDGMENTS

All writers owe a debt of gratitude to hundreds of people – the teachers, friends, acquaintances, and strangers who have shaped their understanding of language and the way it works. In my case, there are far too many for me to number or name but that does not lessen my gratitude. A few people, though, should get a special shout out: first Kate and Emily and the team at Dark Ink. Not many publishers take chances on unknowns but you did. I am grateful.

Two people now gone deserve special recognition: first, my late father, Lee Farrell, who told a good story, and loved books and words, and taught me to love them, too. And next my late brother, Jim Farrell, whose patient encouragement when I was young and my writing only half good kept me at it. Thanks to both of you. I look forward to seeing you again.

And finally, thanks to my wife, Barbara Thrall. Without her quiet presence and dogged support my writing life would not be possible. If there are angels in the world, she is mine.

Follow me on social media.

facebook.com/thekatherineanderson
@PoisonedPenner
@katebroderick

www.ingramcontent.com/pod-product-compliance
Lightning Source LLC
Chambersburg PA
CBHW020248030426
42336CB00010B/675